FIELD ENGINEERING

FIELD ENGINEERING

An introduction to development work and construction
in rural areas, compiled and edited
by Peter Stern and others, from
an original work by
F. Longland

1983
INTERMEDIATE TECHNOLOGY PUBLICATIONS

Published by Intermediate Technology Publications Ltd,
9 King Street, London WC2E 8HW, UK.

*The Intermediate Technology Development Group
gratefully acknowledges the financial support of the
Overseas Development Administration of the British
Government in the printing of this book.*

ISBN   Hardback 0 903031 87 6
       Paperback 0 903031 68 X

Photoset and printed by Photobooks (Bristol) Limited

Contents

Figures

Tables

Preface

This book has been produced to meet the needs of all who are concerned with development programmes involving what are, in effect, simple engineering works in rural areas. It is hoped that it will be useful to District Officers, Extension Workers, Development Agents, non-Government organizations and to volunteers who do not have ready access to professional and technical assistance. At the same time, it should be of practical help to anyone trying to do, or to plan, development work on his own—on, say, a smallholding, a homestead, or a farm.

The text has been written on the assumption that readers have received some education in English to at least, say, Diploma level and therefore understand arithmetic, and can use simple formulae, tables, graphs and technical drawings.

In the knowledge that many readers will not have had a technical education, the subject matter has been treated as simply as possible. It should be recognized, however, that field engineering is a technical subject and that there are inherent risks in putting do-it-yourself technology into the hands of people who have no understanding at all of technical matters. Where there is a chance of a little knowledge being a dangerous thing the reader is urged to seek technical or professional advice. This applies particularly to the building of structures where an accidental failure could cause serious injury or loss of life. It is also important to emphasize that, in any country, it is necessary to check with local government the legal ground-rules for construction and development work. It is recognized that some of the over-simplifications may distress the professional reader, but this has been inevitable in covering such a wide range of subjects and a list of references for further reading is included.

A major source of material for this work was Longland's *Field Engineering*, first published in Tanganyika (now Tanzania) in 1936. It was revised and republished as a second edition in 1942, reprinted again in 1943, 1944 and 1948 and the last revision and reprint appeared in 1952. During this period it became a popular, practical handbook throughout East and Central Africa. Thirty years have now elapsed since the last revision and while much of the basic technical wisdom is as relevant today as it was when it was written, so many changes were necessary to bring the subject matter up to date that a new book has emerged, but one which should acknowledge its inspiration. A major task has been the conversion of measurements and quantities from Imperial to metric units, because although some present-day readers will still be more conversant with feet, inches, pounds, gallons and acres, the metric system has been adopted in the text because it is now accepted internationally, and conversion tables are provided in Appendix I. A great deal of additional information has been derived from recent experience in field engineering. This has included extensive additions in particular to the sections on survey and surveying, engineering materials, building construction, water development, sanitation and roads and bridges.

As editor and principal author of this revision, I should like to acknowledge the contributions and assistance received from many different quarters. The operation has been financed jointly by Intermediate Technology Industrial Services with funds from the Overseas Development Administration, and by Gifford and Partners.

The section on roads in Chapter 6 was contributed by John Howe of Intermediate Technology Transport Ltd. Gifford and Partners, in addition to meeting the major cost of this work, provided extensive professional services in the form of specialist advice on the contents of Chapter 2, Engineering Materials, and Chapter 3, Buildings. Chapter 5 was compiled by Stuart Jones and all the figures and sketches were drawn by Harry Faircloth, both of Gifford and Partners. Contributions to the text have also been made by John Burton, John Collett, Henry Mann, Jonathan Sakula and Hugh Stapleton. We have gathered background information from a wide range of books and publications and these are included in the references at the end of the text.

Finally, I should like to acknowledge the support given by Frank Solomon, recently Editor and Director of Intermediate Technology Publications, who conceived the idea of this book and by his successor, Neal Burton, whose joint constant encouragement facilitated its completion.

PETER STERN
Gifford and Partners
Southampton
April 1983

ACKNOWLEDGEMENTS

I would like to acknowledge the following sources of illustrations: Francis Barker & Sons Ltd (Figures 1.6, 1.9, 1.10 and 1.12); Hall and Watts Ltd (Figures 1.13 and 1.15); Pitman Books Ltd (1.16 and 1.19). Figures 5.4, 5.5 and 5.7 are from Wagner and Lanoix; 5.8, 5.9, 5.10 and 5.11 from Feachem and Cairncross; and Figure 5.6 after Pradt. Figure 1.1 has been reproduced from Directorate of Overseas Surveys map DOS 425, Sheet 1131B1, Edition 1-DOS 1964, by permission of the Controller of H.M. Stationery Office.

CHAPTER 1
Survey

1.1 PLANS AND MAPS

1.1.1 Site Plans

For most activities in field engineering it is necessary to draw a plan of the proposed work. Plans and drawings are the most convenient method of describing what is proposed—and of ensuring during construction that what has been planned and agreed is actually built. A general plan shows the existing land and features, together with the proposed works or construction superimposed upon it. For a simple operation a general plan is all that is needed. For a more complicated work, additional drawings will be required to show particular detail.

1.1.2 Maps

The basis of a site plan may well be an existing map. A common scale for maps available now in most countries of the world is 1/50 000. At this scale, 1 millimetre (mm) on the map is equal to 50 metres (m) on the ground; 1 hectare (ha) on the ground would be a square with 2 mm sides on the map; 1 kilometre (km) on the ground would be 2 centimetres (cm) on the map. This scale would be suitable for the outline planning for the alignment of a road or pipeline several kilometres long, or for the development of an area covering several hundred hectares. A portion of a 1/50 000 scale map is shown in Figure 1.1.

For greater detail, showing individual buildings or fields, maps at scales of 1/10 000, 1/5000 and 1/2500 are used, but maps at these scales are usually made for special purposes, and they only exist for very limited areas.

In addition to plan (or planimetric) detail it is usually necessary also to have information about heights. This is particularly important for road works and pipelines but may also be essential for many other field engineering projects. Height information is always measured to a common base or 'datum' and wherever possible the datum for maps is 'mean sea level' (msl). (If msl is not known, or is unnecessary, an assumed height for the datum may be used instead.) By taking msl as

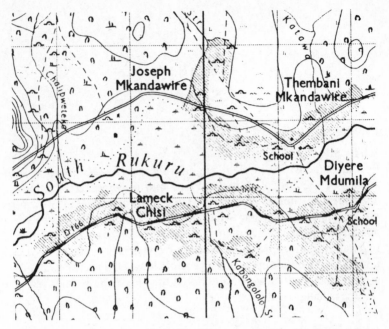

Figure 1.1 Portion of 1/50 000 scale map. © *(Crown Copyright)*

zero height all the heights are shown as positive when above sea level and negative when below sea level.

Contour lines are lines joining points of equal height. Contour lines are usually drawn at equal vertical intervals, which may be any value from 0·25 m to 50 m depending upon the nature of the topography and the scale of the map. On 1/50000 maps contours may be at 50 m intervals in mountainous country, and at 10 m or 5 m intervals in flat country. When contour lines are close together, the land surface is relatively steep; when they are wide apart it is relatively flat. In Figure 1.1 the contour interval is 50 m.

Contours on maps are very useful in describing the topography. Because the Earth is a continuous surface, all contours must close upon themselves, though not necessarily on one map sheet. Concentric contours which increase in elevation towards the centre indicate hills. Valleys normally have 'V-' or 'U'-shaped contours. A contour can never branch into two contours or cross another contour, and the contour line is always at right angles to the direction of maximum land slope.

1.1.3 Aerial Photography

'Aerial photographs' are photographs of the land surface taken vertically downwards from an aeroplane flying at a constant height. They are therefore photographic maps to scale which can be calculated from the height of the aeroplane and the optical dimensions of the camera. Aerial photographs can be very useful for initial field planning because of their clarity and detail and because they can be used in areas previously unmapped, or mapped with insufficient detail, or with details now out of date. They are also used extensively for the preparation of survey maps by means of *photogrammetry* which is the science of mapping from aerial photogaphs. By means of surveyed ground control, which is the accurate identification of points on the ground whose heights are known or can be measured, contours can be traced on maps from aerial photographs. Figure 1.2 is an example of an aerial photograph.

Figure 1.2 Aerial photograph.

1.1.4 Field Survey

Survey in the field consists of taking measurements from which maps and plans can be drawn. For engineering surveys the information required is made up of distances, heights and angles, and survey instruments measure these quantities in various ways.

1.2 ENGINEERING SURVEY INSTRUMENTS

1.2.1 Chains, Bands and Tapes

Distances are measured directly by chains, bands and tapes. Chains are made of tempered steel wire, 20 m or 30 m long with links 200 mm long (though chains may still be found which have a length of either 100 ft or 66 ft, each divided into 100 links). Bands are made of steel strip 6 mm wide and 30 m, 50 m or sometimes 100 m long, marked in metres, tenths and hundredths of metres. Bands are wound on an open frame with a spindle and handle for re-winding. Tapes may be made of steel or synthetic materials 10 m, 20 m or 30 m long, marked in metres, tenths and hundredths of metres, and are wound into a case with a handle for re-winding.

Distance can also be measured by tacheometry (see section 1.3.8) and by various micro-wave systems (Ref. 5).

1.2.2 Measurement of Heights

Small vertical heights can be measured by a suspended weight (plumb line) and tape measure. The difference in height between two points on the ground is measured by a *level*, so named because it gives a truly horizontal or level line. Heights of points are then measured by their vertical distances above or below this level line.

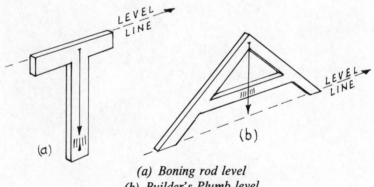

(a) Boning rod level
(b) Builder's Plumb level

Figure 1.3 Plumb-line levels.

Levels depend on the action of gravity on either a plumb line or on a liquid surface. Two simple plumb-line levels are shown in Figure 1.3; while Figure 1.4 shows methods of using liquid levels.

Height differences can be measured by the use of a graduated staff held vertically which is observed along the level line. Figure 1.5 illustrates how the depth of the bottom of a ditch can be measured in

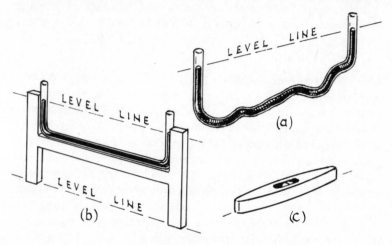

(a) & (b) U-tube levels (c) Spirit level
Figure 1.4 Liquid levels.

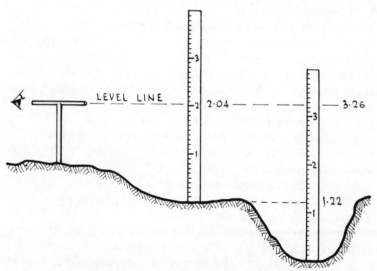

Figure 1.5 Measuring height differences.

this way. The level is set up so that the staff can be observed first standing near the ditch at ground level and then at the bottom of the ditch. The intersections of the level line on the staff at the two positions are observed, and the difference between the two is the difference in heights required. In this example the difference is 3·26 – 2·04 = 1·22 m.

Both *Abney levels* and *clinometers* can be used as levelling instruments. As they are primarily instruments for measuring vertical angles they are described in sections 1.2.8 and 1.2.9.

1.2.3 Surveyor's or Engineer's Level

An instrument used for accurate levelling is the surveyor's or engineer's level which is essentially a telescope fitted with cross wires attached to a levelling device mounted on a tripod. The telescope and cross wires enable the line of sight to be observed on a staff at a much greater distance than is possible by the naked eye. In the more old-fashioned instruments the line of sight is made horizontal by means of a sensitive spirit level and fine-threaded adjusting screws. In modern instruments, known as automatic levels, the line of sight is brought to the horizontal by means of one or two moveable prisms which are suspended so that they swing under gravity. Figure 1.6 shows a modern surveyor's level.

1.2.4 Aneroid Barometer

The pressure of the atmosphere at different places varies with their altitudes, or heights above sea level: the higher the altitude, the lower the atmospheric pressure. Thus the measurement of atmospheric pressure can be used to measure height. As the atmospheric pressure at any place also varies with temperature, the temperatures at the two places must also be taken into account when using atmospheric pressure differences to measure differences in altitude.

Atmospheric pressure is measured by means of a barometer. The most accurate instrument for measuring pressure is the *Fortin* barometer, in which the height of a vertical column of mercury is measured. This is difficult to use in the field because it is not easily portable, and so the instrument commonly used for field work is the *aneroid* barometer. The aneroid barometer consists of a shallow cylindrical box of about 75 mm diameter, from which air has been evacuated. The thin sides of the chamber are prevented from collapsing by a spring which is connected to a system of levers. Small movements of the sides of the chamber under variations in

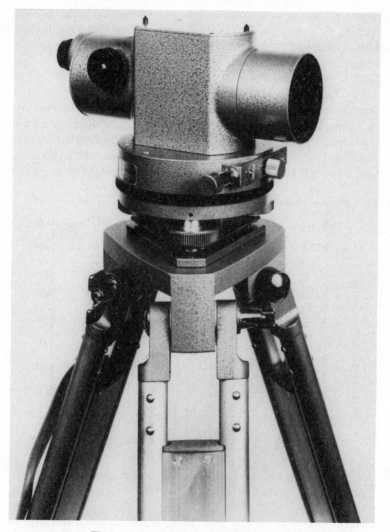

Figure 1.6 A modern surveyor's level.

atmospheric pressure are translated by the levers to a needle moving over a scale graduated in pressure or altitude.

If at one place the reading of a barometer is recorded hour by hour it will be found to vary considerably, largely due to temperature variations. For example the reading at 10 a.m. may be found to be some 40 m lower than that at 4 p.m. at the same place. These daily variations follow a characteristic pattern and this is illustrated in

Figure 1.7. An observer should make his own daily variation curve by reading the pressure at one place at hourly intervals during the day. Most modern instruments are supplied with tables of corrections to be applied to observations.

1.2.5 Angles

Angles are measured to determine the difference in direction between two lines. This can be done by direct measurement with a protractor if the lines can be drawn on any flat surface. But in the field the lines are more likely to be lines of sight or optical lines, and the angle to be measured will be the angle between two lines of sight from a fixed

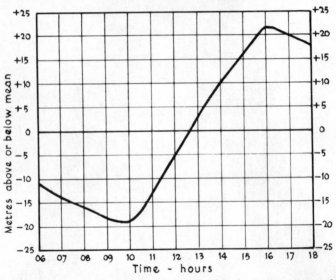

Figure 1.7 Typical correction curve for height measurements by barometer (altimeter).

observation point. Angles may be measured in any plane, but in survey work it is usual to distinguish between horizontal and vertical angles. Figure 1.8 illustrates the horizontal angle between the lines of sight to two distant objects (a telephone pole and the corner of a building).

The accurate measurement of both horizontal and vertical angles is done by means of a theodolite, which is an instrument with a telescope for sighting which can rotate both horizontally and vertically, with a graduated circle for each plane of swing. The use of the theodolite is described in textbooks (Refs 4 and 5). Angles can be measured with fair accuracy by drawing lines on a plane table and measuring with a protractor.

1.2.6 Prismatic Compass

Horizontal angles can be measured fairly accurately with a prismatic compass. A compass is an instrument which uses the property of a magnetized needle which, if allowed to swing freely, points to magnetic north. In a compass a magnetized needle is attached to a card or ring marked in a clockwise direction round its periphery in

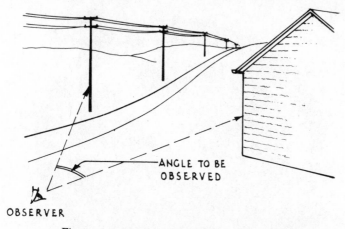

Figure 1.8 Measurement of a horizontal angle.

degree graduations, which are usually 360° to make the full circle. The prismatic compass (Figure 1.9) consists of a round glass-topped case containing the pivoted needle and card or ring, with a prism and sighting wire in a frame at opposite ends of a diameter of the case. The prism holder has a fine slit at the top and when the instrument is held at eye level with the prism towards the observer, a distant object can be sighted by lining it up with the slit and the sighting wire. At the same time the degree graduations on the ring or card can also be observed and read. Since the needle points to magnetic north, the reading on the card under the prism gives the angle between magnetic north and the line of sight. This is known as the *magnetic bearing* of the object from the point of observation. A second bearing can then be taken on a second object and the difference between the two bearings will give the angle between the two lines of sight.

A small prismatic compass 50 mm in diameter can be read to an accuracy of about half a degree. A surveyor's prismatic compass 114 mm in diameter, for example, may be read to an accuracy of 15

Figure 1.9 Prismatic compass.

minutes (or 0·25°). As a 15 minute error in a distance of 1000 m represents a deviation of 4.4 m, prismatic compasses cannot be used for very accurate measurements.

1.2.7 Surveyor's Level with Horizontal Circle
Horizontal angles can also be measured by a surveyor's level, to a similar degree of accuracy, if it is equipped with a horizontal circle graduated in degrees. The angle between the lines of sight from an observation point to two distant objects (Figure 1.8) can be measured

in the following way. Set up the instrument at the observation point, sight on the first object and take a reading on the horizontal circle. Swing on to the second object and take a second reading on the circle. The difference between the two readings gives the required angle. Unless a very expensive instrument is used, this method is no more accurate than compass measurements (as described above).

1.2.8 Abney Level

The Abney level (Figure 1.10) is a useful pocket instrument for approximate measurements of vertical angles. It can also be used as a hand level. It consists of a sighting tube attached to a graduated semi-circle. An index arm, pivoted at the centre of the semi-circle, carries a small spirit level, the arm being at right angles to the axis of the level. By means of an inclined mirror mounted in one half of the sighting tube, the bubble in the spirit level can be observed in one half of the field of view when looking through the tube. The semi-circle is graduated in degrees from 0 to $+90°$ and $-90°$, and when the axis of the spirit level and the axis of the sighting tube are parallel, the index arm reads 0 on the scale.

The main advantages of the Abney level are its size and convenience, but it is not an accurate instrument, and should only be used for sighting over short distances.

To use as a hand level the index arm is set at 0 and the instrument is sighted on a distant object and raised and lowered slowly until the image of the bubble is seen in the mirror. A horizontal sighting wire in the sighting tube indicates the axis of the instrument and when this wire is seen to bisect the image of the bubble, the line of sight is horizontal. In this way the instrument can be used for measuring height differences as indicated in Figure 1.5.

To measure the vertical angle between two points in a vertical plane the instrument is sighted first on one point and adjusted so that the bubble is intersected by the sighting wire in the sighting tube, and the position of the index on the semi-circle is read. The instrument is then sighted on the second point, readjusted and the index is read again. The difference between the two readings gives the vertical angle between the two points observed. The method of measuring vertical angles is illustrated in Figure 1.11.

1.2.9 Clinometer

A *clinometer* is the name normally given to any instrument which measures vertical angles to measure the shape of land. Thus an Abney

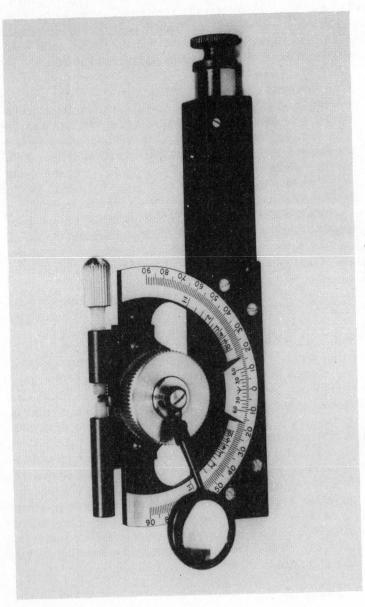

Figure 1.10 Abney level.

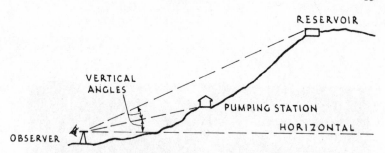

Figure 1.11 Measuring vertical angles.

level is a form of clinometer. Usually, however, the name is given to a small pocket instrument which is used in exactly the same way as the Abney level for measuring slopes and vertical angles, but depends upon a suspended pendulum for establishing vertical and horizontal zeros instead of a spirit level bubble. A combined sight compass and clinometer is illustrated in Figure 1.12.

Figure 1.12 Sight compass and clinometer.

1.2.10 The Plane Table

The *plane table*, as its name implies, consists of a drawing-board mounted on a tripod (Figure 1.13). It differs from other surveying

Figure 1.13 Plane table.

instruments in that the map or plan is prepared in the field without direct measurement of any angles. Its accessories consist of an *alidade*, a *spirit level* and a *trough compass*. These are illustrated in Figure 1.14.

The alidade is a sight rule with folding sights at each end. One sight has a narrow vertical slit, while the other consists of a vertical wire stretched across an open frame. The spirit level is used for levelling the table so that it is truly horizontal and the trough compass is used to orient the table in relation to magnetic north. The use of the plane table in surveying will be described in section 1.3.5.

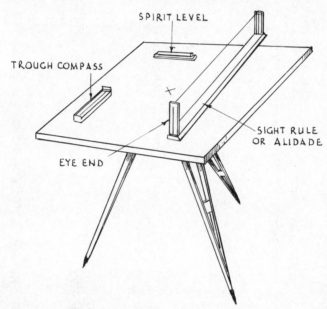

SPIRIT LEVEL

TROUGH COMPASS

SIGHT RULE OR ALIDADE

EYE END

Figure 1.14 Plane table accessories.

1.2.11 Other Survey Instruments

The *sextant* is another surveyor's instrument for measuring vertical angles. Its description and use may be found in standard text-books on survey (Refs 4 and 5).

The *levelling staff* (see sections 1.4.1 and 1.4.3) is an essential accessory to the surveyor's level. Several types of staff are available. The most common is the telescopic staff, made of mahogany or aluminium alloy, 3 m, 4 m or 5 m long on extension. The staff is graduated in metres, 100 mm and 10 mm intervals. An example of a telescopic staff is shown in Figure 1.15.

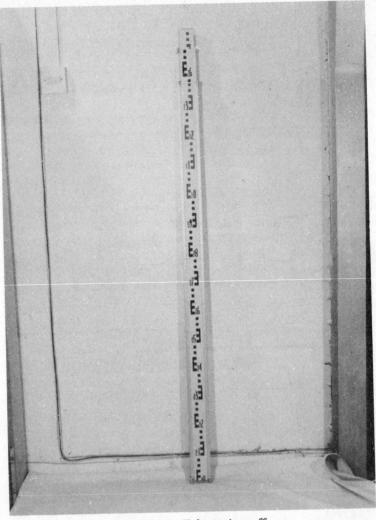

Figure 1.15 Telescopic staff.

Ranging rods, or range poles are poles of circular section 2 m, 2·5 m or 3 m long painted with alternate red and white bands, usually 0·5 m long and usually tipped with a pointed steel shoe to enable them to be driven into the ground. They are used for setting out lines and for marking points on the ground which need to be seen.

A *cross staff* is a most useful sighting instrument for measuring or setting out right angles. Figure 1.16 shows two versions of cross staff. The staff head in Figure 1.16(a) consists of an octagonal brass box with sighting slits cut at right angles; while Figure 1.16(b) shows the foresight and backsight system.

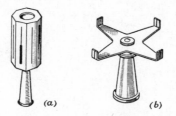

Figure 1.16 Cross staff.

An *optical square* is also an instrument for setting out or measuring right angles. There are two types of optical square, one using two mirrors and the other a prism for turning a ray of light through a right angle. In the mirror type, the two mirrors are set vertically and at 45 deg to each other. One mirror is completely silvered, and the other is silvered to half its height, the other half being plain glass. The instrument has an eyehole and two viewing windows, one in line with the eyehole and one on a line at right angles to the line through the eyehole. When the instrument is held and viewed with the line of sight on some distant object, this object will be visible through the plain part of the half mirror, while the view through the lower half of the mirror will be of objects approximately at right angles to the line of sight. If a marker or range pole is moved about in this field of view, an exact right angle is constructed when the image of the marker in the mirror half is exactly in line with the view of the distant object through the un-mirrored half.

The prismatic type of optical square fulfils the same functions with a prism instead of mirrors, and is rather more accurate than a mirror square. For more details of optical squares see Ref. 5.

Boning rods are rods with 'T'-shaped heads for setting out and checking horizontal or sloping lines in the field, such as a road surface or pipe or channel alignment. They are usually made locally.

1.3 PLAN SURVEYING

1.3.1 Compass Traverse

The prismatic compass can be used in conjunction with a chain or tape for surveying an irregular enclosed area of land such as is shown by ABCDEA in Figure 1.17. First the area is walked over and the stations A, B, C etc are located and marked with ranging rods. If

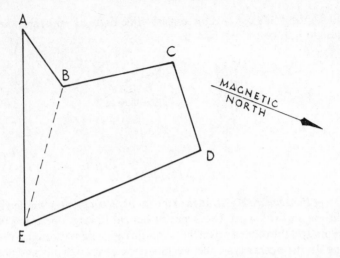

Figure 1.17 Example of compass traverse.

necessary vegetation is cleared so that points A and B, B and C, etc are mutually visible.

Assuming that A is a convenient point at which to commence operations the traverse is carried out as follows. From A the magnetic bearing of point B is taken with the prismatic compass. Wherever bearings are observed they are taken over the centre of the station, the ranging rod being removed for the purpose. After taking bearings it is important that the ranging rod is replaced in its correct position. The bearing from A to B is termed a 'foresight'.

The distance AB is then measured, and from B, stations A and C are observed with the compass. The bearing of A from B is termed a 'backsight', while the bearing of C from B is a 'foresight'. The survey is then continued by the measurement of the distance BC. At station C a backsight and foresight are observed and the distance CD then measured, and so on until each point on the traverse has been visited and the bearings and distances recorded.

If the land being surveyed is flat the horizontal distances will be the distances measured along the lines. But if the land is sloping, the slope of each line must also be measured, uphill or downhill, and the horizontal distance calculated by trigonometry or geometry. An alternative method for obtaining the horizontal distance is shown in Figure 1.19.

In the course of the traverse it may be that stations other than the immediate backsight and foresight can be seen from an observation station: for example, stations D and E may be visible from B. In this case bearings BD and BE should also be observed although distances need not be measured. These observations will serve as a useful check on the work.

Observed magnetic bearings should be booked in a field book, showing both forward and back bearings for each leg of the figure. The back bearing of each line should differ from the forward bearing by 180°, so that by comparing the two, errors can be detected, including, in particular, the presence of local magnetic influence which may distort the readings of the compass. Table 1.1 shows an example of the results of the bookings for the area in Figure 1.17.

Table 1.1 'Booking' a compass traverse.

From	To	Distance	Observed Bgs (Mag)			Accepted Bgs (Mag)	
Sta	Sta	(m)	Fwd	Back	Diff	Fwd	Back
A	B	325	33	212	179	$32\frac{1}{2}$	$212\frac{1}{2}$
B	C	615	327	140	187	327	147
C	D	490	45	231	186	51	231
D	E	1080	$136\frac{1}{2}$	$315\frac{1}{2}$	179	136	316
E	A	1070	248	67	181	$247\frac{1}{2}$	$67\frac{1}{2}$

It will be seen that for two of the lines, BC and CD, the differences between the forward and back bearings are significantly greater than 180°, and therefore there must be errors in the observations at either B, C or D. But since the differences between the forward and back bearings for the lines AB and CD are reasonably accurate, stations B and D can be assumed as free from error, thus locating the error at C. By discarding the observations at C and taking the means of forward and back bearings where there is tolerable agreement, we obtain the 'accepted' forward bearings which are tabulated in the last column of Table 1.1.

In any closed polygon (many-sided figure) of n sides, the sum of all the internal angles is equal to $(2n-4)$ right angles, or $180n-360°$. There are five internal angles in this figure and their values are obtained by taking the differences between the bearings of the two lines forming the angles. Thus the internal angle at A is the difference between bearing AE and AB. Table 1.2 shows the results of calculating the internal angles for the figure. These add up to 540°, which is correct, thus: $180 \times 5 - 360 = 540°$.

Table 1.2   Sum of internal angles.

Station	Bearings	Internal angle	
A	AE–AB	$67\frac{1}{2}$–$32\frac{1}{2}$	= 35
B	360–(BC–BA)	360–(327–$212\frac{1}{2}$)	= $245\frac{1}{2}$
C	CB–CD	147–51	= 96
D	DC–DE	231–136	= 95
E	ED–EA	316–$247\frac{1}{2}$	= $68\frac{1}{2}$
		Total	540

To draw or 'plot' the survey on paper a *protractor* is used, which is a drawing instrument graduated in degrees. The most convenient form of protractor is the circular protractor graduated from 0° to 360°.

On a sheet of drawing paper draw any line to represent the magnetic meridian, or north–south (NS) line. The direction of this line must be chosen so that the whole survey can be drawn on the paper; it is of little importance if the NS line is not parallel with the edge of the paper. To plot an angle with this meridian, or in other words to plot a compass bearing, the protractor is placed on the meridian line on the paper with its centre of radius over a marked point on the line and its 0°/180° axis coinciding with the NS meridian line. The angle to be plotted is marked with a tick on the paper at the edge of the protractor. The bearing is then plotted by ruling a line through the marked point on the meridian line and the tick.

Referring to Figure 1.18, choose some convenient point on the paper to represent station A, or the starting point of the survey. With the protractor on the NS line plot the mean bearing of station B as described above. Through point A draw a line parallel to the bearing so plotted, then along this line and from A, scale the distance AB. Point or station B has now been reached. Repeat the process by plotting the mean bearing of BC, on the NS line, and through B draw a line parallel to it. From B scale BC to reach point C. And so on for points D and E. The bearing EA and the distance EA, when plotted, ought to cut point A (i.e., the commencing point), exactly if a strictly accurate survey has been made and plotted. It is most probable that there will be some difference between the two positions of point A (i.e. EA will not cut point A).

If squared, or sectional, paper is available it is much easier to plot a survey by protractor. One set of lines is chosen as the north and south lines and the protractor can be used without further difficulty.

The difference in the two positions of A is called the 'closing error'.

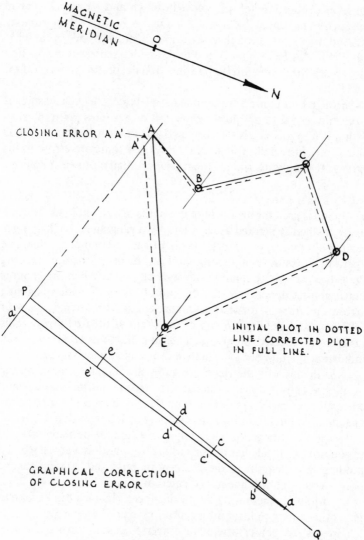

Figure 1.18 Plotting a compass traverse.

In Figure 1.18 the dotted lines represent the survey as initially plotted, ending with a point A' which ought to have coincided with A. AA' is therefore the closing error.

To adjust this difference, draw a line through AA' as indicated in Figure 1.18, and at point P on this line, conveniently clear of the plot, draw a line PQ at right angles to AA'P. Along PQ, scale off Pe equal to or in proportion to AE; and ed, dc, cb and ba equal to or in proportion to ED, DC, CB and BA. On AA'P, scale off Pa' equal to AA', join aa', and through e, d, c and b draw ee', dd', cc' and bb' parallel to AA'P. The lines e'e, d'd, c'c and b'b represent in direction and length the corrections to be applied to the plotted points, E,D,C and B.

Through B as plotted draw a line parallel to AA'P and measure off a distance equal to and in the direction of b'b. This point, marked with a dot in a circle, is the corrected position for B. Similarly C,D and E are corrected. This process does not eliminate errors in the survey. It simply distributes them proportionately to each station.

1.3.2 Chain Survey

The chain is used for measuring the lengths of straight lines. The line to be chained is marked at each end by a ranging rod. Chaining is carried out by two operators. Starting from one end of the line, one operator drags the chain along the line, the other operator holding the other end of the chain at the starting point. When the chain is taut, the first operator marks the end of the chain with a chaining arrow and moves forward a chain length, the second operator following and holding his end of the chain at the first arrow. This process is repeated along the line, the number of arrows used indicating the number of complete chain lengths measured.

Used in this way the chain measures the actual distances on the ground. As all final measurements are made in the horizontal plane, corrections to measured distances on the ground must be made if the ground is sloping. Land which is sloping at 1:100, or flatter, may be treated as flat. For greater slopes the correction can be made either by trigonometrical calculation or, where the land is very steep, by holding short lengths of the chain horizontal and locating change points with a plumb line as indicated in Figure 1.19.

In addition to measuring simple distances, chaining can be used to give other topographical information by recording the distances or 'chainages' of points where the traverse crosses features such as

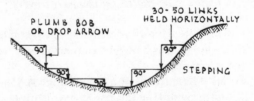

Figure 1.19 Chaining over steep ground.

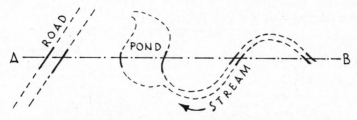

Figure 1.20 Chaining to locate topographical information.

boundaries, the two edges of a road or track, the banks of a stream, and so on (Figure 1.20).

A chain traverse can also be used to locate features visible from the line of the traverse but not lying on the line. This can be done in two ways. The first is by the method of triangulation by which a point can be located in relation to two fixed points if its distances from the two fixed points are known. In the example in Figure 1.21 points A, B and

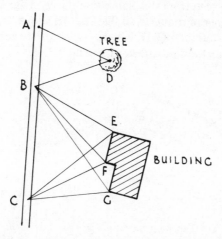

Figure 1.21 Locating detail by triangulation.

C are fixed points on a road, and features on the side of the road can be located by measuring AD, BD, BE, BF, BG, CE, CF and CG. More will be said about triangulation in section 1.3.4.

The second method of locating features adjacent to a traverse line is by means of *off-sets*. An off-set from a traverse line to a point is the perpendicular distance of the point from the line. In this method, the chainage of each off-set is recorded and its length is measured. Figure 1.22 illustrates off-sets, and methods for setting out right angles in the field are given in section 1.3.9.

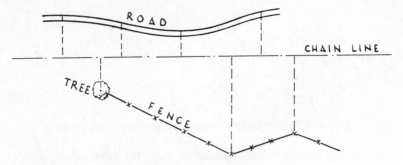

Figure 1.22 Locating detail by off-sets.

By taking a number of suitably chosen traverses over an area, and chaining along each traverse picking up features on each side of the line as the chaining proceeds, a detailed topographical plan of the area can be made. An example of a chain survey is shown in Figure 1.23. It will be seen from this figure that the chainage lines form the sides of a number of triangles, so that starting with a known baseline AB, the other stations—C, D, E and so on—can be established by the triangulation method described in section 1.3.4.

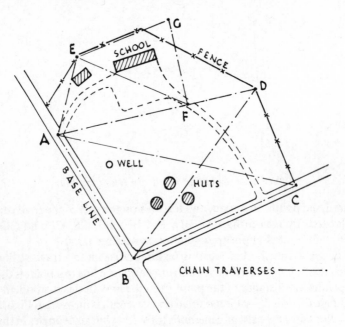

Figure 1.23 Example of chain survey.

The 'booking' of a chain survey is usually carried out in a special chaining field book which is bound like a reporter's or secretary's notebook and which has two parallel lines about 12 mm apart or a single line ruled down the centre of each page. Booking starts at the bottom of the page and all points and distances on the chain line are entered between the lines or on the line in the centre. Offset detail to the left of the traverse (moving along the line) is entered on the left-hand side of the page and detail to the right on the right-hand side. The line being booked must be clearly marked in the field book and a new page should be started for each line. Before leaving the field a sketch should be made of the framework of the survey showing clearly the positions of all the lines in the traverse with their end points identified by letters. An example of booking is shown in Figure 1.24.

1.3.3 Intersection
The position of a point in relation to two or more known points can be fixed by *intersection*. If Figure 1.25(a) represents the positions on a plan of three known points A, B and C, the position of a fourth point D can be plotted either by taking compass bearings of D from A, B and C, or by measuring the distances AD, BD and CD.

By the first method three lines are drawn from A, B and C representing the bearings AD, BD and CD, and where they intersect will be the location of D. In practice it is unlikely that there will be perfect intersection and the three rays will form a small triangle, so that D can be located in the centre of the triangle.

By the second method three circular arcs are drawn with a drawing compass centred at A with radius AD, at B with radius BD and at C with radius CD. D will then be located in the area of intersection of these three arcs.

1.3.4 Triangulation
Triangulation is another method for locating positions and depends upon the trigonometrical principle that a triangle can be defined and therefore drawn on paper from the following information:

(a) the length and direction of one side and the lengths of the two other sides; or
(b) the length and direction of one side and the values of two internal angles.

This is illustrated in Figure 1.25(b) and (c), where the side AB is known in length and direction. In Figure 1.25(b) lengths AC and BC

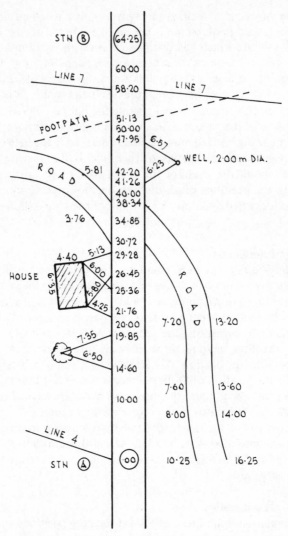

Figure 1.24 Booking a chain survey.

are known, and in Figure 1.25(c) the internal angles BAC and ABC are known. In each case the position of the apex C is determined by the method of intersection described above.

Triangulation consists of locating a number of points over an area by building up triangles which can be plotted in this way. Referring to Figure 1.23 and taking AB as the base line for the survey, point C is established by intersection from A and B. Having completed the

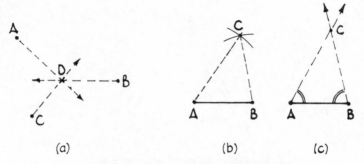

Figure 1.25 Intersection and triangulation.

triangle ABC, the point D can then be fixed in relation to A and C thus constructing the triangle ACD. Points E and G can be located with reference to A and F (which is a measured distance from A) by the same method of triangulation. Once the framework has been established and the key points located, then detail can be filled in either by compass traversing or chain traversing as already described, or by plane tabling (see section 1.3.5).

1.3.5 Plane Tabling

The *plane table* can be used in two different ways. It can be used for the complete production of maps and is a very useful instrument for rapid map-making in exploratory surveys. Alternatively it can be used to fill in detail after control points have been fixed by some other method such as triangulation. The great advantage of plane tabling is that the map or plan is produced as the survey proceeds without measurements and bookings, thus reducing the chance of important features being omitted. The disadvantages of the method are that work is impossible in persistent wind or rain and that the scale of the map or plan must be determined before the work begins.

To survey the area indicated in Figure 1.26 by plane table the following operations are carried out. On the table top, stretch and secure by drawing pins a stout piece of drawing paper, or—having damped the drawing paper—stretch it and secure the edges with drawing pins under the board. This prevents the paper from moving, and the wind from getting underneath. The survey is to be commenced from point A and the table is therefore set up over A, the table top being rotated so that the paper is in such a position that the whole area to be surveyed can be drawn on it. At this point it is necessary to decide on the scale of plotting, and to ensure that the most distant point can be located on the paper. Clamp the table top

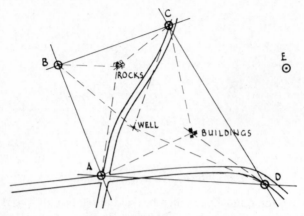

Figure 1.26 Plane table survey.

and level it with the aid of the spirit level. Place the box compass on the paper, with the compass needle pointing to the centre division of its scale, and draw a pencil line along the outside of the trough. Repeat this procedure on another part of the paper. The lines so drawn represent the magnetic meridian and are marked with a north point. If a military type prismatic compass is used it is opened until the lid is flat on the paper and the compass is then rotated until the north point coincides with fixed markings or lines on the compass case and the north line can then be transferred to the paper.

At a convenient point on the paper choose a point to represent station A and mark it on the paper with a finely sharpened pencil with a dot in a small circle labelled A. To observe other stations B, C, D etc. from A these other stations must be clearly visible features, or marked by ranging rods. Next place the alidade on the board with its ruled edge intersecting point A, the eye end towards the observer and the object end towards station B. Use of the alidade can be greatly facilitated by placing a pin or fine sewing needle at point A on the board. The alidade can then be swivelled round the pin. The alidade is moved until the hairline in the object end coincides with the rod or other feature at B. Draw a pencil line on the paper along the bevelled edge of the alidade through A. This line is the direction of AB. The distance AB is then measured by chaining, taping or pacing and, using the chosen scale for the plot, B is plotted on the board and marked with a dot and small circle and labelled B.

The plane table is now transferred to station B on the ground and set up over it. Level the table, lay the compass along or on the NS line drawn on the paper, rotate the board until the compass needle comes to rest at the centre of its scale and then clamp the table top. Press a needle into point B. Lay the alidade along the line BA as drawn on the paper and sight through the vanes. If the hairline in the object end of the rule does not cut the ranging rod at station A, *do not* draw a new line. Make sure that the alidade is resting along the pencil line BA exactly, unclamp the table top and move it slightly until the hairline cuts the rod at A. Clamp the table. Rotate the alidade about the needle at B, intersect the rod at station C, and draw a line along the bevelled edge. Measure the distance BC and plot station C on the paper. The table is now carried forward to station C and exactly the same process is repeated.

The instrument in every case is first set up *roughly* by compass and then exactly by sighting back along the line drawn from the last station. This method is called 'setting by back rays'. Each station having been visited and the distances having been measured and plotted, it will probably be found that the final ray will not cut the starting point exactly, in other words there is a 'closing error'. The closing error can be adjusted by the method described in section 1.3.1. In this way the plane table has been used to establish the main control points of the survey.

The plane table can then be used for plotting as much detail as is required on the survey by setting it up at each station in turn and locating features by intersections. Figure 1.26 shows examples of intersection rays from the four control stations to locate detail such as rocks, a well and buildings. No point should be considered satisfactorily fixed until it is intersected by at least three rays, except those points which are comparatively near to the base of the survey.

1.3.6 Resection

Sometimes after completing plane table observations at a number of control stations it is found that a further control is needed. Referring to Figure 1.26 (in which the controls A,B,C and D have been established and triangulation has been completed), suppose it is now found that a fourth control station E is required. E can be fixed and plotted by *resection*, which amounts to setting up the plane table at point E, observing A,B,C and D and drawing rays from their respective plotted positions. The four rays so drawn will intersect giving a location on the plan for station E.

1.3.7 Triangle of Error

It often happens that the rays from control stations observed either by compass bearings or by plane table plotting do not intersect exactly. In Figure 1.27 the rays from three control stations, A, B and C were shown for two observed points X and Y, X being within the triangle ABC and Y outside it. The small cross-hatched triangular area in each case is called the 'triangle of error'.

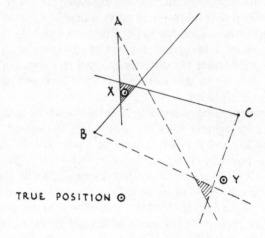

Figure 1.27 Triangle of error.

The following are the rules for the correction of this error:

(a) If the triangle of error is inside the triangle formed by the three points from which the rays have been drawn, the true position of the point is inside the triangle of error. If the triangle of error is outside the triangle formed by the three fixed points, the true position will be found to be outside the triangle of error.

(b) If the observed point is outside the triangle of error, its true position will be either to the right or left of all the rays when facing the fixed points.

(c) The true position must be located so that its distance from the rays is proportional to their length.

Following these rules the true positions of X and Y are indicated in Figure 1.27.

Having selected the true position of a station X, a trial is then made to see if it has been plotted correctly. The plane table is set up over the station and the alidade is placed so that its rule edge lines up the station X as plotted and one of the control stations A, B or C. The table top is unclamped and rotated until the selected control station is intersected through the sight vanes of the alidade. The table top is then clamped and the alidade placed over point X and each of the remaining stations, being moved if necessary to obtain a correct sighting. Rays are then re-drawn from each of these other control stations and if X has been plotted correctly, these rays will now all intersect at one point. If the correction is not correct a smaller triangle of error will appear and the process can be repeated.

1.3.8 Rapid Distance Measurement

Distances can be measured by the solution of an isosceles triangle (a triangle with two equal sides intersecting at the 'apex', the third side being known as the 'base'). If the distant object is conceived as at the apex of a triangle, the base of which is known, it remains to measure the angle at the apex or the angles at the base in order to find the distance from apex to base. Rangefinders measure the angles in various ways and translate the measure into distance. The base length may be at the point of observation or at the distant station. This method of measurement is known as tacheometry.

If the apex of the triangle is at the point of observation, the angle *sub-tended* by the base at the distant station can be measured by a theodolite or sextant. The base itself must be at right angles to the line to be measured. The angle sub-tended between the ends of the base is then observed. If this angle is denoted by a the distance, D, is given by the formula:

$$D = \frac{B}{2 \tan a/2}$$

where B is the length of the base.

For sub-tended angles up to 5° the following approximation can be used. Reduce the observed angle to seconds (1° = 60 min, 1 min = 60 sec). If the base is measured in metres then:

D in metres is equal to 206 265 × base divided by the angle in seconds

Example

Observed, the angle sub-tended by a base of 2 m to be
$$5° = 5 \times 60 \times 60 = 18\,000 \text{ sec.}$$

$$D = \frac{206\,265 \times 2}{18\,000} = 22.92 \text{ m}$$

*Table 1.3 Distances by sub-tense angles for 2 m base.**

Angle ° '	Distance (m)	Diff per 1' (in m)	Angle ° '	Distance (m)	Diff per 1' (in m)	Angle ° '	Distance (m)	Diff per 1' (in m)	Angle ° '	Distance (m)	Diff per 1' (in m)
5 00	22·90	0·08	4 00	28·64	0·12	3 00	38·19	0·22	2 00	57·29	0·50
4 55	23·29	0·08	3 55	29·25	0·13	2 55	39·28	0·23	1 55	59·78	0·54
4 50	23·69	0·08	3 50	29·88	0·13	2 50	40·44	0·24	1 50	62·50	0·60
4 45	24·11	0·09	3 45	30·55	0·14	2 45	41·66	0·26	1 45	65·48	0·65
4 40	24·54	0·09	3 40	31·24	0·15	2 40	42·96	0·28	1 40	68·75	0·72
4 35	24·99	0·09	3 35	31·97	0·15	2 35	44·35	0·30	1 35	72·37	0·80
4 30	25·45	0·10	3 30	32·73	0·16	2 30	45·83	0·32	1 30	76·39	0·90
4 25	25·93	0·10	3 25	33·53	0·17	2 25	47·19	0·34	1 25	80·88	1·01
4 20	26·43	0·10	3 20	34·37	0·18	2 20	49·10	0·36	1 20	85·94	1·15
4 15	26·95	0·11	3 15	35·25	0·19	2 15	50·92	0·39	1 15	91·67	1·31
4 10	27·49	0·11	3 10	36·18	0·20	2 10	52·88	0·42	1 10	98·22	1·51
4 05	28·05	0·12	3 05	37·16	0·21	2 05	55·00	0·46	1 05	105·77	1·76
4 00	28·64		3 00	38·19		2 00	57·29		1 00	114·59	

*Table 1.3 gives distances in metres for sub-tended angles from 5° to 1° at intervals of 5 min for a base length of 2 m.

1.3.9 Setting out Right Angles

There are two situations to be considered in setting out right angles:

(a) dropping a perpendicular from a point to a line; and
(b) setting out a line at right angles from a point on a line (see Figure 1.28).

Case 1
(a) If P is the point from which the perpendicular is to be drawn (Figure 1.28(a)), place the end of a tape or chain at P and describe an arc with the tape or chain to cut the line at A and B. Bisect AB at Q and the angle PQA will be a right angle. If the ground is smooth and the tape can be swung freely, Q can be located by swinging the tape and noting the minimum reading at which it crosses the line. This occurs when the tape is perpendicular to the line, which gives the position of Q. Q can also be found by shortening the tape until the arc just touches the line.

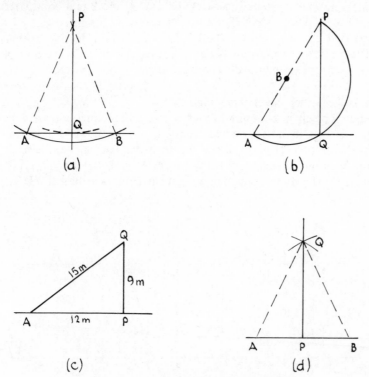

Figure 1.28 Setting out right angles.

(b) Referring to Figure 1.28(b), run the tape from P to any point A on the line. Bisect PA at B, and with centre B and radius BA strike an arc to cut the line at Q. Then the angle AQP is a right angle being the angle in a semi-circle.

Case 2

(a) Cross staff. Set up a cross staff at the point on the line at which the right angle is to be set out and turn the staff until a site is obtained along the line and a second site at right angles to it.

(b) Optical square. This is used in a similar manner to the cross staff, by siting along the line and perpendicular to it (see section 1.2.11).

(c) A triangle with sides in the proportion 3:4:5 has a right angle opposite to the longest side. To construct a right angle at P (Figure 1.28(c)) a triangle of sides 9 m, 12 m and 15 m can be constructed as follows. From P set out 12 m along the line to point A. With the zero of the tape at P and the 24 m mark on the tape at A, pull the tape out in the direction of Q. Take the 9 m mark on the tape in the hand and ensuring that the tape is securely held at A and P pull both parts taut to Q. The angle APQ must, as a result, be a right angle.

(d) Referring to Figure 1.28(d), take A and B on the line so that PA = PB. Strike arcs from A and B with equal radii to intersect at Q. As a result the angle APQ is a right angle.

1.3.10 Setting out Building Plots

Suppose that it is required to set out seven building plots each 40 m × 20 m, with a 12 m roadway running through the plots, as shown in Figure 1.29. The direction of the line ABCD having been selected on the ground, ranging rods are set up at A and D. Intermediate rods are set up by siting through or 'ranging in' from A to the rod at D. At

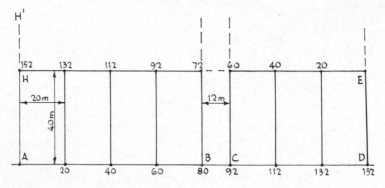

Figure 1.29 Setting out building plots.

A, a right angle with the line AD is set out by one of the methods described in the previous section.

The direction of the right angle is marked by a rod at H' and the distance of 40 m is measured along the line AH' and a rod is set up at H, 40 m from A. Measurements are now made along the line ABCD and pegs driven in at 20 m, 40 m, 60 m, 80 m, 92 m, 112 m, 132 m and 152 m. At points B, C and D, right angles with the line ABCD are set out. On the perpendicular line from D measure 40 m to give point E. Range a line with rods from E to H. Starting from E, measure distances towards H and drive in pegs at 20 m, 40 m, 60 m, 72 m, 92 m, 112 m, 132 m and 152 m. The pegs at 60 m and 72 m should lie on the perpendiculars from C and B and the peg at 152 m should coincide with H. It will be found that there will be some differences caused by the inequalities of the ground and by unequal pull on the tape. If the differences are large the setting out must be checked but if they are small they can be adjusted between plots.

1.3.11   Inaccessible Distances

Case 1 in Figure 1.30 may be a pond or standing crops, where visibility along the line AB is not obstructed but it is not possible to measure the line directly. At C and D set out two equal off-sets CE and DF perpendicular to AB. The distance EF is then measured to supply the missing length CD. As a check further off-sets GK and HL can be off-set on the other side and KL measured to determine GH.

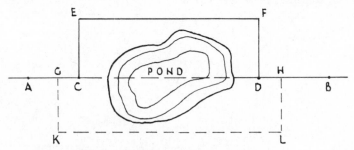

Figure 1.30 Distance across a pond.

Case 2 in Figure 1.31 is the case of an obstacle such as a river which cannot be taped or chained across, but where points can be seen from both sides. The figure shows four different ways of measuring distances across the river. In the first three the required distance GH is shown as the perpendicular distance across the river and in the fourth it is an oblique distance. All four methods can be used for

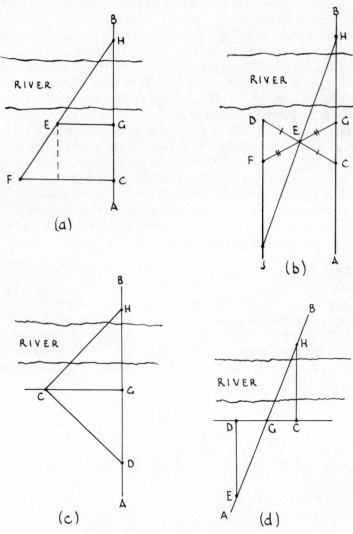

Figure 1.31 Distances across a river.

measuring distances across the river in any direction and need not necessarily be the perpendicular distances. In each case the direction of the line of measurement is indicated by AB.

In the first case (see Figure 1.31(a)) the line HG is produced back to any point C using ranging rods. Set out lines at G and C at right angles to line AB. On the perpendicular from G select a point E and from the perpendicular at C locate F so that H, E and F are in line. Measure the distances GC, GE and CF. Then the required distance is given by:

$$GH = \frac{GE \times GC}{CF - EG}$$

In Figure 1.31(b) produce HG back to a point C. Choose another point D at about the same distance from the river bank as G. Measure the distance CD and mark the centre of CD with a ranging rod at E. Range a further point F in with E and G and make the distances GE and EF equal. On the line DF (extended) locate point J so that H, E and J are in line. Then GH =JF.

In the third example (see Figure 1.31(c)) a line GC is set out at right angles to AB, C being chosen at a convenient point. At C set out another line CD at right angles to HC, D being the point of intersection with AB. Measure the distances GC and GD. Then:

$$GH = \frac{(GC)^2}{GD}$$

In the fourth method (see Figure 1.31 (d)) select a line through G parallel to the river bank and locate point C so that CH is perpendicular to this line. Measure the distance CG and locate D a convenient distance on the other side of G. From D set out a perpendicular DE to intersect AB at E. Then:

$$GH = \frac{EG \times GC}{GD}$$

1.3.12 Determination of True North
True North can be determined from the Sun by using a watch, but this method is not suitable in the tropics (i.e., too near the equator). Lay the watch flat with the hour hand pointing to the Sun; in the northern hemisphere a line halfway between the hour hand and 12 noon runs True South. In the southern hemisphere point 12 noon to the Sun and True North is halfway between this and the hour hand.

True North can also be found using a plane table. After levelling the plane table and securing paper to the board, a 'style', or marker can be made in the following manner: press the blunt end of a well-sharpened pencil, or a ball-pointed pen, into some heated sealing wax which has been dropped on a fairly large round coin. When the 'style' is complete the pencil must stand quite 'plumb' on the centre of the coin. Place the 'style' on the plane table with a pencil mark around the edge of the coin. Remove the style and find the centre of the circle so defined. Replace the style exactly. In the morning, say at about 9 or 10 a.m. Sun time, make a pencil mark on the paper at the tip of the shadow made by the style. Remove the style, rule a straight line from the mark just made to the centre of the circle. Take a pair of compasses, and with the centre of the circle as centre and the distance from it to the mark of the shadow as radius describe an arc of a circle. Replace the style. In the afternoon at about 2–3 p.m. Sun time examine the shadow, watch it until the apex of the shadow just cuts the pencil arc. Mark this point and draw a line from the centre of the arc to a point exactly half way between the two shadow points. This line is on the true meridian (i.e., it runs exactly north and south). This method is fairly accurate if carefully done.

The 'magnetic variation' is the difference between north as located by a magnetic compass and True North. This variation varies over the Earth's surface with variations in the Earth's magnetic field. On many maps the magnetic variation is given and therefore True North can be determined in relation to compass north.

If this information is not available an approximate method for determining it may be useful. With a prismatic compass observe the centre of the Sun's disc as it appears over the horizon at sunrise and again observe the Sun's disc as it disappears at sunset. The observations should be taken in flat open country. Subtract the bearing of the evening reading from 360, and then add to this difference the reading of the morning's bearings. Take half of this sum and compare it with the morning's reading. If the morning's reading is greater than half of the sum the difference is the variation west, if the bearing is less, the difference is the variation east. This is a very rough method, but it gives an approximation which can be useful on occasions.

1.4　LEVELLING

1.4.1　Uses of Levelling

The term 'levelling' in survey means using a levelling instrument to determine heights with reference to some common datum. For this purpose a level is used in conjunction with a staff, as described in section 1.4.3. Levelling is carried out for one or more of the following purposes:

(a) To determine the differences in heights between specific points, as might be required in the preliminary survey for a road or pipeline.

(b) To define the profile of the land surface along a given line, which might be the longitudinal section of a road alignment or the cross-section of a valley.

(c) To describe the topography of an area by levelling on a grid or on spot heights, for plotting on a map or plan, with contours if required.

Levelling starts from a starting point with a known or assumed height and follows a traverse, finally closing on the starting point, which thus provides a check on accuracy. The traverse may be a *closed* traverse in which the route followed is a circuit, or an *open* traverse to the end of a line and back.

1.4.2 Setting up the Instrument

When using a level it is essential that it is properly set up on its tripod. A position should be chosen such that there are no obstructions on the line of sight of the telescope towards the points to be observed, and if possible at such an elevation that the line of sight will be neither above nor below the staff at all the points to be observed. To ensure steadiness, the tripod legs should have a fairly wide spread, and on sloping ground two legs should be placed downhill.

There are three principal types of level, the dumpy, the tilting and the automatic level, and the setting up procedure is different for each type:

(a) *Dumpy level.* The ordinary dumpy level consists of a telescope which is rigidly attached at right angles to a vertical spindle that can rotate in a bearing carried in a levelling head with three or four levelling screws. The telescope contains a screw-focusing eye piece and diaphragm with cross hairs or lines, at the viewing end. The cross hairs must be made clearly visible by focusing the eye piece. A focusing thumbscrew, usually on the side of the telescope, adjusts the telescope for viewing distant objects. A bubble tube is mounted on top of the telescope and in line with it, with a small bubble tube at right angles. Before finally pressing the legs of the tripod into the ground the instrument is brought nearly to the level in all directions by moving the tripod legs in or out, or by swinging them laterally. This preliminary levelling will be sufficiently accomplished when the whole of the large bubble is visible in any position of the telescope. The legs are then pressed in firmly, and the final and accurate levelling is carried out with the levelling screws. This is done by placing the telescope parallel to two levelling screws, levelling up with these screws and then placing it at right angles to this direction and levelling up again with the other screw or screws. The main bubble should now stay in the centre of its travel through 360° of rotation of the instrument.

(b) *Tilting level*. The telescope focusing is the same as for the dumpy level. For tilting instruments with levelling screws, the procedure for levelling is the same as for the dumpy level, except that instead of using the main bubble on the telescope as a guide, the level is set approximately by using a small circular bubble. For instruments with a ball-and-socket base the approximate levelling is also done with reference to the small circular bubble by tilting the head on the ball-and-socket and then fixing the clamp. Exact levelling of the main bubble is then achieved by adjusting a tilting screw on the telescope for each separate sight on the staff.

(c) *Automatic level*. The telescope is focused as before. The automatic or self-setting level needs only to be set up using the small circular bubble, accurate levelling on the line of sight being obtained by the action of gravity on a suspended mirror system in the telescope. The instrument will not work unless it is within the range of its automatic travel, and this is indicated by the proper centring of the circular bubble.

1.4.3   Method

The instrument is set up in a convenient position and at a convenient distance from the starting point, on which the staff man holds the staff. The reading on the staff (where the cross wires cut it) is noted and entered in the special level book in the column headed 'back-sight'. The staff man then takes his staff to various points indicated by the surveyor, the levels of which are required, and the readings of the staff are recorded in the 'intermediate' column with appropriate notes in the 'remarks' column. When no more information can be obtained from this set-up the instrument must be moved; before moving the instrument the staff man is directed to a convenient spot, the staff reading is taken and recorded in the 'foresight' column. The staff man stands fast and the surveyor moves his instrument to some convenient position, sets up the instrument and records the reading of the staff under 'back-sight'. The staff man then moves to other positions, the readings are recorded as intermediate, the last 'shot' is recorded as foresight and the process continues in this manner until all levels are taken.

1.4.4   Booking

There are two systems of booking in common use: the line of collimation method and the rise and fall method. Examples of the two methods are given in Table 1.4. In each case the back, intermediate and foresights have been entered as described. Levelling is usually carried out in metres, and the height of the starting point in this example has been assumed at 100·000 m which is entered in the book in the column headed 'reduced level'.

In both methods of booking, the levels are *reduced* or correlated to the assumed datum of starting level. In the *line of collimation* method (I in Table 1.4), there is a column for the 'Height of instrument'. For the first position of the instrument this is obtained by adding the backsight on Station A to the assumed height (i.e., 100·000 + 2·326 giving 102·326 m as the height of the instrument). From the height of the instrument all intermediate readings are subtracted as well as all foresight readings. The results will give the level relative to the starting point of the points on which the readings were taken. Thus 102·326 − 3·784 = 98·542 m is the level of the bed of the stream. 102·326 − 0·835 = 101·491 m is the level of the farm gate. 102·326 − 0·924 = 101·402 m is the level of the point B round which the instrument was moved. To this last level the backsight on B of 3·792 must be added to give the new height of instrument 105·194 m, from which the intermediate and foresight readings taken from B will be subtracted. The process continues until the 'book is reduced'. The rule is: intermediate and foresights are subtracted from the height of instrument. The backsight is added to the last reduced level to get a new height of instrument.

Table 1.4 Examples of level booking.

I. *Line of collimation*

Station	Backsight	Inter-mediate	Foresight	Height of instrument	Reduced level	Remarks
A	2·326			102·326	100·000	Assumed height of starting point
		3·784			98·542	Bed of stream
		0·835			101·491	At gate to farm
		2·640			99·686	Road junction
B	3·792		0·924	105·194	101·402	Corner of field
		3·821			101·373	Centre of road
			2·773		102·421	Foot of telephone pole
	6·118		3·697		102·421	
	3·697				100·000	
Rise	2·421			Rise	2·421	

II. Rise and fall

Station	Backsight	Inter-mediate	Foresight	Rise +	Fall −	Reduced level	Remarks
A	2·326					100·000	Assumed height of starting point
		3·784			1·458	98·542	Bed of stream
		0·835		2·949		101·491	At gate to farm
		2·640			1·805	99·686	Road junction
B	3·792		0·924	1·716		101·402	Corner of field
		3·821			0·029	101·373	Centre of road
			2·773	1·048		102·421	Foot of telephone pole
	6·118		3·697	5·713	3·292	102·421	
	3·697			3·292		100·000	
Rise	2·421		Rise	2·421	Rise	2·421	

The arithmetic in the line of collimation method can be checked by adding the backsights and adding the foresights, and subtracting one total from the other. The difference should be equal to the difference between the first and last reduced levels.

In the *rise and fall* method (II in Table 1.4), there are two columns headed 'Rise' and 'Fall', and the bookings are reduced in the following way.

The difference between the backsight on A and the intermediate sight on the bed of the stream is 2·326 − 3·784 = − 1·458 m. The negative sign indicates the bed of the stream is lower than A and the fall of 1·458 m is entered in the Fall column. This fall is subtracted from the assumed level at A to give the level at the bed of the stream; thus 100·000 − 1·458 = 98·542 m.

The difference between the first intermediate sight and the second intermediate sight at the gate is 3·784 − 0·835 = +2·949 m. This is positive, is entered in the Rise column and is added to the previous reduced level to give the level at the gate; thus 98·542 + 2·949 = 101·491 m. The third intermediate sight is a fall of 1·805 m giving a reduced level (RL) of 99·686 m, and the foresight on station B is a rise of 1·716 m, giving the level at station B as 101·402 m. After moving the instrument the RL of the next intermediate sight at the centre of the road is found from the difference between the backsight on B and the intermediate sight reading, or 3·792 − 3·821 = − 0·029 m. This fall is subtracted from the RL of B to give the RL of the centre of the road (101·402 − 0·029 = 101·373 m). The reduction of levels continues in this way.

The arithmetic in the rise and fall method can be checked by adding the backsights and foresights as in the line of collimation method. It can further be checked by adding the rises and adding the falls, and again the difference between the totals should be equal to the difference between the first and last reduced levels.

The rise and fall method is a little more laborious than the line of collimation method, because it involves more computation. But it is a method favoured by many surveyors because in a closed traverse of a series of stations which can be levelled twice, once on the outward journey and once on the return, the sums of the rises and falls in each leg between successive stations should be equal. Thus levelling errors can more easily be located.

1.4.5 Closing Error

In a closed levelling traverse which returns to its starting point there will usually be a small difference between the assumed level of the starting point and its reduced level at the end. This is known as the *closing error*. The greater the distance levelled the greater the closing error is likely to be. The amount of permissible error will depend upon the degree of accuracy required. For topographical survey work, accuracy is defined in terms of the total distance levelled from a starting point and back to the starting point. If the total distance, measured in km is d, the permissible error in mm can be expressed as $k\sqrt{d}$, where k is a factor depending upon the order of accuracy required. A normally accepted value for k is 20.

For many field operations a lower order of accuracy is adequate. For example, suppose levelling is carried out for the design of a pipeline from a source in the hills to a point in a valley below, with the following results:

Starting point in valley, assumed	100.000 m
Level at source	208·560 m
RL at starting point	100·274 m
Distance levelled, one way	5 km
Closing error	274 mm

Here the closing error is 274 mm in a total fall of 108 m; an error of 0·25 per cent. For the hydraulic design of the pipeline this magnitude of error can usually be accepted. In this case the error would have fallen within a limit defined by $100\sqrt{d}\,(= 100\sqrt{10} = 316$ mm$)$.

For levelling over flat country, say for the design of an irrigation channel where the total fall over a distance 5 km might be about 600 mm, a closing error of 316 mm would clearly not be acceptable, and much greater accuracy would be needed. Here $20\sqrt{d}$ or even $10\sqrt{d}$ would be more appropriate.

CHAPTER 2
Engineering Materials

2.1 EARTHWORKS

2.1.1 General

Earthworks is the word used for all operations involving excavating, moving and placing earth or ground materials. This includes excavation for foundations, for laying pipes or other equipment or for cuttings, channels, waterways and similar work. It also includes laying and placing material to form platforms, embankments and other structures raised above ground level.

2.1.2 Type of Ground

Ground material is described as 'hard', 'medium' or 'soft' in relation to the ease with which it can be excavated. Solid rock is usually impossible to break and move without mechanical equipment or explosives. Highly compacted gravels, sands and clays can be very hard to work. Soft soils such as soft clays, marls, silts and sands are usually easy to work by hand. Apart from hard rock most ground in areas that support vegetation consists of a layer of top soil which contains a high proportion of organic material and which is not suitable for engineering use. Below this the sub-soil contains much less organic constituents and can be used for engineering work. Many soils contain stones and boulders and when these are very large they can cause great difficulties in moving and handling.

2.1.3 Physical Properties of Soil

Soil is produced by the disintegration of rocky portions of the Earth's crust. This disintegration is brought about by weathering, which may be caused by the effects of frost, rain and temperature change, or by the movement of particles by wind, ice or water; or it may be caused by the chemical action of weak acids in solution in water in the soil. The final product of these physical and chemical activities is the clay, sand, marl, gravel or other soil which can be used to support or make structures. Soils may be divided into three main classes:

(a) Coarse-grained or non-cohesive soils.
(b) Fine-grained or cohesive soils.
(c) Organic soils (e.g., peat).

Coarse-grained soils are composed of rock fragments varying in size from boulders down to gravel and sand. Quartz, because of its hardness, is the predominant mineral in the composition of many gravels and sands. Fine-grained soils include the types generally known as silts and clays. Clays are fine-grained soils which possess plasticity, especially when moist. The top soil at any site nearly always contains organic matter which occurs partly as partially decomposed vegetable matter and partly as humus, a dark amorphous material derived from the decomposition of organic material. Peats and organic soils should generally be avoided for construction purposes. The ideal foundation materials are sands, gravels, stiff clays, cemented soils and rock, although rock may not be satisfactory because of the expense of excavating it.

2.1.4 Tools
The most common tools used in hand earthworks are the spade, pick-axe, shovel and, in many parts of the world, the hoe. The most useful carrier for moving materials is the wheelbarrow, but in many countries this sort of work is done with head pans or baskets. For shifting large stones and boulders the crowbar is a useful implement.

2.1.5 Excavation
Excavation may be temporary (e.g., for foundations) or permanent (e.g., for cuttings or channels). In most firm soils temporary excavations can have vertical sides. For permanent work in soft soil the sides should be sloped. If the sides are in contact with water as in a canal, the slopes should be flatter than if the sides were dry. Suitable side slopes for average soils would be 2:1 (horizontal:vertical) for cuttings, and 3:1 for channel sides in contact with water. For heavy clays these slopes can be steeper, and for loose sandy soils they should be flatter.

2.1.6 Fill
Earth placed to form a raised mound or embankment is known as 'fill'. When natural material is excavated, its volume usually increases owing to the presence of voids or empty spaces, so that when it is placed to form an embankment it needs to be compacted to restore its natural stability and bearing capacity. Compaction can occur

naturally with time through settlement, or it can be brought about artificially by placing the material in layers and watering and rolling. Compaction and settlement will bring about a reduction in volume so that the top of any placed earthworks should be higher than its required final height. The amount of reduction in height will vary with the type of material and its condition, but usually about 5 per cent additional height should be allowed before compaction and settlement.

2.1.7 Mud Walls

Mud, or earth consisting of fairly uniform silty clay, is a popular material for walls in many parts of the world. In arid regions where there is little rainfall it is an amazingly durable material and has relatively good heat insulation. The excavated silty clay is mixed with water to the consistency of a stiff paste and is either placed in handfulls to build the wall, or it may be used to make Sun-dried bricks or blocks, subsequently to be used for the construction of the wall with wet mud mortar. To reduce cracking when drying, straw is often included in the mud mixture (see also section 2.2.1).

2.2 BRICKS

2.2.1 The Manufacture of Bricks

Brick earth may be clay, loam, or even such a material as ant heap. A firm rule is that materials must not be taken from places where salt water is found; salt, being soluble, makes poor bricks. Sand mixed with clay in the proportion 1 sand: 4 clay may be suitable, if the clay is particularly prone to cracking. All roots, gravel, lumps, etc. must be removed. To test if earth is suitable for brick-making, mould a trial brick, and place it in shade until dry; if it hardens without cracking, this is a fair indication of suitability. About 2 m³ of brick earth are required for 1000 bricks.

Brick earth is mixed in a pit with water. People can work the mass with hoes and can (and often do) trample and tread it with bare feet to make it plastic, though some simple equipment is now becoming available to make it plastic.

Moulds are made of any hardwood, 25 mm thick, and can be arranged as in Figure 2.1. The internal dimensions of the mould must be about 10 per cent larger than those of the brick required as it contracts on drying. Some experimentation may be necessary here. The length of a finished brick should equal twice its width, plus the thickness of one joint of mortar. Example: 215 mm × 102·5 mm × 65 mm. Good bricks must be moulded on a table; rough bricks are often moulded direct on the ground.

Sun-dried, 'green' bricks, mud bricks, or 'adobe', etc., are made and dried in the same way as ordinary bricks, but are often moulded on the ground and not on a table. Sun-dried bricks measure 305 mm × 215 mm × 215 mm, or 305 mm × 200 mm × 200 mm, or 305 mm × 150 mm × 150 mm. In Kenya 305 mm × 150 mm × 200 mm brick has been used, in other places a 460 mm × 215 mm × 215 mm. Large bricks can be too large and heavy to handle, and they can only be made with particularly amenable clay.

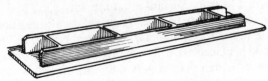

Figure 2.1 Brick mould.

The mould must be cleaned before use, either by dipping in water or by sprinkling with fine sand on the inside. The tempered material is pressed and crammed into the mould by hand, and any surplus material is then swept off by pushing a wooden bar, or striker, along the top of the mould. Care is needed in removing wet or 'green' bricks from the mould, or they will twist.

A piece of ground is prepared as the drying ground. It is cleared of all growth, carefully levelled, drained and sprinkled with sand. The green bricks are turned out from the mould onto this floor, and left until they are dry enough to turn on edge. Protect green bricks from the sun by covering with grass, or by building long low sheds, which can be roofed with grass, or any other locally available covering. When green bricks are dry enough to handle, stack as Figure 2.2, and leave for 6–10 days in order to dry thoroughly. Test by breaking a brick occasionally: and note if it has dried through to the centre.

Improved, simple methods of brick-making have been developed resulting in much more accurately moulded bricks than can be made by the wet process described above. If used with a suitable releasing agent such as sawdust, clay can be prepared much dryer, and hence is less liable to crack and shrink during drying.

A range of simple hand-operated moulding aids also exist to improve productivity, and methods of increasing the efficiency of clamp-firing, to improve the yield of fully burnt bricks, and reduce firewood consumption have been developed.

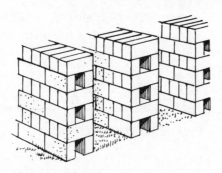

Figure 2.2 Green bricks stacked for drying.

2.2.2 Labour for Brick-making.

It has been estimated that to turn out 1000 moulded bricks a day, the labour requirements are:

Five men digging and tempering
Four men filling moulds
Three men carrying moulds to drying ground
One man removing brick from moulds
One man cleaning and washing moulds
One man sanding moulds
Total: 15 men per 1000 green bricks a day

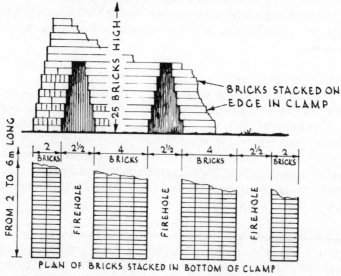

Figure 2.3 Bricks stacked in clamp for burning.

Figure 2.4 Completed clamp.

2.2.3 Burning

Bricks are burnt in kilns or 'clamps'. Kilns are permanent structures. Clamps are described here: select a solid piece of ground and then carefully level it. If possible cover the site with old bricks set on edge. Place the bricks on edge as in Figure 2.3. Continue stacking until the pile resembles Figure 2.4. The long passages in Figure 2.3 between the bricks are the fire holes. Plaster the sides and ends of the pile, or 'clamp', with clay. Kindle wood fires in the fire holes.

Fire slowly at first. Clouds of steam will rise from the top and sides of the clamp. Continue to increase the intensity of the fire until it licks through the top of the clamp. Then cover the top with a layer of earth 15 cm thick. Firing continues from three to six days and nights. When firing ceases, brick up, or block up, the fireholes. Leave the whole mass to cool. Roughly 3–4 m^3 of firewood are required to burn 1000 bricks. Clamps should not be exposed to the wind. A brick thoroughly burnt will give a clear ringing sound when struck, and should be of uniform colour.

2.2.4 Pisé de Terre

Pisé de terre is carefully selected earth, mixed with a little chopped straw and water. It is rammed within shuttering, as described for concrete cast *in situ* (see section 3.3.8), and allowed to become firm before the shuttering is removed. The face of a *pisé de terre* or sun-dried brick wall must be protected from piercing rains by verandas or good projecting eaves. The top of these walls should be protected by a damp-proof course of some kind (see section 2.8.15). Foundations are as for sun-dried bricks.

2.2.5 Stabilized Soil

Stabilized soil has come into use during recent years particularly on aerodromes and military works. In brief it is soil mixed with Portland cement or lime, asphalt, or other bitumen emulsion. Practically any soil may be used. Cohesionless sands and fat clays are not very suitable, but they may be improved by mixture. Most suitable soils are sand or gravel firmly held together by clay binder. Soil should be dry but not too dry; when several lumps are squeezed together in the hand they should just fail to form one lump. Soil is broken up and passed through a sieve (some advocate 12 mm sieve) and to it is added 4–7 per cent of cement for a sandy soil, or 6–10 per cent for a clay soil. Proportions are by weight. The materials are mixed on a platform, and a small amount of water added. (It is important that too much water should not be used.) If a handful of the mixture, after water is added, is taken and squeezed it should just, and only just, form a large lump. To test if soil and cement content is suitable make several blocks (say 450 mm × 300 mm × 150 mm) with mixtures 1 cement : 20 soil (5 per cent mixture), 1 in 15, and other mixtures, also a block without cement. Do not let them dry too quickly. After a week wet them well, then expose to sun; repeat treatment daily for a week. Note which block stands up to this treatment.

Stabilized soil can be rammed in shuttering, or forms, as *pisé de terre*. It should be placed in layers not more than 100 mm thick and well rammed from the face inwards. The shuttering, or form, can be removed immediately. Stabilized soil can also be cast into blocks in the same way as concrete blocks.

If lime is used in place of Portland cement for stabilizing soil, approximately double the amount, by volume, is needed. This may be economical in some places. In Java, the local volcanic ash, a pozzolana (see section 2.5.1), is used for making blocks by mixing with lime in the ratio 1:5, by volume, lime–ash.

Simple compression moulding equipment such as the Cinva Ram has been developed in order to aid the rapid production of stabilized soil blocks. These machines are cheap and portable, and in their simplest form produce pressures of about 0.2N/mm^2.

2.3 STONE

2.3.1 Selection of Stone
For building purposes there are two requirements:

(a) durability; and
(b) ease of working.

The major classifications of rocks are igneous, metamorphic and sedimentary. The igneous rocks, the granites and granitic rocks are usually durable. They are also difficult to quarry, except by blasting, and hard to work to shape. The sedimentary rocks, sandstones, etc., are more easy to quarry and to work. Rocks which occur in definite beds, the sedimentary, should be laid in the work on natural beds (i.e., the grain of the rock should be horizontal to the pressure and not vertical to it). Examine specimens of the stone exposed to the weather in the locality of the proposed quarry before beginning work. Some stones look dull and earthy on fracture; they will probably disintegrate when exposed to weather. The best situation for a stone quarry is on a hillside—for ease both of access and excavation, and often for that matter, of removal.

Rock can be cracked by lighting a fire on it, and after the surface is heated, by pouring water over it. Another method is to drill holes in the rock and to drive in wooden wedges and pour water on the wedges. The wedges swell and crack the rock. A 'drill' or 'jumper' is a steel bar with a chisel point. The drill is about 1–1·2 m long, and it is held by one man, while a second man strikes it with a hammer. After each blow the drill is turned slightly about its long axis.

2.3.2 Blasting
The instructions issued with the explosive to be used must be carefully followed. Dynamite and gelignite are exploded by means of detonators. Detonators are not dangerous if properly handled, but highly dangerous in careless hands. Figure 2.5 is a sketch of a dynamite or gelignite cartridge prepared for use. Figure 2.5 also shows the cartridges in a hole, which must be cleared of all dust before the cartridge is introduced. Fuse burns at the rate of 0·6 m in 1 min. Always test the rate of burning of a fuse.

The 'tamping' is clay, or earth. It is pressed down with a wooden rod. On no account must a metal rod be used, as *any* spark can cause an explosion.

2.3.3 Rubble Masonry
Local masons can usually build walls in rubble masonry to between 300 and 500 mm thick. Figure 2.6 represents such a wall. Note the corner stones or 'quoins' which give strength to the wall. Quoins can also be made of cast concrete, or in brickwork. The stones in the wall should be solidly bedded, and small stones used as filling should be fitted roughly in place in the spaces between larger ones. No hollow spaces must occur. Large stones must not rest in an unstable position on small stones. Stones must break joint (i.e., be staggered, as with bricks) as much as possible. It is wrong to build up the inside and outside of the walls and fill in with small stones. Large stones, or

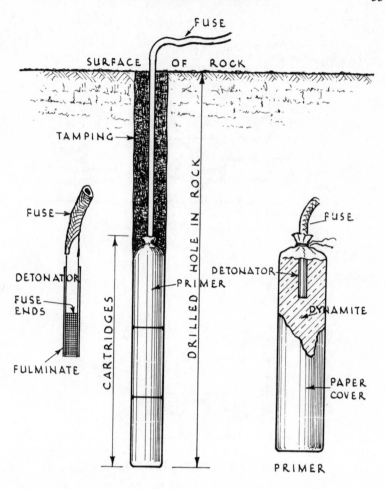

EXPLOSIVES

Figure 2.5 Arrangement for blasting.

'bond' stones, running nearly through the wall must be introduced at frequent intervals. A quarter of the area of the face of the wall should be bondstones. 'Through' stones run completely through the wall. In damp climates 'through' stones are liable to conduct the moisture through the wall. All the walls of a building should be built together (i.e., the work must progress round the circuit of the walls). Stones should be soaked in water before being embedded in mortar. Lime mortar is used in stone walls, and mud mortar where lime mortar is

ELEVATION AT CORNER

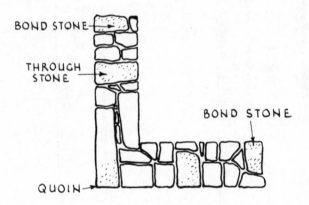

PLAN AT CORNER OF WALL

Figure 2.6 Rubble masonry.

not obtainable, but it is said to be better to build foundations in cement or without mortar, rather than in lime. Long strands of barbed wire, or wire mesh, built into the length of the wall greatly improves its strength.

A stone wall is provided with footings in the same manner as brick walls. Footings should be constructed of large through stones. Large stones in the same course in the footings should be of the same height, but each course need not be equal in height. The projection of each course is from 75 to 100 mm.

The width of footings should *as a general rule* equal twice the thickness of the wall. The base of a stone wall up to plinth level (floor level) is usually 150 mm, or more, wider than the wall proper. In dwellings the plinth is 600 mm above ground level and may be much more. Where the rainfall is not excessive and when time allows, masonry walls may be built up to plinth level and the enclosed space can be filled with earth, before the rains, and then left. The walls and the filling then settle down, for rain is an excellent consolidator.

Pointing masonry or brickwork consists in scraping out the joints for a depth of about 25 mm and refilling with lime or cement mortar (see section 2.5.2).

2.3.4 Quantities for Rubble Masonry

The materials required to produce 1 m^3 of finished rubble masonry wall will be 1·25–1·5 m^3 in volume when loose. The volume of the material when placed in the wall is reduced because in properly constructed masonry all voids or spaces are filled.

The approximate quantity of materials required for 1 m^3 of masonry wall is as follows:

With lime mortar

Large stones	0·5 m^3
Small stones	0·7 m^3
About 20 bond stones	
Lime	0·2 m^3
Sand	0·3 m^3

With mud mortar

Large stones	25
Rubble	1 m^3
Earth	0·24 m^3
Sand	0·12 m^3

2.4 LIME, MORTARS AND PLASTERS

2.4.1 Production of Lime

Lime is obtained from limestones, coral, shells and nodules of 'kunkar'. A simple test for a limestone is to put a chip of stone in a little weak hydrochloric acid; if it is a limestone effervescence will take place. The quality of the lime varies considerably, as it is a natural and not a uniform product—varying from kiln to kiln, and with the quality of the limestone. Hydraulic lime is obtained from some limestones. The Indian Standards Institution has published a wide range of standards dealing with all aspects of lime production, kiln construction, and the use of lime. (Ref 9).

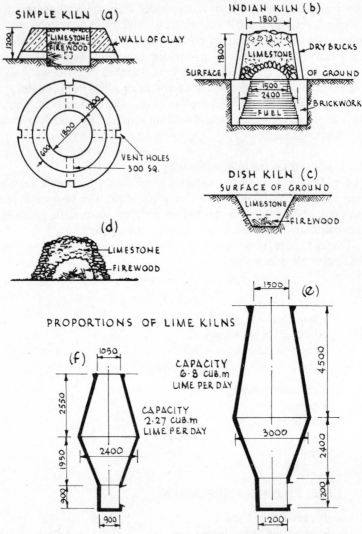

Figure 2.7 Lime burning. (Measurements are all in mm.)

Figure 2.7(a) shows a section of a small kiln for burning lime, as used in India. Four vent holes are provided, each 30 × 30 cm. The bottom of the kiln is covered with dried grass, the kiln is half filled with wood, and then completely filled up with broken stone. Fire is lighted at the vents, and the top of the kiln is plastered with mud; firing is then continued until the stone is calcined. This method does not produce a very good lime. If the kiln is made as Figure 2.7(b), a better lime can be produced, but kilns can, in effect, be made in a great variety of shapes, the general rule being that a greater height in relation to breadth encourages efficiency of burning. Figures 2.7(e) and (f) show only two possible designs. For quick burning the stone can be burnt in a pit or 'dish' kiln (see Figure 2.7(c)) or by making a clamp of limestone (Figure 2.7(d)). In any case the product of the lime kiln is called 'quicklime'.

Quicklime should not be slaked a long time before use, as it deteriorates. Mortar made of freshly slaked lime is stronger. To slake add small quantities of water to quicklime which is spread in a layer of about 150 mm. The lumps of quicklime expand and burst. The process should continue until all the lumps are reduced to a whitish powder. The residue is then screened and reburned. Six to twelve hours should be allowed for slaking. It is absolutely essential that every particle of quicklime is thoroughly slaked before being used in any work. Rich, pure or fat limes (i.e., those which slake easily, set slowly in air, and not at all under water) are not suitable for building work, except when mixed with a proportion of Portland cement. Fat limes should be used for ceilings and whitewash (i.e. for lime washes and for plaster). Hydraulic lime slakes fairly slowly, sets slowly in water, and does not increase in bulk when slaked in the way pure lime increases.

2.4.2 Lime Concrete
Concrete may be made of lime as well as cement. Materials for 1 m³ lime concrete are as shown in Table 2.1.

*Table 2.1 Materials for lime concrete.**

Mixture	Lime m³	Sand m³	Stone m³
1 : 2 : 4	0·23	0·46	0·92
1 : 3 : 6	0·16	0·48	0·96

*Lime weighs from 800 to 1000 kg per m³.

2.4.3 Mortars and Plasters
Lime mortar is made from 1 slaked lime: 2–3 clean sand. About 0·16 to 0·2 m³ of lime is required for every 1 m³ of brickwork and 0·2 m³ for every 1 m³ of stone walling. In Egypt a good mortar is made by mixing 2 sand : 1 *homra* (i.e., well burnt brick pounded to a powder) : 2 lime.

It is claimed that coarse sugar (*goor*, or *jagree*) in proportion of 1 kg added to every 10 l of water with which mortar is mixed, adds greatly to its breaking and cohesive strength; but this should not be used with Portland cement.

To make lime mortar from quicklime, spread the quicklime on a prepared floor, pour water over it until it will absorb no more, turn it over in a heap with a shovel and let the lime expand and burst. Take three times the quantity of clean sand and cover the lime with it. Let the lime slake until it becomes a powder, then mix the sand and the lime. Afterwards, screen or sift the whole to take out the underburnt stone. The mortar should not be used for some days.

Mud mortar is earth and sand mixed in proportions of 1–2:1, or even earth itself. It is much used in the tropics.

Mud plaster can be prepared in this way: clay is dried in the sun, then powdered. Chopped straw and cow dung is added and thoroughly mixed while the clay is dry. Water is then added. The mass is left to soak for 2–14 days. After this it is thoroughly mixed, more water being added as necessary. The plaster is spread over the surface of the wall not more than 20 mm thick. Cracks are filled in with liquid cow dung.

Plaster, or rendering, for walls is usually made of cement, lime and sand. Typical mixes are:

Cement:lime:sand   1:1:5–6, by volume
Cement:lime:sand   1:2:8–9, by volume
Cement:lime:sand   1:3:10–12, by volume

Mortar is now made of similar mixes provided that the lime is of good quality and the sand is clean.

2.5 CEMENT AND CONCRETE

2.5.1 Cements

The principal constituents of Portland cement are calcareous material (such as chalk and limestone) and argillaceous material (such as clay, mud, shale), mixed together in proportions of 75 per cent calcareous material : 25 per cent argillaceous. The hard materials are ground to powder.

Soft materials are reduced in water. After reduction the materials are burned in a slow-moving rotary kiln. The clinker formed by burning is ground to a fine powder and 3–4 per cent gypsum is added. The powder is ordinary Portland cement.

Ordinary Portland cement is supplied in bags or in bulk. A bag of

Portland cement weighs 50 kg. When stored in air-tight containers it can be kept indefinitely. In bags it must be kept in a dry place and should not be kept for long periods as it absorbs moisture from the air and may become lumpy. The lumps are thrown out if too hard to be squashed in the hand.

Rapid-hardening Portland cement is similar to ordinary Portland cement, but it is more finely ground, and gains strength more quickly.

Coloured cements. Ordinary Portland cement is made in a variety of colours by the addition of pigments.

Natural cement. Before the manufacture of Portland cement was perfected, natural cements were much used. A pozzolana is a material which, although not in itself cementitious, can react with lime, in the presence of water, to make cementitious products. Examples of pozzolanas naturally occurring are volcanic ash, pumice and certain kinds of earths. The name 'pozzolana' comes from the village of Pozzuoli near Naples in Italy, where the local volcanic ash has been used in building for many centuries, but natural pozzolanas are also found in many other parts of the world.

Pozzolanic materials generally have a high content of fine silica and alumina, and can be produced artificially by burning and grinding certain kinds of clay, or vegetable waste such as rice husks. Pulverised fuel ash (pfa), the ground ash from coal-fired power stations, is the most commonly used industrially produced pozzolana.

Pozzolana can be used in concrete in two ways:

(i) *Portland-pozzolana.* In this mixture, pozzolana is partially substituted for Portland cement. This is not only more economical but also improves the quality of the resulting concrete, making it more resistant to sea water or other chemical attack, more plastic, lowering the heat of hydration and raising its long-term strength. If pfa is used, about 20–30 per cent is normally substituted for Portland cement in this way. This is the major use of pozzolana in the world.

(ii) *Lime-pozzolana or 'pozzolime'.* This is a mixture of pozzolana and lime which can be used as a substitute for Portland cement for plaster, mortar and most types of unreinforced concrete construction. The proportion of lime to pozzolana can be varied from 1:1 to 1:3 (by weight). The materials so obtained have a strength of about half that of Portland cement-based materials. Their setting and hardening are much slower than of Portland cement and great care has to be taken to prevent premature drying-out of the material. Good curing is thus extremely important. With these precautions, excellent buildings can be and have been produced using pozzolime. Pozzolime mortars are in many ways superior to Portland cement mortars.

2.5.2   Cement Mortar and Plaster
Nowadays cement mortar is sparingly used except for floor surfaces.

1 cement : 4 clean sand, for most purposes
1 cement : 3 clean sand, for finishing floor.
1 cement : 5, 6–8 clean sand, for wall plaster.

Plaster is 13–20 mm thick, and 0·25 m³ of loose cement to 0·75 m³ of sand will cover roughly 35 m², 20 mm thick. In addition, 0·25 m³ cement to 1 m³ of sand will cover about 40 m²; 0·25 m³ cement to 1·5 m³ of sand will cover about 47 m². If joints are finished in cement mortar (i.e., 'pointed' in cement), 1 m² of brickwork requires about 4·5 kg of cement. Cement mortar is 'harsh working'. Bricks or stones must be soaked in water before cement mortar is used. Surfaces to be plastered must be liberally sprinkled with water.

2.5.3   Concrete
For concrete the following are required: cement (or lime), sand, and broken stone, brick, ashes, gravel or burnt clay. The 'aggregate' is the broken stone, etc. The proportions of cement concrete are described as 1 : 3 : 6, or 1 : 2 : 4, etc. This means the mixture (or mix as it is called) contains 1 part cement, 3 parts sand and 6 parts aggregate; or 1 part cement, 2 parts sand, 4 parts aggregate. The sand should be clean and sharp with no clay, earth, mould or roots. A very fine sand is not satisfactory. The stone should also be angular if possible, clean, free from clay, mould etc. Natural 'ballast' containing pebbles and sand makes good concrete. For mass concrete, stones up to 63 mm diameter are used: for walls and floors, 25 mm diameter. A better concrete is made from a weak mixture of sand and cement which entirely fills the spaces between broken stone than a strong mixture of cement and sand which does not fill the spaces. Proportions for mass concrete are 1 : 2 : 4 for a strong mixture, 1 : 3 : 6 for a medium mixture and 1 : 4 : 8 for a lean mixture, which is usually considered strong enough for foundations. In mass work large stones or 'plumbs' may be thrown in; the concrete is rammed around them.

2.5.4   Mixing by Hand
A level platform of boards is required on which to mix the concrete. Good concrete cannot be mixed on the bare ground. If the proportions of the mix are to be, say, 1 : 3 : 6 a cement barrel or

measuring box (see Table 2.2 below) is filled with stones six times and the stone is deposited on the platform. The stone is then soaked with water. Three barrels or boxes of sand are mixed on the platform with one barrel or box of cement; both sand and cement are mixed 'dry' (i.e., without water). The mixture of cement and sand is shovelled on to the stone; the whole mass—stone, cement and sand—is turned over dry twice or thrice (i.e., without water being used). After the turning over, water is added from a watering can fitted with a rose, or from an empty petrol tin with holes in the bottom. The wet mass is again turned over several times until thoroughly plastic and the whole is homogeneous in appearance and colour. The mass is turned over by shovelling it from one side of the platform to the other and by twisting the shovel in the hand while so doing. Only just sufficient water should be used to make the concrete thoroughly plastic. Too much water reduces the strength of concrete.

It is often convenient to use a measuring box rather than a cement drum. A measuring box has no bottom; it is placed on the mixing platform, filled with cement or sand or stone, and lifted up so that the material remains on the platform.

Table 2.2   Dimensions of measuring boxes (internal).

mm	Capacity, m^3
400 × 400 × 310	0·05
500 × 500 × 400	0·10
600 × 600 × 550	0·20
800 × 800 × 470	0·30
800 × 800 × 620	0·40
800 × 800 × 780	0·50
1000 × 1000 × 1000	1·00

2.5.5 Laying Concrete

As soon as concrete is mixed it must be used; it must never be allowed to set before use. It is laid in 250 mm layers, or under, and rammed with a wooden rammer. Before new concrete is placed on old or set concrete, the surface of the old concrete must be thoroughly cleansed and wetted with water, and if smooth it must be chipped to form a good key. Old concrete is often painted with liquid cement before being joined to new concrete.

2.5.6   Quantities of Materials in Cement Concrete

Table 2.3   Materials in 1 m³ of concrete.

Mix	Cement (kg)	Sand (m³)	Broken stone (m³)
1 : 1 : 2	536	0·37	0·74
1 : 2 : 4	326	0·45	0·90
1 : 3 : 6	228	0·47	0·94
1 : 4 : 8	175	0·48	0·96

Table 2.4   Proportion of concrete using 1 sack (50 kg) as basis.

Mix	Cement sack	Sand (m³)	Stone (m³)
1 : 2 : 4	1	0·07	0·14
1 : 3 : 6	1	0·10	0·20
1 : 4 : 8	1	0·14	0·28

Cement weighs 1200–1450 kg per m³ when loose. It should be noted that the modern practice is to specify the amount of cement in a 'mix' by weight and not by volume, although this method requires a machine.

2.5.7   Reinforced Concrete

Reinforced concrete is an intimate combination of concrete and steel bars or rods. Concrete is peculiarly suited to resist compression, but it is weak in resisting forces which tend to pull it apart. Steel is introduced to make good the defect. Knowledge of the forces which act and react in structures is necessary in order to assign the correct relative positions and proportions of the concrete and the steel in a beam, wall, or other structure. Some simple examples of reinforcement in beams, lintels and pillars are given in Figure 2.8. Wooden moulds or shuttering have to be made for the concrete.

2.5.8   Reinforcement

Reinforcement in concrete is most commonly plain round mild steel bars, but medium-tensile and high-tensile steels are also used, which are stronger than mild steel. Other high strength bars are cold-worked bars which may be twisted ribbed or twisted square bars and drawn mild steel wire. Fine bars or wires may be welded or woven into fabric reinforcement for floor slabs and roads.

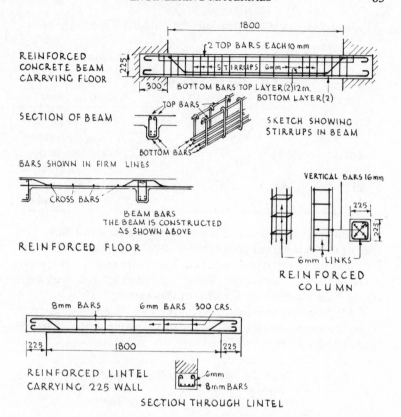

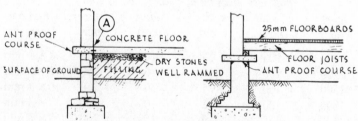

Figure 2.8 Reinforced concrete.

For round bars the usually available diameter sizes are 6, 8, 10, 12, 16, 20, 25, 32 and 40 mm. The lengths, sizes, numbers and positioning of the bars are determined from the design calculations for a reinforced concrete structure (see Ref 8).

Reinforcement should always be adequately covered by concrete. Unless otherwise specified the cover should not be less than the diameter of the bars being covered.

Table 2.5 gives some dimensions for reinforced concrete lintels.

Table 2.5 Lintel to carry 225 mm wall (see Figure 2.8).

Clear span (mm)	Length (mm)	Depth (mm)	Thickness (mm)	Reinforcement
1800	2250	150	225	4 × 8 mm bars, 2 hooked, 2 cranked
2400	2850	200	225	4 × 10 mm bars, 2 hooked, 2 cranked
2750	3200	225	225	4 × 12 mm bars, 2 hooked, 2 cranked

Concrete is 1 : 2 : 4, and a cover of 25 mm is given to all bars. Steel wire of 6 mm is wound about the top bar, taken round the bottom bars and up to the second top bar. These wire stirrups are placed every 300 mm along the beam. The cranked bars are bent at an angle of 45° from a point over the edge of the opening.

Table 2.6 gives some dimensions of reinforced slabs of single span. These dimensions are incorrect if the slab is continuous over several supports. Concrete is 1 : 2 : 4.

Table 2.6 Simply supported slabs.*

Span (mm)	Thickness of slab (mm)	Bearing at ends (mm)	Main bars (run in direction of span) dia. (mm)	centres (mm)	Cross bars No. × dia.
900	100	75	†10	250	4 × 8 mm
1200	100	115	10	250	5 × 8 mm
1500	100	115	10	250	6 × 8 mm
1800	120	115	10	200	7 × 8 mm
2100	135	150	10	200	9 × 8 mm
2400	150	150	10	200	7 × 10 mm

* These slabs would be suitable for domestic floors.
† The minimum diameter for longitudinal steel should be 10 mm and for transverse steel 8 mm to avoid distortion during placing of the concrete.

2.5.9 Concrete Blocks
There are numerous machines on the market for producing hollow concrete blocks by pressure. Blocks are made in many different sizes

and some common dimensions (length × height) are: 390 mm × 90 mm, 390 mm × 190 mm, 440 mm × 190 mm, 440 mm × 290 mm, 590 mm × 190 mm, 590 mm × 215 mm. Thicknesses may be 75 mm, 90 mm, 100 mm, 140 mm or 190 mm. The concrete is usually a dry mixture (i.e., only sufficient water is added to moisten the ingredients). With a dry mixture the block may be taken from the mould directly after the pressure has been applied. If the concrete is 'wet', the block must be allowed to harden. Strength depends on the mixture and the compaction, but great damage can be done—especially in hot dry climates—if the mix is too dry. The proportions of the ingredients for a good solid concrete block are 1 cement : 2 sand : 4 stone, or 1 cement : $2\frac{1}{2}$ sand and 5 stone, or even 1 : 5 : 8. The stone is crushed fine enough to pass through a 13 mm mesh.

In hollow blocks the cavities should not exceed one third of the bearing surface; the material round the cavities should be at least 60 mm thick.

Blocks made by machines must be 'cured', as, of course, must hand-made blocks. Curing is effected by protecting the newly made blocks from sun and wind for seven days, or longer, and by sprinkling them with water from time to time in order to prevent them from drying too quickly. The blocks are then removed to the open air and are allowed to remain for a month before being used. Insufficient curing has caused much disappointment in this class of work.

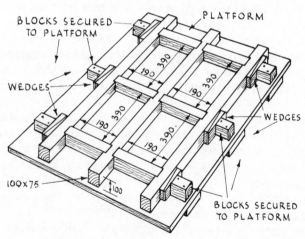

Figure 2.9 Mould for concrete blocks.

Concrete blocks are also made by hand and cast in wood or metal moulds; a wooden version, which can be made easily, is shown in Figure 2.9. The blocks can be made to any size—the mould in the figure is for blocks 390 mm × 190 mm × 100 mm. The best proportions for the concrete are 1 cement : 2 sand : 4 stone, or 1 cement : 2½ sand : 5 stone, and 1 cement : 3 sand : 6 stone. The size of stone is 13–20 mm. The mixture is made fairly wet and is carefully tamped or rammed in the mould. The interior of the mould is wiped with oil, or soft soap, to prevent the concrete from adhering to the sides. The concrete must set before the moulds are removed. Allow twenty-four hours at least. In this process many moulds are required as the manufacture of blocks is much slower than by machine.

2.6   TIMBER

2.6.1   Selection of Timber

Local inhabitants usually know the best local woods to resist white ants, borers etc. Their advice should be sought. If time allows, a tree should be ring-barked and allowed to dry out through the normal evaporation via the leaves, before felling. After felling, the bark of the tree is stripped off. The tree trunk is then cut into thick slabs. Slabs should be stacked carefully under cover. Place a batten or strip of wood between each slab. Slabs must be kept level or they will twist. Timber, to be thoroughly seasoned, requires months or even years of drying. The object of seasoning is to get rid of the sap which, if it remains, causes decay. Most of the timber usually sold is under-seasoned. Trees when felled are sometimes placed in running water for a week or 14 days with butt (or root end) up stream. The running water helps to soak the sap out and aids seasoning. The timber is taken out, cut into slabs and dried as above. It has been said that timber is well seasoned when it has lost one-fifth of its weight, and that it is then fit for normal use, and carpentry; and that it is fit for joiner's work and framing when it has lost one-third of its weight.

The signs of a good, sound timber are the narrowness of annual rings, when they occur (which denotes slow growth), a clean-cut appearance (without woolliness, or clogging the saw), dark rather than light colour, heavy weight, little resin or sap in the pores, and little sapwood. The signs of unsound timber are radiating cracks, circular cracks between the annual rings, crippled fibres, and hollows and spongy places, indicating incipient decay.

In buildings timber should be kept dry and well ventilated. Damp earth, damp walls, lime mortar, and lack of air hasten decomposition. Preservation against moisture should be by oil paint, Solignum, or similar preparations, but the timber must be dry before being painted. It is good practice to char the lower ends of posts or poles used in wattle and daub huts; it helps to prevent rot. Cooper's Dip also preserves poles from attacks by white ants. In fitting timber to the job there is 10 per cent waste.

2.6.2 Cutting

To cut the best beam from a log (see Figure 2.10) divide diameter d into three parts, $d,1,2,m$, (see Figure 2.10(a)). From 1 and 2 draw lines at right angles to dm, 1–4 and 2–3. Join $d3$, $m4$. The heavily lined portion is best beam. To cut the stiffest beam divide the diameter into four parts instead of three (Figure 2.10(b)).

Logs are felled trees with the branches lopped off. Balks are logs roughly squared. Balks are cut into small dimensions for building purposes. In converting timber to workable sizes 20–40 per cent waste occurs.

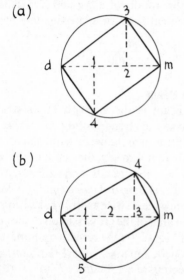

Figure 2.10 Cutting timber.

2.6.3 Weights of Timbers

Table 2.7 shows the specific gravities of several African timbers. (The specific gravity of a solid is the ratio which its density bears to that of distilled water). The weight of 1 m³ of water is 1000 kg. If the decimal point in the numbers in the table given below is moved three figures to the right, the number will indicate the weight in kg/m³.

Table 2.7   Specific gravities of African timbers.

	Average specific gravity
East African cedar	0·63
Camphor	0·625
Muhugwe	0·97
Podocarpus	0·58–0·66
Ngwe	0·94
Mkomohoyo	0·86
Mninga	0·63
Mvule	0·70
Douglas fir	0·41
White pine	0·37

2.6.4 Cubic Content of a Log

If P is the girth at the middle of a log and L is its length (both in metres), the cubic content is given approximately by:

$$\frac{8L \times P^2}{100} \text{ m}^3$$

2.6.5 Strength of a Beam

The strength of a beam is the strength of its weakest place. In mathematical language the strength of a rectangular wooden beam varies directly as the breadth of the beam, as the square of its depth, and inversely as its length; that is to say, the depth of the beam is of great importance in relation to its strength and stiffness, and the strength decreases rapidly with its length. Under similar conditions a beam 150 mm deep × 75 mm wide is twice as strong as a beam 75 mm deep × 150 mm wide, yet the area of the cross-section of the beam (150 mm × 75 mm = 11 250 mm²) is exactly the same. To compare the strength of beams of the same length and load, square the depth and multiply by the width. Thus to compare a 150 mm × 75 mm with a 75 mm × 150 mm beam:

$$150 \times 150 \times 75 = 1\,687\,500$$
$$75 \times 75 \times 150 = 843\,750$$

The former has twice the strength of the latter. For more details concerning beams see Appendix IV.

Rough formulae for rectangular beams: b = breadth of beam in mm. d = depth of beam in mm. L = length in mm. FS = factor of safety = 5 (see section 6.7.5). W = load in kg which beam will carry. c = for deal 2·1; teak 3·2; oak 2·8–3·5 kg/mm^2.

(a) Load distributed over whole length of beam:

$$W = \frac{c \times b \times d^2}{L \times FS}$$

(b) Load concentrated at centre of beam:

$$W = \frac{c \times b \times d^2}{2 \times L \times FS}$$

(c) Cantilever (beam supported one end only). Load distributed:

$$W = \frac{c \times b \times d^2}{4 \times L \times FS}$$

(d) Cantilever. Load concentrated at end:

$$W = \frac{c \times b \times d^2}{8 \times L \times FS}$$

So little is known of the ultimate strengths of local timbers (which depend on their seasoning) that accurate figures for the value of c cannot be given.

2.6.6 Plywood

Plywood is made by gluing together an uneven number of thin layers of wood. Alternate layers are placed with the grain running lengthwise and crosswise so that the tendency to warping and splitting is minimized, and the top layer may be of a more expensive wood, giving a decorative wood at relatively low cost.

2.7 STEEL

2.7.1 General

Steel has been one of the most popular engineering construction materials since the middle of the nineteenth century. It is strong, tough, malleable and durable and with modern tools it can be cut, drilled, shaped and welded fairly easily. It is used extensively for major structures such as bridges, large buildings, ships and in railway and industrial engineering. It is also a common material for farm and domestic buildings and structures.

2.7.2 Availability

The properties of steel vary with its composition, and quite small variations in the quantities of carbon and other elements make a significant difference to its properties. The most common form of steel is mild steel and this is manufactured in sheets, plates, beams, strips, bars and rods of various cross-sections.

2.7.3   Applications

The design of steel structures is based on the properties of the steel and structural theory, and information about this will be found in appropriate text books (Ref 9). Many structures such as water tanks, towers, roof trusses, building frames, gates and fencing are pre-fabricated for installation or erection on site. It should be remembered that steel is a heavy material with a density of 7840 kg/m^3, and special lifting and handling equipment may be needed. Because of its weight care must be taken to avoid accidents.

2.8   ROOFING MATERIALS

2.8.1   Thatch

The material for thatching must be carefully chosen. Grasses or reeds should be round in section and at least 1 m long and ought to be dried before use. The roof-life of grass thatch may be doubled if leaves and other debris are removed by combing. A comb can be simply made with a few wire nails driven into a wooden frame.

Grass is laid on the roof in courses or layers, commencing at the eaves, to a thickness of about 300 mm. It is beaten into place with a grooved board to produce a tight and even surface. The steeper the roof, the longer the thatch will last. Although thatch will decay faster in a hot moist climate, it need not be considered a temporary roof covering. Good grass thatching in tropical South East Asia, for example, is weathertight for 25 years, though palm leaf thatch everywhere cannot be expected to last more than five years. Both will last longer if they are soaked for 24 hours in a decay-retardant. The current recommended mix is a 3 per cent solution of copper–chrome–arsenite multisalts, commonly known as Tenalith NCA or Celcure AN.

Fire-proofing solutions, though attractive in principle, are all expensive, and water soluble. They are not recommended. Since most house fires start internally, lining the underneath of the thatch with an incombustible ceiling is recommended. Additionally, where sufficient water is available, a sprinkler pipe laid along the ridge can be used to soak the roof when there is a risk of fire.

Finally, the roof structure should be capable of supporting the thatch. 10 m^2 of grass thatch weighs approximately 300 kg.

2.8.2 Tiles

The clay for tiles requires to be stronger than for bricks. Tiles will crack in drying if exposed to wind and rain. Moulds are made to suit the design of tile. There are many designs. Tiles are dried on edge and burned on edge as with bricks. They can be burned in a clamp (see section 2.2.1) suitably modified—the outer edges of the clamp being made of bricks.

The following is from an old book on tile burning:

> The fire is gentle at first, till the disappearance of all white steam from the smoke, then it is raised till the flues appear red hot, then slackened for six hours, then raised till the flues are white hot and kept so for three hours, again slackened six hours, then raised to white heat for four hours, flues filled with fuel, their mouths stopped with brick and mud, and the fires allowed to burn out. The burning generally takes altogether 72 hours.

Figure 2.11 shows a tile in position viewed from the underside. Note the lug at the upper edge. This hooks on the batten and secures the tile. The spacing between battens is known as the gauge.

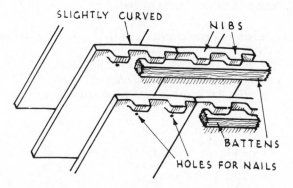

SLIGHTLY CURVED

NIBS

BATTENS

HOLES FOR NAILS

Figure 2.11 Plain tile (from underside).

Locally made tiles vary in shape and size; little information can be given concerning them. The English 'plain' roofing tile (270 mm × 165 mm × 13 mm) weighs about 1 kg. To cover 10 m² of roof area at 100 mm gauge, 599 tiles are required, 100 m of battens and 0·8 kg of nails. Pan tiles (338 mm × 245 mm × 13 mm) weigh about 2·25 kg each. To cover 10 m² requires 180 tiles at 75 mm lap. Add 10 per cent for waste. Both plain and pan tiles should curve in their length.

2.8.3 Shingles
Shingles are wooden tiles and are much used in countries possessing straight grained timber. Sizes vary from 300 to 460 mm long × 75 – 150 mm wide × 6 mm thick. American shingles of white cedar are said to last 40–50 years in the Northern States. They are 686 mm long × 150–180 mm wide × 6 mm thick. Shingling, like tiling, is commenced from the eaves and continued upwards.

2.8.4 Galvanized Corrugated Iron Sheets
Corrugated iron sheets are manufactured from steel sheet of various thicknesses. Common thicknesses in standard wire gauge (swg) and millimetres are:

swg	16	18	20	22	24	26	30
mm	1·626	1·219	0·914	0·711	0·559	0·457	0·315

Roofing of 10 m² with sheets 0·65 m wide require 53 galvanized roofing nails and washers: the nails (112 mm) weigh 0·018 kg each or 0·95 kg per 10 m² of roof, and the washers 0·006 kg each or 0·32 kg per 10 m² of roof. Table 2.8 gives number of sheets 0·65 m wide and different lengths to cover 10 m² of roof.

Table 2.8   Number of corrugated iron sheets to cover 10 m² of roof – sheets 0·65 m wide.

Length of sheet (m)	50 mm side lap 150 mm vert lap	125 mm side lap 150 mm vert lap
1·80	9·78	11·21
2·10	8·21	9·50
2·40	7·20	8·23
2·70	6·35	7·26
3·00	5·68	6·58

To find the number of corrugated sheets 0·65 m wide in one row on a roof:

For side lap   50 mm : divide length of roof by 0·6
For side lap 125 mm : divide length of roof by 0·525

Table 2.9 shows the approximate number of sheets per tonne for different lengths and gauges.

Table 2.9 Number of corrugated iron sheets per tonne, for 18 and 24 swg sheets.

Length of sheets (m)	Number of sheets per tonne			
	18 (swg)		24 (swg)	
	*	†	*	†
1·80	74	64	158	132
2·10	64	55	135	113
2·40	56	47	118	99
2·70	49	42	105	88
3·00	44	38	95	79

* Sheets 650 mm wide, eight corrugations.
† Sheets 800 mm wide, ten corrugations.

Corrugated sheets are laid as Figure 2.12. In laying corrugated iron sheets the nails must always be driven through the ridges and not in the valleys. Large punches (to make holes for nails) should not be used. The nails should not be driven in too hard.

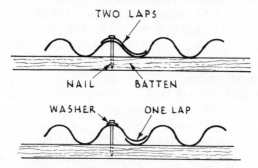

Figure 2.12 Fixing corrugated sheeting.

The length of ridging for corrugated iron is usually 1·8 m and the girths are 300–900 mm. The gauge is 16–26. Valleys are made of galvanized ridging reversed and secured to battens which are themselves fastened to rafters. The ridging is opened out as necessary.

2.8.5 Corrugated Aluminium Sheets
Corrugated aluminium sheets are often used in preference to corrugated iron because they are lighter, not liable to rusting and have a shiny heat-reflecting surface. Aluminium is not as strong as iron and requires more careful handling. Numbers of sheets required for 10 m² of roofing are as in section 2.8.4.

2.8.6 Corrugated Asbestos Cement Sheets

These are another alternative to corrugated iron, but because asbestos-cement is a weak material compared with iron, the sheets are much thicker and therefore heavier. A swg 24 corrugated iron sheet is 0·56 mm thick and its weight is about a quarter of the weight of a 6 mm thick asbestos cement sheet of the same surface area.

2.8.7 Ridges and Valleys for Tiled and Asbestos Cement Slate Roof

Tiled roofs, or roofs of asbestos slate, are provided with specially made tiles for the roof ridge, for lines of intersection between roofs, or valleys. There are various designs for ridge tiles which are usually 300 mm in length.

Galvanised iron ridging may be used for valleys for want of better materials. Tiles have to be cut to fit. It is this fact which makes it essential to make tiled roofs as simple as possible. A long straight roof without valleys is best for the types of buildings here described.

A mixture of sand, cement and chopped sisal fibre can also be used to make corrugated sheets and tiles. The major advantage of this material is that with the use of simple equipment, the sheets or tiles can be made on the building site, using semi-skilled labour. This material can also be used for plastering on to mud walls, and for making gutters, lintels and other permanent frameworks.

2.8.8 Ruberoid Roofing

This type of roofing is laid on 13 or 19 mm boards and is secured by special nails supplied with the material. The joints between the sheets are made tight by painting them with special ruberoid cement. Ruberoid is sold in half rolls and rolls. The width is 1 m; the length of a half roll is 11 m and that of a roll is 22 m. The area of roof covered by one roll is approximately 22 m². The material is supplied in half-, one-one-, two- and three-ply. There are two colours, grey and red. Ruberoid roofing is used on flat roofs or roofs of small pitch. It should not be used on steep pitches.

2.8.9 Roofing Felts

Roofing felts consist of a sheet of felted material (wool, hair, cotton, jute, flax or asbestos fibre) saturated with bituminous water-proofing composition. The felt is passed slowly through a bath of bitumen and then squeezed through heated rollers. On flat roofs of permanent buildings two or three layers of the material are used. They are bonded together with hot bitumen. The surface is finished off by sanding or gritting, but the surface has to be periodically coated with bitumen and sanded. The chief enemy of felts is bright sunshine which causes the bitumen to be hard and brittle. The sanding protects the material.

Roofing felts are laid on 13–19 mm boards. There are various makes. The rolls are from 0·8 to 1 m wide and contain from 10 to 25 m. Felts are largely used under other coverings. On steep pitches the felt tears away from the nails.

2.9 MISCELLANEOUS MATERIALS

2.9.1 Building Boards

Building boards for lining walls and ceilings are available in various materials, including plywood (see section 2.6.6), asbestos-cement sheets (see section 2.8.2), fibre boards, wood-waste and wood-wool slabs, laminated plastic boards, hardboard and plasterboard.

2.9.2 Asbestos Cement Sheets

A common size is 2440 mm × 1220 mm × 6 mm thick. When used for partitions or walling the vertical supports or studding of 75 mm × 50 mm timber are placed about 600 mm apart in good work. Asbestos sheets are very brittle and a smart blow will shatter them.

2.9.3 Fibre Boards

Fibre boards are made from waste cellulose material; wood; refuse from sugar making (*bagasse*), waste paper and the like. Sisal waste has been used. The process of manufacture is analogous to paper making. Hardboard is pressed in a heated press and usually bears the pattern of the screen on which it is pressed. Laminated board is built up in piles which are stuck together. It must not be confused with plywood. Plaster board (for ceilings) is in the main plaster of Paris between two sheets of stout paper.

There are numerous brands of fibre boards on the market such as Ten Test and Celotex. The sheets are 2240 mm × 1120 mm, and are secured to the underside of the rafters or ceiling joists and the joints are covered with a batten or paper strip. The ceiling joists must not be more than 0·6 m apart or the sheets will sag and pull apart at the joints. Fibre boards can also be used for partitions.

2.9.4 Expanded Metal

Special expanded metal such as Expamet can be used instead of laths. The sheets are 2·7 m × 0·6 m × 10 mm mesh × 26 gauge with an approximate weight of 2 kg per sheet, or 2·7 m × 0·6 m × 20 mm mesh

× 24 gauge, with an approximate weight of 2·7 kg per sheet. The metal must be well painted and secured by staples to ceiling joists which ought not to be more than 450 mm apart. It is best to use cement plaster as some limes will attack the metal lathing.

2.9.5 Mosquito Gauze

Mosquito gauze is often used in ordinary door and window openings, but this has the effect of making a room stuffy and uncomfortable. The gauze is heated by the sun and warms the air which passes through it. It also retards the passage of air. In proofing old buildings these disadvantages have to be endured, but in designing new buildings it is necessary to allow for larger window and door openings than would be necessary, if gauze is to be used. Mosquito gauze is sold in rolls of 30 m × 1 m wide. A mesh of 10 holes to 18 mm with wire 30 swg will exclude mosquitoes.

2.9.6 Fencing Wire

Wire netting made up of wire from 14 to 20 swg and galvanized wire is usually supplied in 25 m or 50 m rolls, of various widths, from 0·5 m to 2·0 m.

Barbed fencing wire is sold in 25 kg reels. Ordinary galvanized wire, 8 swg (4 mm diameter) and 1100 m weighs about 100 kg.

2.9.7 Lightning Conductors

Lightning conductors are of copper tape 25 mm × 3 mm, low buildings 19 mm × 3 mm or iron telegraph wire No 5 swg. The tape is secured by clips 1 m apart. The point of the conductor is at least 1·5 m above the building. The base of the conductor should be let into ground which is permanently wet, or connected with a water main. Should these things be impracticable, a shallow trench at least 5 m long should be dug and the copper tape or telegraph wire should be connected with some old chain or old iron and laid in the bottom of the trench. The chain is covered with powdered charcoal, and the drier the ground the longer the trench will be.

2.9.8 Paint

To mix a paint the following ingredients are required: white lead or oxide of zinc, linseed oil, drier, and a pigment (e.g. black, blue, yellow, red, etc.). White lead, zinc, etc., is supplied in drums ready ground in oil. Lead is the best base for paints, but when carelessly used there is a danger of poisoning; oxide of iron and zinc are often used in its place. Linseed oil is either 'raw' or 'boiled': raw for internal work; boiled, which is thicker and heavier, for external work. 'Driers' are of various substances; 'litharge' (oxide of lead) is commonly used in England. Linseed oil is added to white lead or zinc to make it workable, and driers or litharge is added. Litharge in the proportion of a heaped teaspoonful to 4·5 kg of paint pigment is then added. Turpentine which is now largely replaced by a product of petroleum known as white spirit is mixed with linseed oil to give the paint a flat surface as opposed to a shiny finish; only a little should be used. First coats are made thinner than the succeeding coats.

The approximate quantities required are as follows. For the first coat, 1 kg of prepared paint will cover about 8–9 m^2. For subsequent coats 1 kg will cover about 12 m^2. For painting iron roofs 1 kg oxide of iron paint covers about 15–20 m^2.

A mixture of 5 l of tar with 0·5 kg of pitch, for water-proofing walls, will cover 10 m^2 as a first coat and 15 m^2 as an extra coat.

In varnishing 1 l of oil varnish will cover 3·5–4 m^2. Table 2.10 gives the results of some recent research in areas covered by paint.

Table 2.10   Superficial metres covered by 5 l of paint.

Ironwork	
Red lead, priming	80
Second coat	110
Smooth woodwork	
Stain	100
Tar	20
Oil paint priming	90
Second coat	110
Third coat	120–130
Solignum carbolineum	40
Rough woodwork	
Creosote	20
Tar	10
Plaster	
Oil paint, priming	70
Second coat	100

Water paints (distempers) cover 7 m^2 in a first coat, and 14 m^2 in a second coat, per kg.

Before woodwork is painted, the knots are treated, so that the resin cannot exude. Ordinary knotting for this purpose is made by mixing ground red lead with glue size. It is applied hot. An extra coat of red lead thinned with boiled oil and turpentine is then applied.

When lime knotting the knot must be covered with hot lime and left for twenty-four hours, after which it is scraped off and the surface is coated with red lead and glue size. For painting plaster work, it is good to apply first a coat of plain linseed oil. Finally it must be remembered that stopping (i.e., filling up the nail holes, etc.), with putty, is done after the first coat of paint is applied.

2.9.9 Whitewash
An Indian recipe for whitewash is as follows:

    50 kg clean white lime
    6·5 kg salt dissolved in hot water
    3·8 kg rice pounded and boiled to a thick paste
    0·7 kg glue

Ingredients are well mixed and brought to the required consistency by the addition of hot water, then allowed to simmer over a fire for a few hours; they are then strained and put on hot. This whitewash is said to be hard to rub off (see *PWD Handbook*, Bombay).

A little manioca flour boiled and added to the ordinary lime and water mixture improves it, and whitewash itself minimizes the absorption of heat on an iron roof.

To make whitewash adhere to stone, iron or glass, mix 10 per cent common vegetable oil with lime when slaking (the lime is weighed dry). If the oil does not saponify and incorporate with the lime it must be boiled a little, and castor oil must not be used in any case. The oil forms an insoluble soap, which will not wash off and this is then strained and applied in the usual manner (see *PWD Handbook*, Bombay).

2.9.10 Putty and Glue
Putty is made from raw linseed oil and very fine whiting well mixed by hand. A little white lead may be added.

The glue that resists moisture is made by melting 1 lb of glue in two quarts of skimmed milk. To make a strong glue add powdered chalk.

2.9.11 Metal Casements
These can be purchased in standard sizes, which vary in different countries. Casements are manufactured in the horizontal bar and small pane types. They can be supplied with metal or wooden frames (see section 3.1.5). Metal casements should be fixed as far towards the

interior of the wall opening as possible. Satisfactory fixing depends on a mastic joint between frame and masonry. When ordering casements state if they are to open inwards or outwards.

2.9.12 Glass
Glass is specified by its weight per square metre. Glass 1.5 mm thick weighs about 6 kg/m^2, 2·5 mm thick weighs about 10 kg/m^2 and 3 mm thick weighs about 13 kg/m^2. Plate glass is 6 mm thick.

2.9.13 Locks, Bolts and Nails
The furniture needed for a single door is:

    1 pair 100 mm butt hinges
    1 150 mm mortice or rim lock with furniture
    2 brass key holes
and sometimes
    1 150 mm cabin hook and eye (to hold door open).

The furniture needed for a casement window with folding sashes is:

    2 pairs 75 mm brass butt hinges
    1 brass flush bolt 19 mm × 100 mm
    1 brass flush bolt 19 mm × 460 mm
    2 casement stays
    2 150 mm hooks to hold window open

Figure 2.13 illustrates the types of hinges, bolts, nails and locks in general use. The bolts are specified by the length of bolt; the butt hinges by their vertical height and the garnet and strap hinges by the length of the strap measured from the joint. Locks are specified by their horizontal length.

Locks of the Yale pattern are quite economical and are not so much duplicated as others.

Table 2.11 Approximate number of nails in 1 kg. (The weights vary with the manufacturer (see Figure 2.13).)

Length (mm)	Cut clasp	Cut brads	Wire nails
25	1250–1300	2200	1470–1560
32	730–880	1100	860–1040
38	590–615	730–790	680–770
50	275–330	440–506	330–450
64	180–200	150–180	230–350
75	110–130	120	140–175
100	55	55	

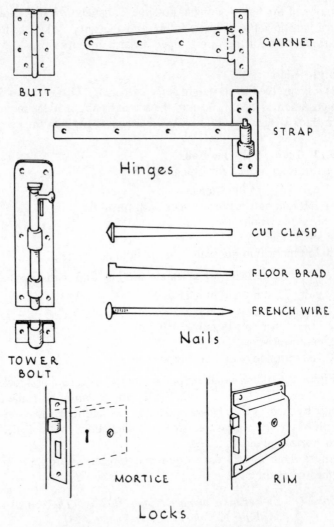

Figure 2.13 Hinges, bolts, nails and locks.

Above 100 mm in length iron nails are termed spikes. There are about ten 150 mm spikes in 1 kg.

Roofing nails of 64 mm weigh 1·5 kg per 100; 76 mm roofing nails weigh 1·9 kg per 100. In the case of the 6 mm bolts used for connecting corrugated sheets, weight per 100 is as follows: 19 mm long, 1·2 kg; 25 mm long, 1·3 kg. Limpet washers for corrugated iron weigh 0·45 kg per 100. Washers for roof bolts, diamond shape weigh 2 kg per 100.

Table 2.12   Weight of screws per 1000 (in kg).

mm	Strong	Middling	Fine
100		9	
88		9	8
75	11	7	7
64	10	7	6·5
50	10	6·5	6
38	9	6	5
25	7	5·5	3·5
19	6	4·5	3
13	3	4	2·7

2.9.14   Ant Resistance

There are many species of 'white ants' (termites). They are not always white and do not appear to be ants. Those which attack buildings are:

(a) Subterranean termites. These always maintain a ground connection. They build covered passages to reach untreated wood which they destroy. Most of the damage to buildings is caused by subterranean termites. Complete insulation of all wood from ground is the answer to their attacks.

(b) Mound-building termites. These enter buildings through wood connected with ground.

(c) Dry wood termites. These fly into buildings and require no ground connection. All timber in a building in a white ant area should be painted with solignum, Cooper's Dip, or some such preparation.

White ants of type (a) above invade the most carefully built walls. Ant-proof courses of cement concrete (section 1.2.4) as shown in Figure 2.8 are introduced to prevent their entrance. The concrete is cast *in situ* (i.e., between boards on the wall itself). The course is 75–100 mm thick. The concrete must be carefully laid. White ants will find their way through cracks and airholes in the concrete. If too much water is used in mixing concrete air holes are formed. In some places it has been found that cow dung defeats white ants. Mud mortar mixed with cow dung, or the bottom of the foundation trench treated with cow dung, is worth a trial. Where ant-proof courses are used damp-proof courses are considered unnecessary.

2.9.15   Damp Courses

For walls of sun-dried, or burnt bricks, 1 part tar to 4–5 parts powdered limestone makes a fair damp-proof course. The tar and limestone are mixed and boiled—or 1 part tar to which is added 1 part sifted lime and 1 part sand. The ingredients are boiled together. Where a thatched roof is used on sun-dried brick walls a damp-proof course should be laid on the top of the walls.

In recent years various emulsions have been produced for coating roads. Such a one is *colas*. Colas is compounded of bitumen and water. It is not necessary to heat this emulsion which is poured from a water can directly on the work, as when the water dries out it leaves a film of bitumen. As far as is known colas has not been used for walls, etc., but it might easily be tried failing other materials. It is suggested that the top of the lower courses of a sun-dried brick wall at a level just above the floor could be coated with colas, also the top of the wall just below the wall plate.

CHAPTER 3
Buildings

3.1 DESIGN OF BUILDINGS

3.1.1 General Principles

In isolated areas, the design of a building depends to a very great extent on the materials which can be found near the site. The type of building also depends on the climate. In the tropics there are varieties of climates; in some areas heating arrangements may be required in the living rooms during the cold season, in others deep continuous verandas are necessary to keep out the glare of the sun or any 'solar gain' through the walls, or driving rain. There cannot be, therefore, a standard type of building suitable for all places. Each design for a building must take into account both the materials available and the climate, and the orientation of the buildings must take note of any prevailing winds.

A plan and section, or sections, of the building should first be drawn, preferably on squared paper because of the ease with which that paper can be used. Without a drawing it is impossible to make an estimate of the cost of the proposed building, and moreover the drawing is merely a diagrammatic working out of a design. When preparing a design for a building, think from the roof down rather than the floor up. As the span of the roof and the span of the ceiling over a room varies with the lengths of timber obtainable, the size of rooms is fixed almost automatically.

When designing a house, consider whether the proposed arrangement of the rooms allows them to be covered or roofed with ease. Roofs of large span are expensive to erect, and so are roofs of irregular shape. The joints between roofs cutting each other at an angle are difficult to make and hard to keep weatherproof (section 2.8.7).

For example, if the design of a house shows a room behind a room, and the rooms are 4·2 m wide then the span of the roof will be 9·0 m (allowing for the thickness of the walls). If it is proposed to use thatch, a material often locally and easily available, the height of the apex of the roof should be at least 4·5 m above the ceiling (see section 3.5.1). A mass of grass, which when wet becomes heavy, crowns the building and dwarfs it. There will be a loft, or void, in the roof, nearly 4·5 m high, which will be practically useless except as a nursery for bats and other vermin. And in addition, the roof as a whole is inflammable. If corrugated sheets are used instead of thatch, the apex could be as low as 1·5 m above the ceiling; the weight of the roof would be much less than with thatch; and so lighter timbers would be used. It would not be so inflammable. Thus, if thatch, or some types of heavy tiles or shingles are used to cover a bungalow, the building should be comparatively narrow. And so, in design, both span and shape of roof must be kept constantly in mind, in relation to the materials available. After all the roof is the most important part of the building. But see also section 3.1.6.

3.1.2 Suggested Dimensions for Some Buildings

Hospitals:	7·5–10 m² per bed
Churches:	Accommodation, including passages, etc., for each person, 0·5–0·7 m². Width of pews: min. of 920 mm
Schools:	2·0 m² of floor per pupil
	Distance of window sills from floor 1·2 m
Garage:	6·0 m long × 3·2 m wide × 2·7 m high
Motor pit:	3·0–3·6 m long × 0·85 m wide × 1·2 m deep
Garage for trucks:	Door opening 3 m, height 4·3 m
Cattle shed:	Average area of building for each head = 10 m². Depth from wall to wall 4·5–5·5 m

3.1.3 Rooms

A good proportion for rooms is: length of room to be equal to one and a quarter times the breadth. The height of a room in the tropics ought not to be less than 3 m; and 3·6 m is better, unless it is well insulated.

The proportions of a dining room depend on the size of the dining table. Dining tables are in general 1 m–1·2 m wide; length 0·75 m per person. Allow at least 1·4 m all round the table for seating and service space. Sideboards are up to 0·75 m wide × 1·7 m long. A dining room to seat six persons in ease will be about 5 m × 4–4·25 m. If a round table is used (1·4 m dia.), then 4·25 m × 4 m will be enough.

In bedrooms it is estimated that twin beds cover at least 2 m × 2 m. A space of at least 0·6 m should be left on each side of beds. Double beds are 1·2–1·5 m wide. Beds should not be placed with long sides against wall. Wardrobes are 500–600 mm deep. Bedrooms should be at least 4 m wide.

3.1.4 Bathrooms

Where there is water-borne sanitation, bathrooms and water closets should be planned in one block to facilitate drainage, and in such a position that they are accessible from all rooms without passing from one room to another.

The minimum size for a bathroom is 1·5 m wide × 1·7 m long; a bathroom and lavatory together should be 1·8 m wide × 1·7 m long. Baths are 1·7 m long × 0·7 m wide. Lavatory basins are 630 mm wide, and 460 mm from front to back.

3.1.5 Windows and Doors

Window and door openings need not be placed in the centre of wall spaces, and generally speaking they should not be so placed. The use of the room should be considered in relation to such openings: in a bedroom, for example, the position of the bed, or beds, should be visualized. Windows and doors should be arranged so that they are in the best positions relative to them and other furniture. Windows should give left-hand light to the most important pieces of furniture (e.g., writing desks, pianos, dressing tables).

It is a general rule that the window area of a room should equal one-eighth to one-tenth of the floor space. Some advocate 20 per cent of the floor space. Window sills need not be too high: 760 mm above floor level is often sufficient, or so that a seated person can see out of the window. In bedrooms and in bathrooms, windows should be set higher in the wall.

Doors and windows placed opposite each other do not ventilate a room, they create draughts. They should be arranged so that beds, at least, are free from draughts. In bedrooms, doors should be arranged to hide the bed when they are opened.

The terms 'doors' and 'windows' do not include their frames. If doors and windows are ordered from a manufacturer it is important to specify if the frames are required as well and whether the window is to open inwards or outwards, or whether the door is to have the lock on the right hand or left hand. The opening in a wall for a single door may be taken to be 2·2 m high by 1·1 m wide. This allows for a door frame 100 mm × 75 mm and a door 2·1 m high and 0·9 m wide. Figure 3.1 shows types of door, including a *mosquito* door, and methods of fixing door panels. All dimensions can, of course, be altered to suit the style of the building. In brick buildings, the height of a door or a

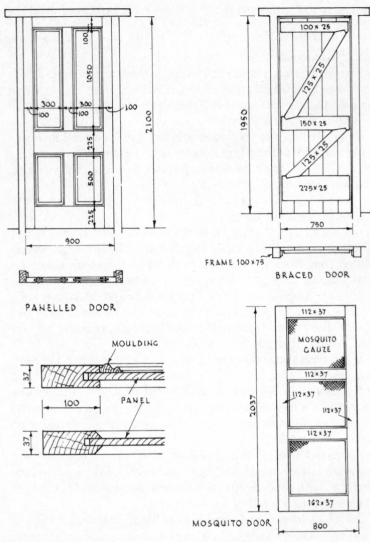

PANELLED DOOR

BRACED DOOR

MOSQUITO DOOR

Figure 3.1 Types of door.

window should be an whole number of courses of bricks, the width so many exact lengths of bricks. The proportion for the height of a door is obtained by adding 1·2 m to its width. In India the height = width + 0·9 m or 1 m. Doors of greater width than 0·9 m are hung folding—i.e., hinged down the middle.

In the tropics, window openings may be 1·8–2 m high. The lower part of the window is often made as in Figure 3.2. An upper part, or 'fanlight', is added which swings about its long axis. Both upper and lower parts are in one frame. A room 5 m × 4 m has a floor area of 20 m², and 20 per cent (see above) of this = 4 m². So in such a case, two window openings each 2 m high × 1·2 m wide would be ample. Window openings should not be too wide or there will be difficulty in supporting the wall above. Figure 3.2 also shows how glass can be fixed.

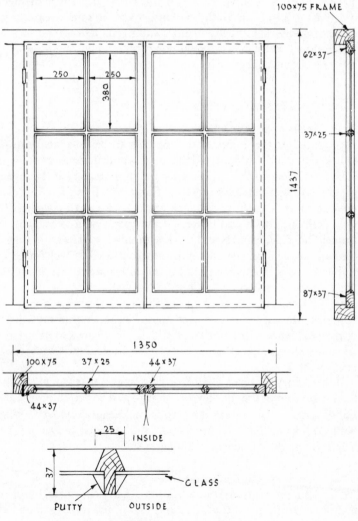

Figure 3.2 Casement.

3.1.6 Estimates of Cost

Estimates for the costs of buildings are often based on rates per m^2 of floor area. For a single storey building the floor area will be the plan area of the building. For buildings of more than one storey, the total floor area is the sum of the floor areas of each storey. Costs of buildings vary very considerably of course with locality and with the type of construction. In general, however, a square plan is cheaper than an oblong. A square building 3 m $\times$ 3 m = 9 m^2. The perimeter is 4 $\times$ 3 = 12 m. An oblong building 6 m $\times$ 1·5 = 9 m^2. The perimeter is (6 + 1·5) $\times$ 2 = 15 m. Both buildings cover the same area, but the oblong building has 25 per cent more walling, though see section 3.1.1 which shows that it may be better policy to build the oblong building in some circumstances.

3.2 SITE PREPARATION

3.2.1 Setting out Foundations

Pegs placed at the angles of the trenches to be excavated can get knocked out and lost. To avoid this, erect wooden frames as in Figure 3.3(a) well clear of the angles of the building starting at the highest part of the site. Stretch a string from frame A to frame B to represent the outer line of the finished wall and mark with a saw cut where the string cuts frames A and B. Repeat the operation for each wall, on frames C,D,E,F,G and H and mark with saw cuts. The outer lines of the walls of the finished building are now indicated on each frame. On frame A, mark the thickness of the wall with a metre rule. Mark also the foundation steps, or footings, in the wall projecting from each side of the thickness of the wall. Finally, mark the projections of the concrete. Make a saw cut for each mark. The top of frame A will now appear as Figure 3.3(b). Repeat on each frame. Strings stretched from the outer marks on the frames will give the lines of the trenches to be excavated.

If the strings are brought into the next marks, or saw-cuts, the lines for the bottom of the footings are shown, and so on. In order to set out the lines of the walls at right angles, make a large wooden triangle with sides which have the proportion of 3 : 4 : 5, as in Figure 3.3(c). The right-angle is opposite the longest side.

3.2.2 Levelling and Boning the Site

To level a piece of ground or the bottom of a trench, a straight edge or a stiff plank with parallel edges, a spirit level, and some 'boning rods' are required. Boning rods are simply 'Ts' of wood in the form of

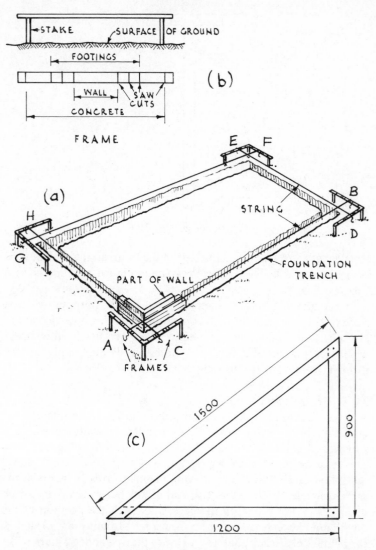

STAKE   SURFACE OF GROUND

FOOTINGS

WALL   SAW CUTS   (b)

CONCRETE

FRAME

Figure 3.3 Setting out excavations for foundations.

Figure 3.4. They may be of any convenient length. The operation of levelling a piece of ground is shown in Figure 3.5(a).

Pegs A and B are levelled by means of the spirit level and straight edge. A boning rod is placed on peg A, the second on peg B, and the top edge of the cross piece of the third is sighted in an exact line with the top edges of the first and second. Provided that the rods are all of

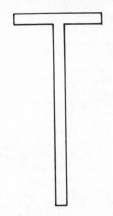

Figure 3.4 Boning rod.

equal length a peg driven at the base of the third, as at C, will be level with pegs A and B. The operation can be continued indefinitely, as in Figure 3.5(b).

In foundations, water channels, or drainage trenches where a surveyor's level is available, the operation of boning is carried out as in Figure 3.6. Sight rails are erected at a given height above pegs which are put in with the level. Boning rods are simply sighted through from sight rail to sight rail.

3.2.3   Setting out a Gradient

A rough method can be used for putting in foundation levels, the gradients of a water channel, or similar excavations where a surveyor's level is not available. Construct a frame as in Figure 1.3(b). The distance between the legs should be a convenient length. Level the frame carefully in the following manner: drive in two pegs the same distance apart as the legs, and at any height relative to each other. Place the frame on the pegs, and mark the position of the plumb line. Reverse the frame on the pegs, and again mark the line of the plumb line. Exactly half way between the first and last mark make a saw cut. When the plumb line coincides with this cut, the feet of the frame are level.

A gradient is obtained in the following way. Say the length between the legs is 4 m, and it is desired to obtain a gradient of 1 : 100. 1 : 100 is as 40 : 4000. Insert a large screw in the top of one of two levelled pegs so that its top is 40 mm above the peg. Place the frame on one peg, and on the screw of the other mark the position of the plumb line with a saw cut as before. Mark this saw cut 1 : 100. Other gradients

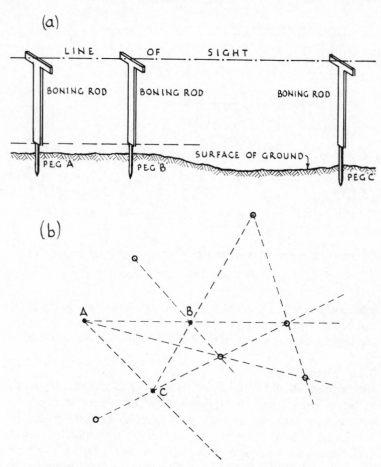

(a)

LINE   OF   SIGHT

BONING ROD   BONING ROD   BONING ROD

SURFACE OF GROUND

PEG A   PEG B   PEG C

(b)

A   B

C

PEGS A, B & C ARE LEVELLED WITH SPIRIT OR
OTHER LEVEL. THE REMAINDER ARE BONED IN.

PLAN   OF   LEVELLING   OPERATIONS

Figure 3.5 Boning.

can be worked out and marked in a similar manner. The frame will
then give various gradients, and boning rods can be used to carry
them forward. The gradient is checked by the frame at intervals. It is
not entirely necessary to construct a frame, as pegs can be driven in on
a gradient by means of a straight edge and spirit level. Pegs are
levelled, and in one a large screw is inserted, the top of which is
adjusted to the gradient, and the boning rods are used to carry the

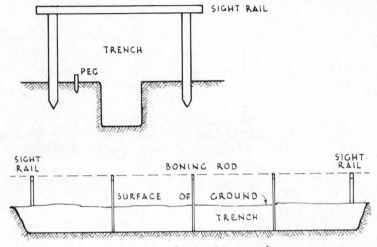

Figure 3.6 Boning in a trench.

gradient forward. The advantage of a frame is that several gradients can be marked, it is always ready for use, and the gradient as carried forward by boning rods can be checked easily and conveniently.

3.2.4 Foundations

Foundations should normally be taken down to at least a depth of 1 m below ground level or to firm rock at less than 1 m depth. In swelling clays such as black cotton soils foundations should be deeper.

Figure 3.7 shows the usual proportions of foundation for a brick wall. Sometimes foundations are carried out as Figure 3.8. Concrete is of cement, 1 : 4 : 8, or lime 1 : 2 : 4. Concrete may be dispensed with; the footings (i.e., the brick steps 56 mm wide) at the base of the wall, as in Figure 3.7, are in that case increased in number to give the wall more spread. Where concrete is used, the foundation trenches are excavated to the full width of the concrete. The concrete is laid directly in the trench and levelled off. Pegs are placed in the trenches and levelled to show the top of the concrete before concrete is deposited.

Foundation trenches must be excavated down to a bed of hard soil. Inequalities in the nature of the bed cause cracks and failures in walls. Where practicable the level of the bottom of the excavation should be the same throughout. Steps in the foundation should be avoided if possible. If soft patches occur in the soil of the bed, cut them out square and fill with concrete. Earth filling should *not* be used to bring

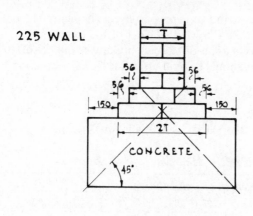

225 WALL

350 WALL

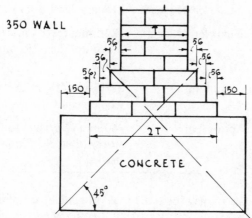

Figure 3.7 Foundation for brick walls.

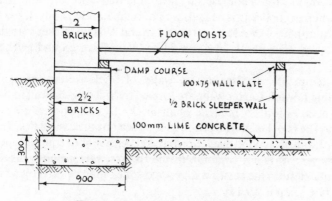

Figure 3.8 Foundation for building.

the surface of the earth to the proper level. The material from the excavations should be thrown well clear of the trenches.

The foundations of a sun-dried brick building should be of stone if possible. The stone should be built up to floor level. See section 2.3.3.

3.3 WALLS

3.3.1 A Guide to the Thickness of Walls for Dwellings

Table 3.1 Minimum wall thicknesses.

Height of walls	Length of wall between partitions	Thickness
Up to 3 m	Whatever its length	215 mm (or 1 brick)
3–4·5 m	Whatever its length	327·5 mm (or 1½ bricks) for 2·4 m up, then 215 mm (1 brick)
4·5–7·5 m	Up to 9 m	327·5 mm (1½ bricks) for whole height
	Above 9 m	440 mm (2 bricks) to first storey, then 327·5 mm (1½ bricks)

Table 3.1, above, may be taken as a guide for minimum requirements. For inferior brickwork, the thickness should be increased by a half or a whole brick, especially in outside walls. Thick walls make for coolness in hot climates and prevent heat loss when the building is heated, in a cold climate. Generally, the wall up to plinth level should be between 115 and 230 mm thicker than the wall above. The plinth level should be 0·6 m from ground level, at least.

In temperate climates 'cavity walls' of brick are customary in dwelling houses. Cavity walls are formed by building the wall in two thicknesses of 102·5 mm (i.e., half-brick) at a distance of 50 mm apart. The two thicknesses are bound together by metal wall ties. This type of wall gives good insulation but is expensive and requires expert bricklayers. It is not common in the tropics where solid walls are general. Besides the cavity is a passage which may be used by white ants (see section 2.9.14).

3.3.2 Brick Walls

The first essential in a well-built brick wall is to obtain a good 'bond'. 'Bond' is an arrangement whereby no vertical joint of one layer or 'course', of bricks is directly over, or under, the one below, or above it. Bricks are bedded in mortar to distribute the pressure evenly over the underlying bricks, as well as to obtain adhesion and to make the wall weatherproof.

Both in the 'footings' and in the wall proper, a 'bond' is maintained. A strong simple system is known as 'English bond'. Figure 3.9 gives details for laying bricks in several thicknesses of walls. A 'header' is a brick with its length running into the wall. A 'stretcher' has its length on the surface of the wall. To lay English bond, first place a corner brick, which is always a 'header'. Next place a brick cut lengthwise, or a 'closer'. Continue with 'headers' along the face of the wall until the corner is reached, and just before the last 'header' (i.e., corner), again lay a 'closer'. The 'closer' is most important and is always the thickness of one half the full breadth of a brick (i.e., just over 50 mm). The next course above is all stretchers. If you can anticipate where you will want to fix nails or pegs, wooden bricks are sometimes built in the wall. English bond can be used in sun-dried brickwork. Burnt bricks must be soaked in water before use if good work is to be done.

Double Flemish bond has headers and stretchers alternately in the same course, both on the outside and inside of the wall. It is economical, but weaker than English bond. In laying Double Flemish bond, first place a header, then a closer as for English bond, then a stretcher, then a header, and continue stretchers and headers alternately. In the next course above, commence with stretchers then follow with a header. No closers are necessary in this course. The third, fifth, seventh, etc., courses are as the first; and the second, fourth, etc., courses are alike.

In Dutch bond, the courses run headers and stretchers but in every alternate stretcher course a header is introduced as the second brick from the end.

Inexperienced bricklayers easily get 'out of bond', and their corners out of level. Build up a corner six bricks or 'courses' high. Mark each course on a rod, or piece of wood, and build up all the other corners to the marks on the rod. Bricklayers fill in between the courses, building up to a string, or line stretched from corner to corner. Care must be taken to avoid pulling out the string. Hoop iron laid flat in the joints and bent down at the ends increases the strength of brickwork.

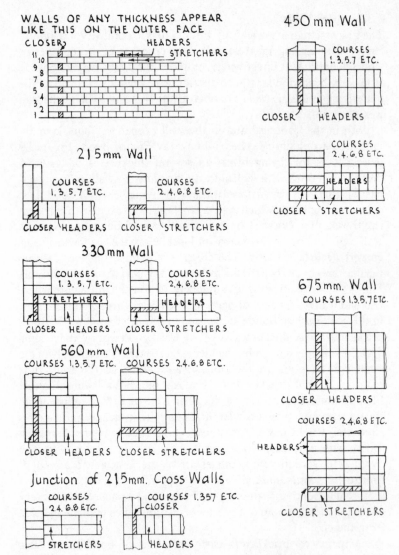

Figure 3.9 Brickwork, English bond.

3.3.3 Brickwork: The Number of Bricks Required

Calculate the cubic contents of all walls (i.e., multiply length of wall by height and by breadth, all in metres). Deduct door and window openings. The size of locally made burnt bricks can vary considerably, and in local brickwork the mortar joints are unusually thick. If a brick, together with the thickness of its joint on the top, on the back and on one end, measures 225 mm × 112·5 mm × 75 mm, then the number of bricks for every cubic metre in the wall equals 553, allowing for 5 per cent wastage. For mud mortar allow 0·3 m³ per 1 m³ of wall. Brickwork of 1 m³ requires 0·15–0·2 m³ of slaked lime, if lime mortar is used. For 1 m² of walling (measured on the face of the wall) the number of bricks required are as shown in Table 3.2.

Table 3.2   Number of bricks per 1 m² of walling.

Thickness of wall	Number of bricks approximate
½ brick	59
1 brick	119
1½ bricks	178

If the outside of a wall of sun-dried brick is coated with two coats of hot palm oil, or 'ghee' (clarified butter fat), it is greatly improved. It is possible that old sump oil for cars or lorries might improve the bottom courses. A mixture of 1 lime : 1 sand or 1 cement : 3–4 sand, brushed on the surface of the wall, will help to preserve it.

The following recipe is claimed to be effective for waterproofing brickwork: 1 kg sodium silicate to 10 l of water, applied to the work on a dry day, preferably by a spray. After 24 hours apply the following—1 kg of calcium chloride in 10 l of water, which should be rain water. The calcium chloride combines with the soluble silicate of soda to reproduce an insoluble silicate of lime which fills the pores of the brickwork.

3.3.4   Brick Arches

Brick arches are turned over door and window openings and other similar gaps in a wall. If arches are not built, wood or concrete lintels are introduced (see sections 2.5.7, 2.6.5 and 3.3.5). A wooden core or 'centre' is first made. A 'centre' usually consists of wooden ribs, 25 mm thick, separated by laths (see Figure 3.10). The bricks are laid on the 'centre' in rings 112·5 mm in thickness (i.e., bricks on edge); two rings for a span of 1 m; three rings for 1·5 m. Add another ring for every 1·5 m span.

If a series of arches is to be built, supported by pillars (as in an arcade) the end pillars, or abutments, must be of greater breadth than the intermediate pillars, or the arches will push the abutments out. A rough rule for arcades: Thickness of pillars are one-sixth of the span

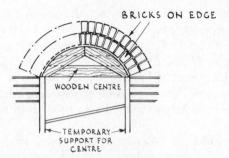

Figure 3.10 Brick arch.

of the arch (but see section 3.3.7). Ends or abutments are one quarter of the span of arch.

In a semi-circular arch the tendency is for the key or crown to fall in and for the next sections or 'haunches' of the arch to be thrust up. If the haunches only are loaded (i.e., well weighted with brickwork in order to keep them in position) the weight of brickwork tends to squeeze the crown and force it up. But if *both* crown and haunches are well covered with brickwork, the movements are neutralized to some extent. Old masons say a loaded arch is the strongest arch.

A good rule for the radius of an arch over windows and doors is to make it equal to the width of the opening.

The wooden centre of an arch should not be removed until the brickwork has been built over the arch (i.e., until the arch is loaded) but it can be gradually relieved by loosening wedges before the mortar is fully set—thus allowing the bricks to settle.

3.3.5 Lintels
For a beam or lintel over a window, door or other opening of ordinary width, where the superimposed masonry is not supported by an arch, allow 26–31 mm of depth to a beam for every 250 mm of the opening. The width of the beam or beams will be the thickness of the wall. The bearing at each end is 150 mm. See section 2.5.7.

3.3.6 Chimneys and Fireplaces
Chimneys and fireplaces are built in brickwork, stone or concrete. An Indian-type fireplace is shown in Figure 3.11. Chimneys should be built at least 1 metre higher than any neighbouring roof ridge, or a full height of 6 m. It is best to build the outside brickwork of chimneys at least 215 mm thick. To avoid gutters behind chimney stacks, the stacks should penetrate the roof ridge, or be built at the gables; see

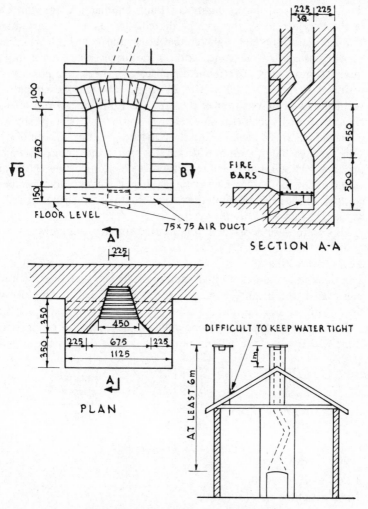

Figure 3.11 Indian-type fireplace.

Figure 3.11. The flue should change its direction in easy curves, as soot accumulates on abrupt shoulders. The size of flues is 225 mm × 225 mm or 225 mm × 337·5 mm. If the interior of the flue is coated with lime and cow dung it improves the construction. In wet or cold climates it is best to build fireplaces on inside walls, in order to preserve the heat.

The following method (Count Rumford's method) of building fireplaces has been used successfully in the USA and the UK. Above the fireplace a bell-shaped chamber is built. The distance from the top of the fireplace to the bottom of the chamber is never more than 150–200 mm. Fireplace and chamber are connected by a 'throat' or 'smoke passage' of the same width as the fireplace and never more than 100 mm across. (Thus the dimensions of the smoke passage = width of fireplace × 100 mm × 200 mm.) The smoke passage is vertically over the position of the fire. The floor, or bottom of the chamber forms a shelf (the smoke shelf) on three sides of the smoke passage (i.e., at the back and on the two sides, but not in front of it). The shelf is 100–150 mm wide, or more. (If the smoke passage opening was 360 mm × 360 mm, the base or floor of the chamber would be 660 mm × 255 mm.) From the shelf, the sides of the chamber contract until they unite with the flue or chimney, which would have, say, a 230 mm × 230 mm opening.

This method of construction has cured smokey chimneys.

3.3.7 Brick Pillars
The thickness of a brick pillar should not be less than one-tenth to one-twelfth the height of the pillar. See Figure 3.12 for details of bond, and see also section 3.3.4.

The same rule applies to stone pillars if they are made of 'dressed' stone. Otherwise stone pillars should be thicker than brick pillars.

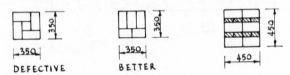

Figure 3.12 Brick pillars.

3.3.8 Concrete Walls
There are three general types:

  (a) Walls built of machine-made concrete blocks.
  (b) Walls of hand-cast concrete blocks.
  (c) Walls of concrete cast *in situ*.

Concrete blocks are laid in mortar, as with bricks (see section 3.3.2). Figure 3.13 shows the method of laying concrete blocks in a wall. See also section 2.5.8.

For walls of concrete cast *in situ* a casing or 'shuttering' is first constructed to enclose the wall, or part of it. The concrete is placed in the 'shuttering' on and in the wall itself, and rammed in position.

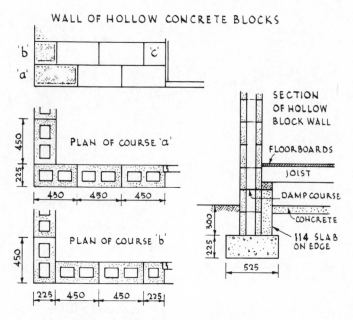

Figure 3.13 Laying concrete blocks.

Load-bearing concrete should usually be reinforced with steel (see section 2.5.7). Except where suitable boards for the 'shuttering' are cheap, skilled labour and good supervision are available, or several buildings of the same size and dimensions are to be erected, this method of construction does not commend itself. 'Shuttering' must be as simple as possible. It must be strong enough to resist the pressure of the concrete without bulging, and must be so designed to allow it to be easily removed. Figure 3.14(a) shows a type of 'shuttering'. 'Shuttering' must not be removed until the concrete is set. Allow 24 hours at the very least. If the 'shuttering' supports a floor, or a beam, allow up to three weeks before removing it. The 'shuttering' may be made of timber or metal. This type of shuttering may also be used as a 'climbing' shutter. In this method, the wall is first completed within the shutter for the entire length of the wall. The shutter is then raised.

Fence posts, lintels, etc., can be cast in the same fashion as hand-cast blocks (see Figures 3.14(b) and (c) for moulds). It is necessary to 'cure' cast concrete in the same manner as described for machine-made concrete blocks.

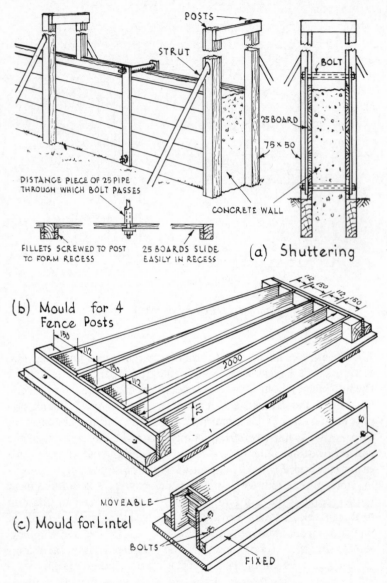

POSTS

STRUT

BOLT

DISTANCE PIECE OF 25 PIPE
THROUGH WHICH BOLT PASSES

25 BOARD

75 × 50

FILLETS SCREWED TO POST
TO FORM RECESS

25 BOARDS SLIDE
EASILY IN RECESS

CONCRETE WALL

(a) Shuttering

(b) Mould for 4
Fence Posts

112   150   112   150

150

112

150

2000

112

112

MOVEABLE

(c) Mould for Lintel

BOLTS

FIXED

Figure 3.14 Formwork for concrete.

3.4 FLOORS

3.4.1 Beaten Lime Floor

A floor may be constructed in the following manner: on a bed of sand, lay a flat course of bricks or stone. On this bed lay about 150 mm of broken brick, small enough to pass through a 20 mm ring, mixed with dry lime. When in position the broken brick is saturated with water, raked well and beaten down. The floor is finished with a thin layer of stiff lime mortar which is beaten down. The final coat is of lime laid on and rubbed in.

3.4.2 Concrete Floor

Concrete floors of 'the Madras type' consist of 20–40 mm of fine cement concrete laid on 100–125 mm of lime concrete. The cement concrete is laid before the lime concrete has set. The surface of the lime concrete must be moistened. The surface of the cement concrete is beaten until the mortar comes to the surface, and the floor is then polished with trowels.

Figure 2.8 on page 63 shows a usual type of floor. The floor is 75–100 mm thick and is laid on a bed of hard core (i.e., stone, or broken brick, well rammed) 150 mm thick. The concrete should be laid in one operation with as little delay as possible. A good floor is also obtained by laying 65 mm of concrete, covering it with wire netting, then laying another 65 mm of concrete. The filling should be sand, if obtainable. Earth filling must be laid in narrow layers, rammed and watered. Ordinary material excavated from the foundations is liable to contract on drying, unless thoroughly consolidated, and the floor sinks and cracks in consequence (see section 2.3.3). Cracks often develop at (A) in Figure 2.8, through which white ants find their way. Introduce a strip of flat galvanized iron sheet at this point. The concrete mix for floors should be 1 : 3 : 6 cement : sand : aggregate—see section 2.5.3). The floor may be finished with a coat of cement plaster (1 : 3), trowelling it to a smooth surface. It is important to clean the concrete surface thoroughly before applying the plaster. If the ant course and floor can be laid in one operation, so much the better.

The floor when laid should be kept damp for a week by spreading wet sand over it, or by any other convenient method.

3.4.3 Timber Floor

The following rules were made when timber was plentiful. Now that timber has become more difficult to buy, it has to be used more economically. It has been found, for example, that floor joists 50 mm × 200 mm of stress-graded timber, spaced 460 mm from centre to centre, will span from 4 to 4·3 m depending on the type of timber. But the timber generally available for such work as contemplated here is not stress-graded, and the following rules should make for sound work. The joists, however, may be spaced 300 mm or more apart, depending on the thickness of the floor boards.

A rough method for sizing floor joists is to divide the unsupported length in millimetres by 24 and add 50 to give the depth of the beam in mm. The width is one third of the depth, rounded up to the next 5 mm.

Example
Unsupported length of beam (span) = 3·6 m
3600 divided by 24 + 50 = 200 mm (depth of beam)
Width = 1/3 depth = 66·7 mm
Size of joist = 200 mm × 70 mm

The size of floor joist required will also depend on the designed loading, and the quality of the timber. Table 3.3 gives some joist dimensions for different load conditions, and spacing for medium grade timber (defined by British Standards as GS, MGS, M50, and M75).

*Table 3.3   Timber joist dimensions.**

| | Joist cross sections (mm) | | | |
| | Dead load less than 25 kg/m² | | Dead load 25–50 kg/m² | |
Span (m)	(400 mm)	(600 mm)	(400 mm)	(600 mm)
2	44 × 100	44 × 125	50 × 100	50 × 125
2·5	38 × 125	44 × 150	44 × 125	44 × 150
3	38 × 150	44 × 175	44 × 150	50 × 175
3·5	38 × 175	44 × 200	44 × 175	50 × 200
4	38 × 200	50 × 225	44 ×200	75 × 200
4·5	50 × 200	75 × 200	44 ×225	75 × 225
5	50 × 225	75 × 225		

* The dead load does not include the weight of the joist itself which is generally small. Imposed loading is not greater than 1500 kg/m². Spacing of joists 400 mm and 600 mm centre to centre.

Long spans over 5 m with timbers 50 or 75 mm thick are not recommended. Long floor joists bend and can cause cracking of the ceilings beneath. Floor joists of all sizes are stiffened to prevent them from twisting. See Figure 3.15(a)–(e).

Where a floor has to cover a large area, the difficulty of long spans for floor joists is overcome by building dwarf walls, or 'sleeper walls' (see Figure 3.8) to support the joists on ground floors, and by the use of 'binders' on upper floors. 'Binders' are wooden beams of large section, or rolled steel joists, and are placed from 1.2 m up to 3 m apart. The floor joists are fixed from binder to binder.

Table 3.4 gives some dimensions for binders for different load conditions and spacing for medium grade timber (defined by British Standards as GS, MGS, M50 and M75).

Table 3.4   Timber binder dimensions *

Span (m)	Binder cross section (mm)					
	Dead load 25 kg/m²: (binder spacing)			Dead load 25–50 kg/m² (binder spacing)		(m)
	(1·20)	(1·80)	(2·40)	(1·20)	(1·80)	(2·40)
1·0	38 × 75	50 × 75	38 × 100	44 × 75	38 × 100	50 × 100
1·5	44 × 100	44 × 125	38 × 150	38 × 125	50 × 125	50 × 150
2·0	50 × 125	50 × 150	50 × 175	44 × 150	38 × 200	50 × 200
2·5	44 × 175	44 × 200	50 × 225	38 × 200	44 × 225	{75 × 200 / 63 × 225}
3·0	44 × 200	50 × 225	75 × 225	44 × 225	63 × 225	
3·5	50 × 225	75 × 225		75 × 200		
4·0	63 × 225			75 × 225		

* The dead load does not include the weight of the beam itself. Imposed loading is not greater than 1500 kg/m². Spacing of binders 1·20 m, 1·80 m and 2·40 m.

3.4.4   Floors and Floor Boards

It is essential that the underside of wooden floors should be well ventilated. Where white ants are known to be present arrange that the floor is high enough from the ground for a man to pass under (1 m at least) so that the joists may be examined. Openings must be left in the walls for this purpose.

Floor boards are normally from 25 to 40 mm thick and 100–230 mm wide, though they may be wider. Details of joints are shown on Figure 3.15(f). If floor boards are ordered to cover a specified area, allow 10 per cent extra for wastage. Floor boards are in reality beams, the greater the distance between joists the thicker they must be.

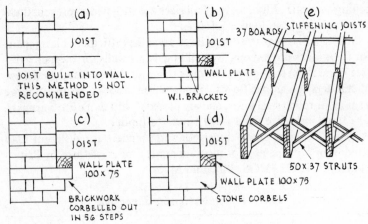

(a)(b)(c)(d) SHOWS METHOD OF SUPPORTING JOISTS ON UPPER FLOORS WHERE THE WALL IS OF THE SAME THICKNESS IN THE LOWER AS IN THE UPPER STOREY

(f) JOINTS OF FLOORBOARDS

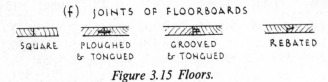

Figure 3.15 Floors.

3.5 ROOFS

3.5.1 Design of Roofs

The dimensions of the timbers in a roof depend on their unsupported lengths, the weight of the roof covering, the uplift pressure of the wind, and, in some climates, on the weight of snow:

(a) Clay tiles weigh 45–80 kg/m².
(b) Thatch weighs about 30–50 kg/m² and is heavier wet.
(c) Corrugated iron weighs 10–15 kg/m².

Thus a tiled roof requires much stronger and heavier timbers than a corrugated iron roof. An asbestos slate roof requires timber of about the same dimensions as a corrugated iron roof. Tiles and thatch need to be laid at a much steeper pitch than corrugated iron or the wind and rain will drive under the tiles, or the wind will get under the thatch and blow it off.

Figure 3.16 shows a 'gabled' and a 'hipped' roof. A gabled roof is usually easier to construct than a 'hipped' roof in that there is no cutting of the corrugated iron or of the tiles. Advantage may be taken of the gable to ventilate and light the interior of the roof; it is more difficult to do these things in a hipped roof.

In simple buildings, provided that the span is not too great, it is better to arrange for a long line of unbroken roof rather than to break it up into ridges and valleys. The intersection of two roofs is often difficult to make watertight with the materials and labour available, and a deep gutter between two roofs is always difficult to maintain in good condition. When this is to be attempted, galvanized iron ridging reversed is used to form 'valleys' (i.e., the line of intersection, between roofs, see Figure 3.16).

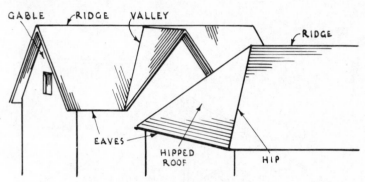

Figure 3.16 Types of roof.

The rise of a roof for different materials is as shown below:

Clay tiles	$\frac{1}{4}$–$\frac{1}{2}$ span
Thatch	$\frac{1}{2}$ span minimum
Shingles	$\frac{1}{2}$ span
Corrugated iron	not less than 1/10th span

To find area of roof, for a gable roof, measure the total length of one rafter on the slope from the plan of the building. Twice this amount multiplied by the length of the building plus the length of projection of the roof at the ends is the area required. For a 'hip' roof, the area is twice the length of one rafter measured on the slope, multiplied by the mean length of roof (i.e., the length of the roof measured half way up the slope) plus the width of roof at the end of the building multiplied by the length of the rafter at the centre of the hip.

3.5.2 General Principles of Construction
The general principles of roof construction are shown in Figure 3.17. Figure 3.17(a) shows a simple roof called a 'couple'. The weight of the

roof covering, the pressure of the wind, etc., cause the lower ends of the rafters to open like a pair of compasses pivoted at P, and the walls tend to be pushed apart and the rafters to sink as shown in dotted lines. To overcome this weakness a piece of timber is secured to the lower end of the rafters at AB (Figure 3.17(b)). This timber AB is called a 'tie'. To the 'tie' the ceiling, if any, is secured; the tie is then called a 'ceiling joist'. No other precaution is necessary in a roof of up to about 4·5 m horizontal span. If these spans are increased, the rafters will tend to bend under the weight which they carry. The

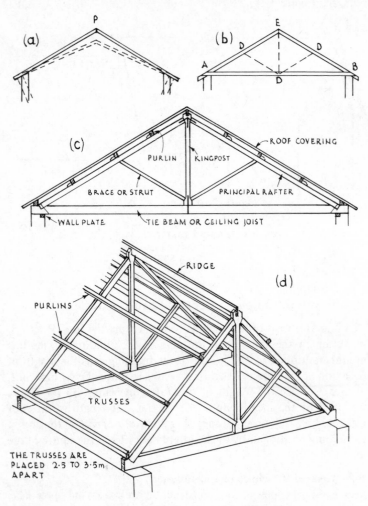

Figure 3.17 Construction of roof.

bending can be overcome by introducing struts as at DD. In spans over 6 m the struts DD will tend to push the tie beam down, and in order to prevent this another piece of timber is introduced at ED. The complete frame as it stands in Figure 3.17(c) is called a 'king post' roof truss. Care must be taken with the joints in a king post roof. The piece of timber ED, in Figure 3.17(b) (i.e., the king post) is in tension. It is not a pillar. It must be secured to AB (the tie beam) so that it can pull (see Figure 3.19(h) and (i)). Such frames, or trusses, are placed from 2·5 to 3·5 m apart (see Figure 3.17(d)). Beams or 'purlins' running in a direction parallel to the ridge of the roof connect the trusses. On the 'purlins' the roof is laid, either by securing corrugated iron to the purlins, or by covering the purlins with boarding and laying the roofing material on the boards, or by making the purlins support other rafters ('common rafters') which carry the roofing material. The elaborations outlined above are not necessary in all roofs, but the underlying principles are the same in all of whatever span. These are:

(a) To keep the timbers which carry the roof covering, or in other words the rafters, rigid.
(b) To prevent the rafters from thrusting out the walls, or disturbing the ceiling.

These conditions can only be accomplished by a frame in the shape of a triangle, and provided the timbers are strong, the roof cannot alter shape (see also section 3.5.10).

3.5.3   Roofs for Rural Types of Buildings

Roofs are often erected as shown in Figure 3.18(a); this method is sometimes dear to rural people, but it is unsound. The centre pole sinks, or the walls settle and there is nothing to prevent the whole structure from twisting. If a beam is fixed to the lower end of the pole rafters as shown by dotted lines, the structure (both roof and walls) will be secure.

In buildings of a rural type which are roofed with thatch, use pole or stick rafters about 75–90 mm dia. which are placed 30–60 cm apart. Long rafters in roofs of large spans must be well supported either by pole 'purlins' secured to trusses, or by braces running down to cross or internal walls as described in section 3.5.5.

A rough truss of round timbers can be made as shown in the full lines at A (Figure 3.18(a)). The trusses are about 3 m apart. For a 6 m span the principal rafters are about 100–125 mm dia. The tie is about 25 cm. The collar (half way up the rafters) is about 100–150 mm dia.

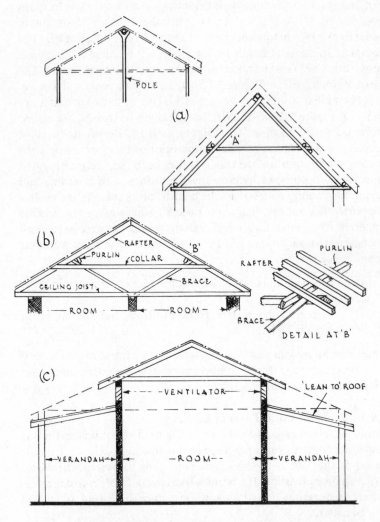

Figure 3.18 Roof supports.

The 'common rafters' carrying the thatch are secured to purlins. The joints of the truss are secured with bolts or iron straps. For a description of principal rafters, tie beams etc., see Figure 3.17(c).

3.5.4 Dimensions of Prepared Timbers in Roof
For a roof covered with clay tiles with a pitch of roof half span Table 3.5 gives the dimensions of the timbers.

Table 3.5   Dimensions of roof timbers

Distance between walls or span (m)	Rafters 0·6 m apart (mm)	Ridge (mm)	Tie beams (ceiling joists) (mm)	King posts (mm)
3	90 × 50	180 × 25	100 × 50	
3·5–4·25	115 × 50	200 × 25	100 × 50 (180 × 50)	100 × 50
4·25–4·5	125 × 50	239 × 25	100 × 50 (200 × 50)	100 × 50

The rafters are 0·6 m apart, centre to centre.

Battens for tiles 60 mm × 32 mm, should be spaced 300 mm centre to centre. Ceilings can be made of a number of materials (see section 2.8). If 'king posts' are not used then the ties, or ceiling joists, must be increased to the figures in brackets. King posts are well nailed to sides of rafters and ceiling joints. A common rule used in India, for example, is 1/24th unsupported length of rafter = depth. A rough rule for the dimensions of ceiling joists is to allow 10 mm in depth for every 0·25 m of span and 50 mm thick.

For corrugated iron roofs the pitch of roof should be between one tenth and one quarter of the span. The same dimensions for roof timbers as listed above are suitable for corrugated iron roofs, only the rafters are placed up to 1·5–1·8 m apart. Each set of rafters with their tie beams becomes a complete frame or 'truss'. Battens, or light purlins 75 mm × 50 mm are secured to the trusses and the corrugated iron is nailed to these. The position of the battens depends on the length of corrugated iron sheets used. The horizontal joints of the sheets are arranged to occur over a batten.

3.5.5   Supports for Roof other than Trusses
The internal walls of buildings can also be utilized to support the roof as shown in Figure 3.18(b). 'Braces' or struts can be brought down from every sixth rafter, approximately, to a division or other wall. The struts support purlins as shown and the purlins support the intermediate rafters. Rafters should also be braced diagonally. Expedients such as these can be adapted to any form of building and as long as the principles of construction laid down above are followed the roof will be sound.

3.5.6   Roofs over Verandahs
In buildings with verandahs it is often simpler to make the roof span

the main rooms only and to give the verandahs a 'lean-to' roof as in Figure 3.18(c), rather than to construct it as shown by the dotted lines. This type of construction assists ventilation of the main rooms. The rafters of the verandah are 100 mm × 50 mm. Verandahs should be 2·4 m high to the underside of beams.

3.5.7 Dimensions of King Post Trusses

A very rough rule for the dimensions of king post roof trusses, spaced 3 m apart, is as follows:

Thickness of the truss in mm should = 20 × span in metres – 23.
Depth of tie beam = 30 × span in metres + 50 mm.

The king post should be square in section in the centre. The top and bottom should be twice the width in the centre. The width of the ends is twice the thickness of the truss.

See Figure 3.17(c) and (d). Table 3.6 gives dimensions for roofs covered with corrugated iron, pitch a quarter of the span and trusses 3–3·5 m apart. The corrugated iron is secured direct to purlins 150 mm × 100 mm.

Table 3.6   King post truss dimensions (pitch quarter span). *

Span (m)	Tie beam (D)	(B)	Principal rafters (D)	(B)	King post (D)	(B)	Struts (D)	(B)
5–6	150	75	125	75	100	75	100	75
6–7·6	200	75	150	75	100	75	100	75
7·6–9	230	100	150	100	100	100	100	100

* *D* = depth (in mm); *B* = breadth (in mm).

Table 3.7 gives dimensions for roofs covered with tiles, with a pitch up to half span and trusses 3–3·5 m apart. Purlins are 200 mm × 125 mm to 230 mm × 150 mm, with common rafters 100 mm × 50 mm.

3.5.8 Composite or Compound Trusses

In a well-designed truss, the king post and tie beam are subject to tensile stress (i.e., these members tend to stretch) or to be pulled apart. Wrought iron or mild steel has a much greater tensile strength than wood, and so wrought iron or steel is often substituted for wood in the tension members. A truss of wood and iron is called a composite, or compound, truss. A composite truss is suitable for

Table 3.7   King post truss dimensions (pitch up to half span). *

Span (m)	Tie beam (D)	(B)	Principal rafters (D)	(B)	King Post (D)	(B)	Struts (D)	(B)
5·0	185	75	105	75	80	75	80	50
5·5	205	75	105	75	80	75	90	50
6·0	230	100	105	75	105	75	90	50
6·5	230	125	125	75	125	75	100	50
7·0	250	125	125	90	125	75	100	65
7·5	260	125	130	90	130	75	105	65
8·0	285	125	130	100	130	100	115	65
8·5	285	150	145	100	155	100	120	75
9·0	305	150	150	105	155	100	130	75

* D = depth (in mm); B = breadth (in mm).

halls, etc.; its disadvantages are that the timber members shrink and the iron expands and contracts.

In place of the king post a wrought-iron rod of 20–25 mm dia., according to the span of the truss, may be introduced. See Figure 3.19(a) for details of fixing a tie beam.

A composite truss to span 7·6 m to carry ordinary roofing has been made of the following dimensions: principal rafter 125 mm × 100 mm; collar (i.e., a timber fixed between the two principal rafters half way up their length see Figure 3.18(b)) 200 mm × 100 mm, notched to rafters; king tie rod 22 mm dia.; tie rods (from feet of principal rafters to meet king rod under the collar) 22 mm dia. (see also section 3.5.10).

3.5.9   Joints in Timbers

Figure 3.19 shows some common joints used in carpentry. Figure 3.19(b) is a 'fished' joint and is suitable for lengthening timber when in compression as in posts or pillars. The length of the 'fish plate' is four times the thickness of the beam. Figure 3.19(c) is a lapped scarf and is a fairly good all-round joint. It is suitable for beams, but not for posts supporting moving loads. It would be improved by the use of fish plates. The length ab of the lap equals $2^{3}/_{4}t$. The form of joint in Figure 3.19(d) is largely used in tie beams. The hard wood wedges in the centre drive the two timbers together. The length of the scarf $ab = 2^{1}/_{2}$–3 times d, or the depth of the beam. Figure 3.19(e) is good either in compression or tension.

The usual dimensions for the joint are shown in the drawing. The

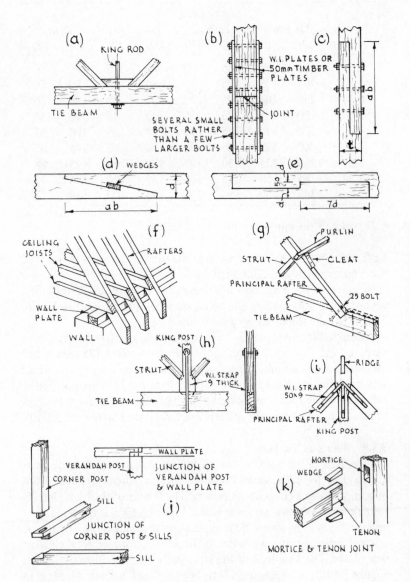

Figure 3.19 Joints in timber.

other drawings in this illustration show the joint between rafters and the wall plate (Figure 3.19(f)), the joints in a king post truss (Figures 3.19(g), (h) and (i)), a halved joint and 'stub tenon' (Figure 3.19(j)) and a mortise and tenon joint (Figure 3.19(k)).

3.5.10 Metal Roof Trusses

Roof trusses made of mild steel or light metal alloy are used in many countries. They may be supplied in standard sizes from spans of about 5 m upwards, or may be fabricated locally to specific requirements. For spans greater than 10 m, trusses are too large to handle except by experienced engineers. With suitable purlins they are placed 2·5–3 m apart when carrying tiles and 3–3·5 m apart when carrying light corrugated iron sheets.

3.5.11 Gutters

Medical authorities are usually averse to standing water, on health grounds, and as fixing gutters to buildings is often very desirable in order to collect water for storage purposes (section 4.2.3) it is important to prevent water collecting in any such system. If carefully hung, with a fall of 8 mm/m and supported so that they do not sag, there is thus every advantage in fixing a gutter to a roof. For ease of transport light galvanized sheet guttering is usually used in the tropics. Asbestos, cement and PVC guttering and pipes are becoming popular.

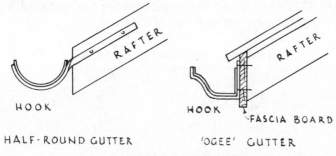

Figure 3.20 Guttering.

Galvanized sheet gutters can be obtained in 2 m and shorter lengths. There are two shapes, 'half round' and *Ogee*, 250–900 mm in girth. Gutters are supported on hooks (see Figure 3.20). Down pipes are 75–250 mm dia., and bends and shoes are also made of the same material. Down pipes are normally made in 2 m lengths. With thatched roofs, wooden 'V' gutters were often used in old buildings.

3.6 MISCELLANEOUS

3.6.1 Ceilings

Split bamboos, 25 mm broad and free from borers, may be used as laths in lath and plaster ceilings. They are spaced about 13 mm apart. Hair is added to the plaster (2 kg/0·25 m³); sisal tow might be used. For the plaster 1 lime : 2–3 sand is used for the first coat which must be thin (not more than 13 mm). The second coat of 13 mm is 1 lime : 1 sand and 'fat' lime (section 2.4.1) is used. Many ceilings fail because the plaster is too thick.

Asbestos sheets (section 2.8.2) and fibre boards (section 2.8.3) are also used for ceilings. Good insulation under corrugated iron has been obtained by covering the upper and lower sides of the rafters with ceiling (fibre) boards. Wooden boards are fixed on the upper surface so that a man can walk in the void of the roof. Bush poles are sometimes laid across a room with a thatched roof. On these, locally made mats are spread and on these again 150 mm of earth, well consolidated. On the underside of the poles, trade calico is stretched and nailed, and it can be whitewashed. If any thatch should burn, it then falls on the earth covering.

3.6.2 Steps and Stairs

Figure 3.21(a) shows the proportions for steps from a verandah.

Figure 3.21(b) shows the construction of wooden stairs. The treads are 230–330 mm wide, and 30 mm thick for steps 1–2 m broad. The accepted proportions are as shown in Table 3.8.

Table 3.8 Dimensions for stairs in mm.

Riser	Tread
140	330
150	305
180	255
190	230

The 'strings' are 50 mm thick. The treads and risers are 'housed'—that is, fitted into grooves cut in the 'strings' and secured by wedges.

3.6.3 Frame Buildings

Figure 3.22 gives some general details of a building built up on a wooden frame.

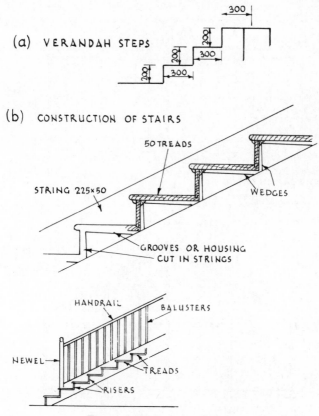

Figure 3.21 Steps and stairs.

Here are some particulars of a wooden bungalow which has actually been erected:

Three rooms each 6 m × 5 m
At end small room 3·7 m × 3 m and bath 3 m × 2·4 m
Verandah 2·4 m wide
Roof principals 2·4 m centres, main rafters 127 mm × 75 mm
Collars (see section 3.5.8 and Figure 3.18) 178 mm × 75 mm
Purlins 114 mm × 50 mm carrying corrugated iron
Under all principals and at corners 100 mm × 75 mm uprights, 100
   mm × 50 mm studs, wall plates, horizontals and sills
Door and window frames 100 mm × 50 mm
Verandah posts 100 mm × 75 mm, 2·4 m spacing
Frames covered with 25 mm boarding

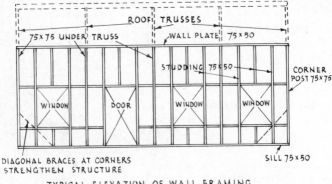

TYPICAL ELEVATION OF WALL FRAMING

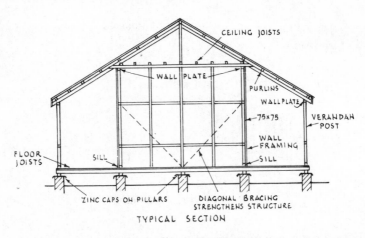

TYPICAL SECTION

Figure 3.22 Frame building.

Studding is the term used to describe the uprights which run from the top beam (wall plate) to the bottom beam (sill) as shown. They are spaced from 0·6 m to 1·0 m or even more apart, depending on the type of building. A frame building may be covered with corrugated iron, flat steel sheets, asbestos sheets, or weather boarding. Wood slabs tend to shrink and so does ordinary boarding, particularly in the sun. The joints between the boards open, and gaps are seen. These gaps can be closed with strips of wood (fillets) nailed over them, but the fillets will split with the shrinkage of the boards if they are nailed both sides of the gap. If possible arrange a verandah to protect boarded walls.

Corrugated iron on the outside of a frame building demands a lining on the inside (see sections 2.9.1–2.9.3 for insulation). Great care is necessary in the use of corrugated sheets. Bats will enter by way of the corrugations between the sheets and lining, and their stench ultimately becomes unbearable.

CHAPTER 4
Water Development

4.1 WATER RESOURCES

4.1.1 Sources of Water

The primary source of fresh water is rainfall, which may be collected directly from catchment surfaces, drawn from streams, rivers and lakes, or recovered from underground through springs and wells. In arid parts of the world some fresh water is manufactured from seawater by desalination processes.

Rainfall is part of the hydrological cycle in which water, evaporated from the oceans, enters the atmosphere as vapour, is carried by winds over the earth's surface and on cooling is precipitated again as rain, hail, snow or dew. On land surfaces this precipitation is disposed of in one of the following ways:

(a) By direct evaporation into the air.

(b) By draining off the land surfaces and collecting in streams and rivers as *run-off*.

(c) By absorption into the ground, to be returned to the air through the transpiration of trees and plants.

(d) By absorption into the ground as ground water.

In very dry uncultivated lands it is probable that the entire rainfall is accounted for under the first head (i.e., by evaporation). There are many places with shallow soil over rock where the entire rainfall is consumed by (a) and (c) combined (i.e., by evaporation and absorption by trees and plants). In other places where the land surface is permeable (such as sands, limestones or deep volcanic soils) a large proportion of the precipitation is absorbed into the ground.

4.1.2 Rainfall

Rainfall is recorded in millimetres of depth of precipitation falling in a period of time, the period being defined as a day, a month or a year. Annual amounts of rainfall vary extensively from one part of the world to another, ranging from zero in desert regions to over 10000

mm in some tropical areas. At any one place the rainfall varies from
year to year, so that average annual rainfalls are calculated for
comparative purposes. (Observations have to be taken for at least 30
years for really reliable long term averages.)

Variations in rainfall are more extreme in tropical and sub-tropical
regions than in temperate zones. As a rule the most arid climates are
subject to the greatest variability of rainfall, with extremes ranging
between 160 per cent and 40 per cent of the long-term average annual
rainfall. The long-term average annual rainfall figures for some
selected places in the world are given in Table 4.1.

Table 4.1 Rainfall at selected places.

Place	Height above sea level (m)	Annual rainfall (mm)		
		Average	Highest	Lowest
Addis Ababa	2408	1183	1937	902
Athens	107	393	846	116
Bombay	11	1807	2918	849
Calcutta	6	1574	2269	1000
Colombo	12	2129	3548	1311
Jerusalem	880	602	1091	181
Khartoum	380	164	382	76
Lagos	3	1829	2921	1016
London	5	611	970	463
Moscow	160	481	744	307
New York	96	1079	1516	731
Rome	50	827	1470	323

4.1.3 Rain Gauges

Rainfall is measured by means of a rain gauge which collects the rain
into a funnel at the top of a container so that it can be measured. A
standard rain gauge is observed at the same time every 24 hours.
Standard rain gauges are usually provided with graduated glass
measuring cylinders which show the measured amounts converted
into millimetres of precipitation. If the precipitation is collected in a
cylindrical container which has not been calibrated to give the results
in millimetres, the amount of precipitation can be calculated as
follows.

Example

If the water collected stands at a depth d mm in a container of diameter x mm, and the diameter of the rain gauge funnel is y mm, the depth of precipitation r in millimetres is given by

$$r = \frac{x^2}{y^2} \cdot d$$

It must not be forgotten that rain gauges are sited to record conditions which are typical of an area, which may be quite large and cover several thousand square kilometres.

4.1.4 Evaporation

Evaporation, like rainfall, is recorded in millimetres of depth in a period of time. It is a process which is occurring continuously from open water and from moist land surfaces in contact with the air. The rate of evaporation varies with temperature, with the relative humidity of the air and with air movement and wind. It is important to distinguish between evaporation from a large body of water such as a lake, from vegetation (which is usually known as evapo-transpiration) and from an evaporimeter which measures evaporation.

The most satisfactory and generally used evaporimeter is the evaporation pan, which measures evaporation directly as a loss of water from the pan. This is known as 'pan' evaporation and is related to open water evaporation and evapo-transpiration by coefficients. If Eo = open water evaporation, ET = evaop-transpiration and Ep = pan evaporation:

$$E_o = K_1 Ep$$
$$E_T = K_2 Ep$$

The values for the coefficients K_1 and K_2 vary with the type of pan used and with local conditions of siting and wind activity. For an 'American Class A' $1 \cdot 2$ m dia. pan above ground the following values may be used:

$$K_1 = 0 \cdot 85$$
$$K_2 = 0 \cdot 75$$

Under arid conditions the annual evaporation from open water may amount to 2–2·5 m. Some figures for open-water evaporation are given in Table 4.2.

Table 4.2 Open-water evaporation at selected places.

Place	Climate	Annual evaporation (mm)
Addis Ababa	mountain	1407
Aswan	desert	2689
Bombay	dry tropical	2447
Entebbe	dry tropical	2111
Georgetown, Guyana	wet tropical	2395
Makurdi (Nigeria)	dry tropical	1451
Mérida, Venezuela	mountain	876

4.1.5 Catchment Area

The catchment area of a drainage system is the precipitation collecting area for the system. In the catchment area of a river and tributaries, each tributary will have its own sub-catchment area, and there will also be some sub-catchment areas which drain directly into the main river. The total catchment area of the system is the sum of the sub-catchments. This is illustrated in Figure 4.1 which shows a river system consisting of a main river R and two principal tributaries T1 and T2, draining into the sea on the coast at a point N.

If the elements of catchment area are a,b,c etc., as shown in Figure 4.1, it will be seen that the catchment area at the point of confluence L of the first tributary with the main river is a + b. Further down stream at M the second tributary joins, but there are also two small elements of catchment, d and e, which drain into R directly or by minor tributaries. So the total catchment area down to the confluence at M is a + b + c + d + e. Between M and the sea at N the river receives some further drainage from areas on both banks, so that the total catchment area to the river mouth at N is a + b + c + d + e + f + g.

The boundary of a catchment (Figure 4.1) defines the limit of drainage into a river system and, because water flows downhill, the boundary line which is known as the watershed (or water divide) follows high ground. In hilly and mountainous country the watershed is easily distinguishable by peaks, crests and ridges. Where the land is relatively flat it is not so easily described. Watersheds can be drawn on a contour map from the pattern of contours as shown in Figure 4.1.

The total quantity of precipitation on a catchment area in a specified time (hour, day, month or year) is the rainfall on the catchment during that time multiplied by its area. Rainfall is measured by one or more rain gauges in the catchment (section 4.1.3).

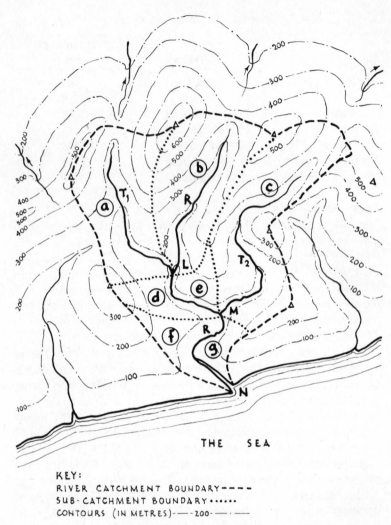

Figure 4.1 Catchment area.

If there are no existing gauges in the catchment, records may be taken from the nearest existing rain gauge, provided of course that it can be accepted as reasonably representative of the catchment area.

4.1.6 Run-off
Run-off is that part of precipitation which flows over the land and is carried away by streams and rivers. The proportion of the total

precipitation which appears as run-off varies greatly for different catchments. The overall average annual run-off on the world's land surfaces is about 35 per cent of the total precipitation, but in some arid catchments it is as little as 3 per cent or less. Some average annual run-off percentages, given in Table 4.3, demonstrate this.

Table 4.3   Average annual run-off as percentage of precipitation.

Area	Run-off %
Volta River Basin, Ghana	10
Uganda (land area)	10
Malawi (land area)	8
Lake Victoria Basin at Owen Falls	7
Tanzania (land area)	7
Kenya (land area)	6

The run-off from a catchment is greatly affected by the condition of the catchment area, particularly as to vegetative cover, at the time of the rainfall—but the existing soil water status, and the intensity of the rainfall, also have their influence. An unusual fall of 56.9 mm of rain falling in 80 min on a catchment area in Northern India, when the area was dry and baked by previous hot weather, only added to the reservoir the amount of water which fell on its water surface. There was no run-off from the catchment area. Later in the year, when the ground was thoroughly saturated by rain which had fallen on 55 days out of 89, a similar fall of 55·9 mm produced a discharge into the reservoir of no less than 98 per cent of the entire rainfall on the ground draining into it within a period of 3 hours. The catchment area consisted of 17 km^2 of largely rocky ground. Table 4.4 relates to this area.

Table 4.4   Monthly rainfall and run-off on a catchment in North India.*

Month	Rainfall (mm)	Percentage of run-off to rainfall
June	172·0	4·7
July	322·6	22·7
August	299·7	55·8
September	202·9	74·4
October	111·0	39·4

* These figures refer to one 'monsoon'.

Table 4.5 gives monthly run-off percentages for normal and above-normal rainfall on rice land on gentle slopes near Calcutta, India.

Table 4.5   Monthly run-off percentages, near Calcutta, India.

Month	Percentage of rainfall flowing off the catchment area	
	In years of normal rainfall	In years when rainfall above normal
June	5	10
July	10	20
August	25	50
September	40	50
October	40	50

These tables demonstrate how the run-off increases as the wet season advances and the ground becomes progressively saturated.

The run-off from a catchment is usually measured as a rate of flow in litres per second (l/sec) or cubic metres per second (m³/sec) and the volume of run-off is this quantity multiplied by a period of time.

This can be illustrated by an example and with reference to Figure 4.2(a) which shows the rainfall and run-off for a catchment in the sub-tropics with a wet half-year followed by a dry half-year. The total catchment area is 100 km² and the rainfall in a year of observation was 1200 mm distributed in monthly amounts as shown in the figure. This gave a total precipitation in the year of 1.2 million m³.

Figure 4.2(b) shows the *hydrograph*, or graph of rate of flow plotted against time for this catchment. The rate of flow is measured at regular intervals which may be daily or every 10 days or at less frequent intervals depending on the local circumstances. If plotted accurately on squared paper the hydrograph can be used to determine the total volume of flow over a period of time. Referring to Figure 4.2(b), it will be seen that each square on the diagram represents 5 l/sec vertically and one-twelfth of a year (approximately one month) horizontally. Multiplying these two quantities together (l/sec × time in seconds) will give a volume in litres. This is the volume or quantity of run-off which would pass if a flow of 5 l/sec were maintained for a month, and amounts to $5 \times 365/12 \times 86400 = 13\,140\,000$ l or 13 140 m³. Multiplying two sides of a square together gives the area of the square, so that in this example the area of one square on the run-off diagram represents 13 140 m³ of run-off.

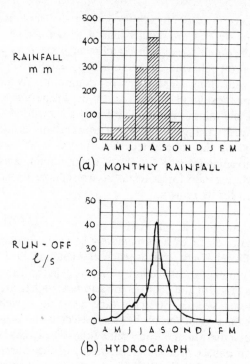

(a) MONTHLY RAINFALL

(b) HYDROGRAPH

Figure 4.2 Relationship between rainfall and run off.

The total run-off passing during a given period of time can be determined by measuring the total area under the hydrograph for this period. In Figure 4.2(b) the area under the hydrograph in July is 1·9 squares, and the total flow during the month was therefore 1·9 × 13 140 = 24 966 m³. The total run-off in the year was found in this way to be 182 646 m³. As the precipitation in the year was 1·2 million m³, 15.2 per cent of this appeared as run-off.

If all the run-off could be stored without loss (to evaporation, for example) and released at a steady rate for a year the steady flow would be approximately 5·8 l/sec. But in practice under conditions such as these with five or six months of dry weather, the evaporation loss from a reservoir could be 1–2 m depth of water and this could reduce the estimated yield of 5·8 l/sec by a third to about 4 l/sec.

The rate of run-off from a catchment depends on its physical characteristics such as shape, ground slope, the land surface material and vegetation cover. Water from a fan-shaped or semi-circular catchment will reach the point of concentration or outlet more quickly than water from a long thin catchment of the same area. It will also concentrate more quickly the steeper the slope. Bare rock obviously yields water more rapidly than deep permeable soil.

The nature of vegetation cover in a catchment area has a significant effect on the run-off behaviour. Vegetation adapts itself to the water it can get. Areas with a long dry season have a comparatively sparse tree cover even when the rainfall is high. The run-off will be high and short lasting. Where the rainfall is well distributed a 'rain-forest' type of cover is produced which grows all the year round and is adapted to use practically all the rain it receives. A dry-type forest cover therefore has to some extent a surplus of water running away in the wet season, while a rain forest tends to arrest more water than is actually needed for its growth.

4.1.7 Stream Gauging: Rough Method

Stream flow can be gauged approximately by using floats. For this purpose select a relatively straight reach of a channel 20–30 m long with a fairly uniform cross-section along its length. Take several measurements of width and depth in the selected reach to arrive at an average cross-section area. Stretch a tape or string at right angles across the stream at each end of the reach selected and measure the distance between these lines. Drop a small float, which may be a cork, a rubber ball or a piece of wood, in the centre of the channel 1–2 m upstream of the start of the measured length, and take the time for the float to cover the measured distance. Do this three or four times to obtain an average reading. The distance divided by the time gives the velocity of the float, which corresponds to the velocity of the water at its surface. The surface velocity is multiplied by a coefficient to give the average velocity over the cross-section. A figure of 0·7 can be used as the coefficient for small streams (Ref. 10).

Thus if d is the measured distance in metres, t is the average time in seconds for the float to cover d, the average stream velocity will be $v = 0·7\ d/t$ m/sec. If A is the average sectional area of the channel in square metres, the discharge Q is given by Av m/sec or $1000\,Av$ l/sec.

For example:

$$\text{If } d = 24 \text{ m, } t = 20 \text{ sec, } \quad \text{then} \quad v = 0·7 \times 24/20 = 0·84 \text{ m/sec}$$
$$\text{If } A = 0·2 \text{ m}^2$$
$$Q = 1000\,Av$$
$$= 1000 \times 0·2 \times 0·84$$
$$= 168 \text{ l/sec}$$

4.1.8 Rectangular Weir

A weir is a structure placed across a stream to raise the water level and control the flow. A rectangular measuring weir consists of a board or plate with a rectangular opening placed across a channel as shown in Figure 4.3. Water flowing through the opening falls freely into the stream channel below.

The flow in the channel is determined by measuring the depth of water flowing over the weir crest. The surface of the water below the weir must be at least 0·25 m below the crest to ensure that there is a 'clear overfall'. The weir plate can be made of metal or wood and the

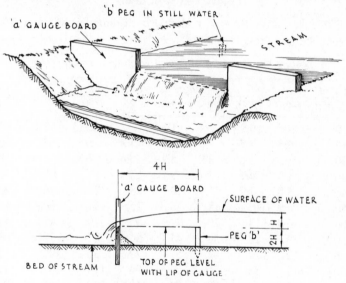

Figure 4.3 Gauging weir.

bottom and sides of the opening should be bevelled on the downstream side. The plate itself should be wide enough and deep enough to be properly embedded in the bed and banks of the stream to ensure no bypass leakage.

Referring to Figure 4.3, the depth of water, H, over the crest is measured at a distance equal to $4H$ upstream of the weir, to avoid the 'draw down' at the crest. The height of the crest above the channel bed should be $2H$ as shown. The measurement of H can be done in two ways. A simple method is to drive a peg into the bed of the channel until its top is exactly level with the crest of the weir, and measure the depth of the water above the top of the peg. Alternatively a post can be driven into the bed of the channel with its top projecting above the highest anticipated water level. A scale is then fixed to the post, so that the zero of the scale is at the same level as the crest of the weir. The depth of water above the crest can then be read directly on the scale.

The flow Q is related to the width of the weir L and the head over the crest H by the following formula:

$$Q = 0{\cdot}0582 \, (L - 0{\cdot}0002H) \, H^{1 \cdot 5}$$

where Q = flow in l/sec;
L = width of crest in m; and
H = head on crest mm.

Table 4.6 gives flows for standard rectangular weirs in 1/sec calculated from this formula.

Table 4.6   Flows for standard rectangular weirs (l/s).

Head,	Length of crest, L (m)							
H (mm)	0·25	0·50	0·75	1·00	1·25	1·50	1·75	2·00
10	0·5	0·9	1·4	1·8	2·2	2·7	3·2	3·6
15	0·8	1·7	2·5	3·3	4·2	5·0	5·9	6·7
20	1·3	2·6	3·9	5·1	6·4	7·7	9·0	10
30	2·3	4·7	7·1	9·5	12	14	17	19
40	3·6	7·2	11	14·5	18	22	26	29
50	4·9	10	15	20	25	31	36	41
60	6·4	13	20	27	33	40	47	54
80	9·7	20	30·5	41	51	62	72	83
100	13	28	42	57	72	86	100	115
120	17	36	56	75	94	113	132	151
140	21	46	70	94	118	142	166	190
160		55	85	114	143	173	202	232
180		65	100	135	170	206	241	276
200		76	117	158	199	240	281	322
250			161	218	276	333	391	448
300			208	284	359	435	511	586
350				354	449	544	640	735
400				428	544	660	777	893
450				505	644	783	921	1060
500				585	747	910	1072	1235

For small flows, a 'V'-notch weir gives more accurate results than a rectangular weir. It is used in the same way, by measuring the head and referring to a calibration table (see Ref. 11).

4.2 SURFACE WATER COLLECTION

4.2.1 Rainwater Harvesting

In arid and semi-arid regions rainfall collected from natural or artificial surfaces provides a valuable source of water. The hard surfaces of bare rock can be used effectively in this way, particularly if cracks and fissures are made good with cement mortar. Channels cut in the rock or formed on the rock with concrete can be used to collect the water and pass it to some convenient storage tank or reservoir. In the porous limestone areas of Jamaica small hillside areas are cleared of vegetation and sealed with concrete to provide impermeable collecting surfaces for domestic water supplies. Rainwater can also be collected from earth surfaces and examples of this can be seen in the desert cisterns of North Africa, some of which are 2000 years old.

4.2.2 Design of Water-collection Systems

The design of a water-collection system involves a study of the climatic conditions and hydrological characteristics of the proposed catchment area, and the purposes for which the collected water is intended to be used.

The steps to be taken in the hydrological design are best described by an example: it is required to provide storage of rainfall to meet the needs of a small rural community and their livestock whose daily consumption is 1000 l for a dry period after the rains lasting a maximum of four months or 120 days. For the remaining eight months of the year the people are able to collect their water requirements from a small spring, but this source dries up during the dry season and they then have to depend upon storage.

A daily consumption of 1000 l for 120 days amounts to 120 m³ of water. If the water is stored in an open reservoir a proportion of the stored water will be lost by evaporation during the dry season. Although the rate of evaporation is known, the amount of the loss cannot be calculated until the size and dimensions of the reservoir are determined. At this stage assume that half the stored water will be lost and therefore $120 \times 1.5 = 180$ m³ should be collected.

A study of local rainfall records for 20 years shows that while the average wet season rainfall over this period was 400 mm, in one year it was only 150 mm. As it is important that the community should not be short of water, this low year is taken as the 'design' year for the proposed system. 150 mm of rain falling on 1 m² of catchment surface amounts to 150 l of water.

The catchment area chosen for this system consists of gently sloping land with light bush vegetation, and for these conditions it is assumed that 5 per cent of the rainfall can be collected which is equivalent to 4·5 l/m². Thus, to collect 180 m³ or 180000 l, the surface area needed will be $180 \div 0·45 \times 100 = 40000$ m² or 4 hectares.

4.2.3 Supply of Water from Roofs

In places where water is scarce the rainfall from galvanized iron, or any other type of impervious roofing, is a valuable addition. The rain is caught in the gutters and passed on to a storage tank or tanks. The tanks may be underground, with the obvious construction and access disadvantages, or can be ordinary corrugated iron tanks set at convenient points. As the first rains of the season wash all the dust etc., from the roof and gutters, arrangements should be made to discharge the first rains away from the tanks. There are various ways of doing this. One arrangement is shown in Figure 4.4. The tanks must be covered and be mosquito proof.

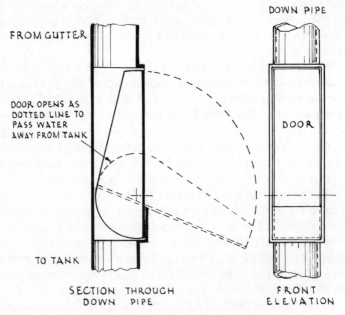

Figure 4.4 Roof rainwater bypass.

4.2.4 Small Storage Systems

Many forms of small storage reservoir are in use in different parts of the world. In this category may be included ponds, cisterns, tanks, *hafirs* and other collections of water often known by local names.

Their capacities range from a few cubic metres to several thousand cubic metres. They are usually constructed, in impermeable soils, by excavating a hole in the ground, using the spoil from the excavation to provide raised banks. Where there is no stream flow, they are filled by direct run off from local catchment areas, but in the Far East they are often fed from existing stream sources.

A simple system using a sand-filled storage is shown in Figure 4.5. The sand reduces evaporation and filters the water as it passes through it. The capacity of the tank is increased by constructing beehive-shaped chambers for the collection of free water (see Ref. 12).

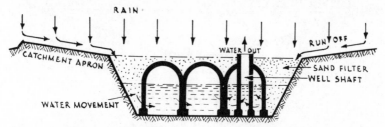

Figure 4.5 Rainwater catchment and sand storage.

4.2.5 Tanks or Hafirs

In these notes a tank or *hafir* means a large excavation (usually rectangular in plan) in solid or impermeable ground. Tanks differ from *infiltration trenches* (section 4.4.5) in that they are filled by the rain, which—falling on a catchment area—is diverted into them or they are filled from the overflow of a stream, hence careful siting is necessary. The best catchment for a tank is rocky, stony, or sandy ground with a definite slope. Clayey ground is often flat and deeply cracked so that the rain is absorbed by the cracks and almost none runs off, whereas rain water runs off copiously from rocky hills. Large tanks have been excavated in impervious ground, as in Figure 4.6. To test if the ground is impervious, dig a trial pit and fill it with water. Tanks are easily constructed with unskilled labour for it is simply a matter of digging. The excavated material or 'spoil' is arranged, well compacted, about the excavation so that it can form a dam to hold still more water.

The water from a tank is drawn off by pumping or by some simple method of raising water (see section 4.6 generally). But because of the height problem, the supply can rarely be taken off by pipes or syphon. In this respect tanks differ from dams as well as in other respects.

In one instance, the bottom of the tank was 2·7 m wide, the depth

2·7 m and the length 9·2 m at the bottom; the side slopes 3 : 1 (i.e., for every 3 m of horizontal distance the side rose 1 m) as in Figure 4.6. The capacity of the tank was about 390 m³, when filled to 0·3 m from ground level. In any tank the side slopes depend on the angle of repose of the formation in which the tank is sunk (see section 6.2.5).

It is advisable to cover small tanks where possible in order to prevent evaporation; to this end they should be made long and narrow, and be thus easily coverable with timber bearers and brushwood or other local and convenient materials.

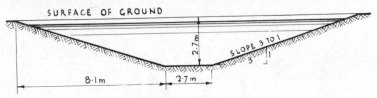

Figure 4.6 Excavated tank.

4.2.6 Small Reservoirs of Masonry or Concrete

Reservoirs may be entirely below the surface of the ground, partly in and partly above ground, or completely above ground. They may be square, rectangular, or circular in plan. Rectangular tanks are the simplest to roof and large circular tanks are the most difficult to cover. Empty reservoirs when built below the level of the ground, have to sustain the weight of the earth on the outer sides of the walls if they are vertical, hence comparatively thick walls are necessary. Walls must be carefully built, as there must not be any settlement in them or leaks will occur. If the excavation for the reservoir is carried out so that the sides have the natural slope of the earth a thinner wall can be used (section 4.2.5). See Figure 4.7 for sketches of reservoirs. The depth of small reservoirs is usually about 2 m, the inlet pipe discharges at the top of the wall, and the outlet pipe should be some 150 mm or so above the floor of the tank. Sediment collects at the bottom of the tank and the floor of the reservoir should therefore slope to a small sump for the collection of sediment. Wherever possible a large valve (sluice valve) should be fitted in this sump so that the sediment may be washed out. An overflow pipe should be provided at top water level. It is usual to provide a bypass so that the water may pass round the reservoir into the outlet pipe while the reservoir is being washed out. For concrete walls use the proportion 1 : 2 : 4. A covered reservoir should be ventilated and the interior surface of the walls are 'rendered' with cement plaster.

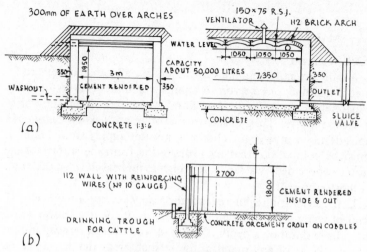

Figure 4.7 Small reservoirs.

4.2.7 Calculating the Capacity of a Tank

Rectangular tank with vertical sides

D = depth (m)
L = length (m)
W = width (m)
V = volume (m³)
$V = D \times L \times W$

Rectangular tank with sloping sides (Figure 4.6)

D = depth (m)
L = (length of top + length of bottom) divided by 2 (m)
W = (width of top + width of bottom) divided by 2 (m)
V = volume (m³)
$V = D \times L \times W$

Circular tank

D = depth (m)
d = diameter (m)
V = volume (m³)
$V = 0.7854 \times d^2 \times D$

4.3 SMALL DAMS

4.3.1 General

A dam generally impounds the waters of a stream and converts an area into a tank or reservoir. A dam can be built of earth, masonry, concrete etc. In an earth dam flood waters are never allowed to overtop the crest. They must be carried off by an overflow channel. In considering a project for obtaining a water supply from a dam, it must be pointed out that the evaporation from the surface of the water impounded by a dam is very high in the season when the water is most required.

In the semi-arid regions evaporation may account for a loss of 12 mm of water a day during the dry season. If the dry season is five months in duration a depth of 1·8 m of water is lost by evaporation alone. To be of any practical use in such areas the dam must be considerably over 3 m in height.

The construction of high earth dams is a work requiring technical skill and experience and should not be undertaken lightheartedly. These notes deal with the smaller dams, of the sort that can be constructed on a farm—say up to 6 m in height.

The following are essential to the design:

(a) The dam must be strong enough to sustain the pressure of water behind it. Properly constructed dams are amply sufficient to resist the pressure of water they hold up. The only way it can and does act prejudicially against them is by infiltration—diminishing their frictional resistance adhesion. The risk of failure lies in the liability of the earthwork itself to slip.

(b) The ends and bottom of the dam must be so constructed that the water does not seep around or under it.

(c) The overflow or waste water channel must be large enough to allow the heaviest flood to run off. Flood water must not be allowed to flow over the top of an earthen dam under any circumstances.

(d) The system of drawing off the water must be simple and accessible.

Long low dams are safer than high dams and they are said to be much cheaper, but evaporation is high in shallow reservoirs, as already pointed out.

4.3.2 Sites for Dams

Wherever possible a site giving the maximum natural basin for minimum expenditure should be chosen. A natural water course or stream bed is ideal where its gradient is least and where it widens out behind some natural restriction. Where natural basins do not exist, however, dams of the horseshoe or 'tank-dam' type can be used.

The requirements for the hydrological design of small dams are similar to those for mini storage works, but because a dam is a much larger project, involving very much greater expenditure, the hydrology of the catchment area, reservoir and drainage system needs more careful investigation. Particular attention needs to be given to estimates of the greatest flood flow which the dam spillway must be designed to pass.

Due regard must be paid to the suitability of the site for a spillway. Natural or uncut spillways are generally to be preferred, particularly if a rocky outcrop can be used. Care should be taken not to spill over badly decomposed rock—especially decomposed granite. In soil, a cut spillway (if well-constructed and covered with grass), is preferable. Attention must be paid to the path the water will follow back to its natural course.

4.3.3 Earth Dams

Earth dams are known as 'gravity dams' because their stability depends upon their weight and consequent resistance to moving under pressure from the water impounded. The design of dams is beyond the scope of this book but properly designed and constructed dams are amply sufficient to withstand the maximum water pressure for which they have been designed (see Refs 13 and 14).

4.3.4 Foundations for Earth Dams

The essential conditions for the foundation of an earth dam are that the soil should be compact, that it will not yield when wet, and that it will not settle nor slip under the weight of the dam. The best foundation for a dam is:

(a) Hard compact rock. The surface should be level, or sloping slightly downward from the down-stream side towards the up-stream side of the dam.

The next best foundations are in the order named:

(b) The softer rocks.
(c) Hard, compact, and solid, gravelly soil.

(d) Hard clay soil.
(e) Brown and red soils.
(f) 'Black cotton' soil.

4.3.5 The Embankment

There are several possible designs for the embankment of an earth dam, depending upon the particular site conditions, but there are certain general considerations which need to be observed. Some countries have regulations governing the design of earth dams and these should be adhered to.

Figure 4.8 shows a cross section of a typical earth dam. The main features are a core consisting of clay or some selected impervious material in the heart of the dam and keyed into the foundation material in a trench. The rest of the embankment material is then placed on both sides and above the core.

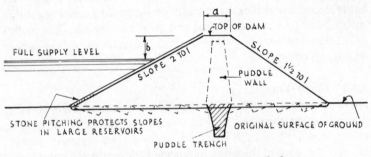

Figure 4.8   Cross section of an earth dam.

The side slopes of the embankment (Figure 4.8) should on no account be steeper than 2 : 1 (2 m horizontal to 1 m vertical) on the upstream side and 1·5 : 1 on the down stream side. If the embankment is made of very sandy or non-cohesive material, or if it is open to severe trampling by cattle, these slopes should be made flatter.

The width of the dam at the top (or crest) should never be less than 2 m. The height of the crest of the dam should always be a certain distance higher than the maximum anticipated water level under extreme flood conditions. This extra height is known as 'freeboard'. The amount of freeboard depends upon the height of the dam and other design considerations. Different authorities have different recommendations about freeboard, but 1 m is a good figure for design purposes.

4.3.6 The Spillway

The spillway acts as a safety valve for a storage system, releasing water when the reservoir is over full so that the dam is not over topped, which could quickly lead to failure. Spillways should be designed to carry extreme floods after intense rainfall so that the water in the reservoir does not rise above the designed high flood level. The spillway for a dam is usually in the form of a weir which is overtopped as soon as the water level in the reservoir rises above the maximum permissible storage level. Natural spillways are generally to be preferred to excavated spillways where possible, and rock spillways are ideal.

In spillway design two main factors must be kept in mind—the spillway must be large enough to carry the maximum flood—but it, and particularly the outfall, must be reasonably secure against erosion. Generally speaking vegetation is the best stabilizing agent for earth spillways and grass which creeps in growth is the best vegetation. The position of the spillway is usually at one end of the dam, or separated from it by intervening ground (see Figure 4.9). The

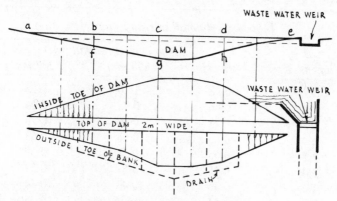

Figure 4.9 Earth dam and spillway.

spillway may be of the drowned type or have a clear overfall. Its width depends on the size of the catchment area which feeds the reservoir, the maximum flood to be escaped and the freeboard at the dam (i.e., the height of the top of the dam above the crest level of the spillway).

The following method for determining the width (W in metres) of spillways has been used in Zimbabwe:

$$W = F \times R \times T$$

where F = Flood discharge factor, depending on the size of the catchment and the freeboard allowed; R = Rainfall intensity factor, depending on the mean annual rainfall and the length of the catchment; and T = Topographical factor, depending on the predominant nature of the soil, the vegetation cover and the overall slope of the catchment.

Tables 4.7, 4.8 and 4.9 give values for these factors for different dimensions and conditions.

Table 4.7   Flood discharge factor (F).

Free-board (m)	Catchment area (Ha)								
	50	100	150	200	250	300	400	500	600
1·00	18	36	54	72	90	108	144	180	215
1·25	13	25	38	51	63	75	101	126	151
1·50	10	19	29	38	48	57	76	94	114
1·75	9	17	25	33	40	48	63	78	94
2·00	8	16	23	29	36	42	55	68	80

Table 4.8   Rainfall intensity factor (R).

Length of catchment (Km)	Mean annual rainfall		
	400 mm	800 mm	1200 mm
0·5	0·98	1·10	1·15
1·0	0·86	0·92	0·94
1·5	0·71	0·76	0·78
2·0	0·63	0·66	0·68
2·5	0·55	0·58	0·59
3·0	0·45	0·51	0·51
4·0	0·40	0·43	0·44
5·0	0·34	0÷36	0·38
6·0	0·30	0·34	0·35

Example
A catchment area of 500 ha is 3 km long and has an average annual rainfall of 800 mm. The area is moderately sloping, heavily grassed and has slowly permeable soils. The dam is to be built with a freeboard of 1·5 m.

From Table 4.7, for a freeboard of 1·5 m and a catchment area of 500 ha

$$F = 94$$

From Table 4.8, for a catchment 3 km long and an average annual rainfall of 800 mm

$$R = 0.51$$

From Table 4.9

$$T = (a) + (b) + (c) = 0.10 + 0.25 + 0.10 = 0.45$$

Therefore

The width of spillway, $W = F \times R \times T$
$$= 94 \times 0.51 \times 0.45 = 21.57 \text{ m}$$

A spillway width of 22 m would therefore meet the requirements.

In selecting the depth of the freeboard for a dam, two points should be remembered:

(a) The greater the depth, the greater the likelihood of erosion in and below the spillway.

(b) The greater the depth, the greater the cost of the dam in relation to the quantity of water stored.

Shallow freeboards are to be preferred, provided this does not make the spillway too costly or unreasonably wide. As a general guide freeboards should not exceed 1 m for dams holding up to 3m of water, or 1.5 m for dams holding up to 4.5 m of water.

Table 4.9   Topographical factor (T).*

Vegetation cover (a)		Soil type (b)		Slope (c)	
Thick bush	0.05	Deep, well-drained (sandy loam)	0.10	Flat to gently sloping, 0–5%	0.05
Heavy grass	0.10	Deep, moderately permeable (loam)	0.20	Moderate, 5–10%	0.10
Scrub or medium grass	0.15	Slowly permeable (clay loam)	0.25	Rolling, 10–20%	0.15
Cultivated land	0.20	Shallow, with impeded drainage (clay)	0.30	Hilly or steep, 20–40%	0.20
Bare or eroded	0.25	Medium–heavy clays, or rocky surfaces	0.40	Mountainous, greater than 40%	0.25
		Impermeable surfaces or waterlogged soil	0.50		

* $T = (a) + (b) + (c)$.

4.3.7   Construction of Earth Dams

The whole of the site of a dam is stripped of all trees, shrubs, grass, loose material, roots and the surface soil removed until a firm natural soil is found. In big dams furrows or notches are excavated as shown by dotted lines in Figure 4.8. The notches are excavated in a line parallel to the axis of the dam.

If an impervious clay core is included in the design, a trench for this is excavated into non-porous material along the axis of the dam. The depth of the trench in non-porous earth is not less than half the depth of water in the reservoir and in any case it is carried down well into non-porous material. The width of the trench at bottom is about 2 m or, in some cases, one-tenth height of dam plus 1 m. Where the dam crosses the bed of a stream concrete is more often used for the impervious core.

The core material, which is the best clay available, is first made plastic with water, and the trench is then filled with plastic clay, or 'puddle'. The puddle is then carried up through the dam as the rest of the embankment material is placed.

All soils that are light and powdery and wanting in cohesion, and all that become slippery or slushy under the action of water, are quite unsuitable for the foundation (as well as for the construction) of a dam. Further, pure black soil swells when wet and cracks when dry and it should therefore never be used alone in an embankment.

The material for the dam is often excavated on the upstream side of it, and the excavation should be well clear of the toe of the slope (a distance of three times height of dam from it). In the construction of low dams, 'dam scoops' and oxen are very useful.

The material, free of all clods, lumps, large stones and rubbish, is spread in layers 150 mm thick over the entire width of dam and well rammed. If the material is too dry it should be damped before being placed in the work. In important works the labourers who carry the soil should not walk in single file over the work. The rammers should work backwards and forwards over the layer until it is consolidated.

The site of large dams is drained by means of dry stone drains (as shown in dotted lines in Figure 4.9). The drains carry away any infiltration from the reservoir and thus preserve the dam.

Where the dam impounds a stream the waters are carried through the outlet pipe (see Figure 4.10) during the dam's construction if this is large enough. If the flow is too great the dam is built in two sections; the water passes between them. The 'closure' or the filling of the gap takes place when the two wings or sections are completed, and when the overflow has been constructed.

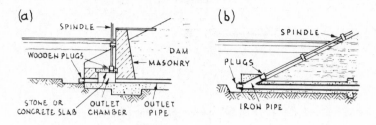

Figure 4.10 Dam outlet controls.

4.3.8   Drawing off the Supply

Figure 4.10 is adapted from *Indian Storage Reservoirs* by Strange. It shows simple methods of constructing outlets to a reservoir. Figure 4.10(a) shows a small masonry chamber at the head of the outlet pipe on the water side of the dam. The top of the chamber is covered by a stone or concrete slab. In the cover slab a tapered hole is cut or cast, and a wooden plug fits into the hole. The plug can be withdrawn or replaced by means of a rod. The plug and hole form the outlet valve. Another pipe passes through the wall at the bottom of the chamber. This is also closed by a plug which is withdrawn when the reservoir is to be flushed out. In Figure 4.10(b) the head of the outlet pipe is fitted with a casting (iron or concrete) in the shape of a *Y*. One arm of the *Y* is joined to the outlet pipe, in the other a wooden plug is fitted which can be taken out or replaced by means of a rod. In the tail of the *Y* is another plug. This is withdrawn when the reservoir is to be flushed out.

4.3.9   Other Types of Dams

Figure 4.11 gives a section of low masonry dam built with stones and cement mortar. The wall must be built solidly (section 2.3.3) and stand on sound foundations of concrete or stone. The proportions usually adopted in such constructions are

$$t_1 = 0.2h, \, t_2 = 0.7h$$

Thus in a wall 2 m high the thickness at the base would be $0.7 \times 2 = 1.4$ m, and at the top $0.2 \times 2 = 0.4$ m. The width at bottom can be reduced to width at top in steps. Dams and weirs are also built of uncemented stones ('rock fill dams'). The stones are carefully piled much as earth in an earthen dam (i.e., with appropriate slopes). The water face of the dam is made as water tight as possible, either by covering it with masonry in cement or even a mass of clay. Rock fill

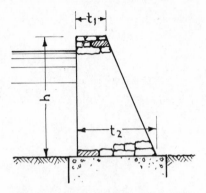

Figure 4.11 Small masonry dam.

dams are not water tight but can be made water tight if an impervious core is incorporated in their construction.

Rock fill dams can also be constructed with the use of gabions. A gabion is a basket made of heavy duty galvanized wire mesh and filled with stone. The function of a gabion is to provide an easily constructed unit which is large enough and heavy enough to remain stable in moving water. Gabions can be made to any convenient size; popular sizes are 2 m, 3 m and 4 m long by 1 m wide by 0·5 m or 1 m deep. The wire mesh is usually made from 2 mm or 3 mm dia. wire, with mesh size from 50 mm to 100 mm.

As gabions are permeable and flexible they generally do not require complex structural design, but if they are to be submerged in water, calculations should be made for their stability under flood conditions. Evenly graded stones should be used so that the gabions are well packed with few empty spaces, and the largest stone should not be more than two-thirds of the minimum gabion dimension. As gabions are usually filled by hand, the manpower available will determine the maximum size of stone used (see Ref 15).

Brushwood dams are also constructed for use in irrigation work for the same purpose as rock fills. They are not very efficient and are only semi-permanent. They need no description.

4.3.10 Sub-surface Dams
Sand rivers are the storm-water drains of some areas. Water can remain in the sand (up to one quarter to one third of the volume of the sand) after the flood waters have passed; and pits can be dug in the river bed to tap it. The water slowly seeps away downstream and the pits run dry. Water can be retained in the sand by building a sub-

surface dam or barrier across the bed of the stream. Clay or rock may be found under the sand, and the object is to bed the dam on solid material. Ant-hill material can be used for the dam, but it is sometimes difficult to open a trench in dry sand, and always difficult to do so in wet sand. In dry sand, bush poles can be driven in on both sides of the excavation, and as the excavation proceeds they are driven in still further. They help to hold the sand up. Ant-hill material is placed in the trench, wetted slightly, and rammed. Corrugated iron has also been used to form a barrier in shallow beds of sand. It can be used in wet sand, but shallow sand beds do not yield much water. In Kenya jet drilling has been used with success. By its means sand is flushed up to the surface by water. When the jet drill pipe reaches the bottom of the sand, a slurry of cement, or lime, or clay is pumped under pressure. The pipe is gradually withdrawn, and the cement, lime, or clay seeps into the pores of the sand and seals them, thus forming an effective barrier. This process is repeated at intervals across the river until a sub-surface barrier of impervious material is formed. The top of a sub-surface barrier should be kept below the surface of the sand or it will be damaged during floods.

4.4 GROUNDWATER DEVELOPMENT

4.4.1 Absorption into Ground

Only a portion, in general, probably not much more than 20 per cent and often a great deal less, of the rain which falls on the earth finds its way into the soil to replenish the subterranean stores of water. In porous limestone 16–24 per cent of the rainfall is absorbed. Figure 4.12 is a diagrammatic section of a portion of the earth's surface illustrating the storage of subterranean water. The rain descends on the outcrops, or places where the various strata are exposed, some of

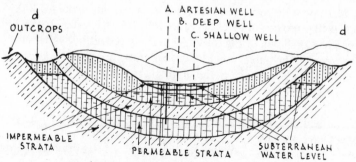

Figure 4.12 Diagrammatic section of strata.

it percolates through the permeable strata. It is held up by the impervious strata. A borehole sunk at A would give an artesian flow (i.e., the water would rise to and above the surface of the bore). At B there is a deep well and at C a shallow well.

4.4.2 Shallow Groundwater

Shallow groundwater sources are not to be despised even if they only yield a limited seasonal supply. A series of shallow wells will sometimes yield surprising results; some may yield a supply while others run dry. Again during another season the good wells may fail and the dry wells yield. Shallow wells are supplied from the sub-surface water and if provision is made for storage they can be made to yield a fair supply.

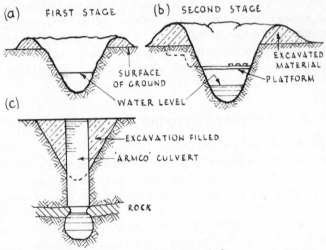

Figure 4.13 Water hole.

Shallow wells are often excavated as shown in Figure 4.13(a). As the water retreats and excavation follows, the water in the hole becomes as shown in Figure 4.13(b). The sides silt in by the wash of the rain and the hole is abandoned. Figure 4.13(c) shows a method of improving a water hole. In the original excavation an Armco culvert (i.e., a culvert made from curved sheets of corrugated steel) has been placed upright. The spoil, or debris, from the original excavation has been filled in around it and the well has been deepened. Cast concrete tubes have been used in place of Armco culverting. The excavation at the bottom of the well is made as large as possible, for storage purposes.

4.4.3 Springs

The water from a spring which appears on the surface of the earth may be conducted by pipes into a tank—and this source of water is the best—where it exists. The tank, which may be of brick, stone, concrete, or galvanized iron, should be of sufficient capacity to contain the flow of the spring for 12 hours.

The rate of flow of the spring can be measured by timing how long it takes to fill a container (say 20 l). The discharge per hour can be worked out and it is an easy matter to calculate the size of the tank to hold 12 hours flow (see section 4.2.7). Twelve hours is taken as the limit of the night flow. The normal daily discharge of the spring, during the 12 hours it is being used, plus the quantity of water already in the tank, doubles the usefulness of the spring when it is used as a public water supply. Springs and gravity-fed pipelines should be the first choice for water development where they are an option.

4.4.4 Infiltration Trenches

Shallow water holes can sometimes be improved in this manner (see Figure 4.14(a)). Let a be a water hole. Dig trial pits about a, as at a^1, a^2, a^3, etc. Observe which way the water, if found, appears to flow. At right angles to the flow excavate a long narrow trench to intercept the flow. The trench can be lined with masonry (Figure 4.14(b)), brickwork (if these linings are used passages or 'weep holes' are left in the walls so that the water can enter freely) or the sides can be revetted with timber and brushwood. In some works the trenches have been filled with big stones through which the water percolates to a sump. The trench should then be covered. An opening for drawing water is treated as a well head. This method is useful near rivers. The excavation is termed as an *infiltration trench*.

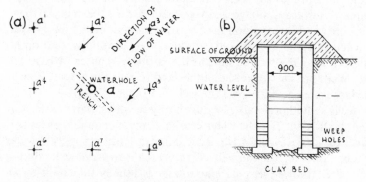

Figure 4.14 Infiltration trench.

Where a flood passes over a porous deposit forming the bed of a stream the water enters the ground and passes down through the pores until it reaches the water table. The zone of saturation is raised by the fresh supply of water and stands at a higher level below the stream than under the surrounding country. The water proceeds to find its own level by moving outwards, the movement is slow and unless the material is extremely porous the water never finds its true level but always remains higher near the stream bed.

4.4.5 Hand-dug Wells

In choosing a site for a well remote from a river, local vegetation including trees should be listed and checked against the nomenclature of plants with roots which reach a water table or aquifer. Such plants which have been given the name *Phreatophytes* are often not only indications of groundwater but capable of giving the approximate depth of the water table. For instance, it is said that:

> In Tanzania the 'Mkuju' tree (Ficus capensis) indicates ground water at a depth of 1·5 to 2 metres, while the 'Schirmakazie' (*Acacia spirocarpa*) indicates the presence of water to a depth of about three times the height of its crown . . . the various acacia are frequently good ground water indicators in the drier parts of Africa, but camel thorn (*Acacia giraffae*) is one of the exceptions. (Keller)

Low ground mists frequently indicate the presence of shallow ground water.

The sanitary aspects of a well should be carefully considered. Contamination of the water emanates from three principal sources namely, surface drainage; seepage from latrines, cesspits, garbage pits, etc.; and internal pollution by using contaminated receptacles, buckets and the like, to extract water. It follows then, that on no account should a well be sited near a latrine, cesspit or garbage pit, etc. Wells near a village should be sited so that the natural flow of surface water is away from the well (see Figure 4.19).

Wells should preferably be dug during the driest parts of the year and should penetrate the water bearing stratum or aquifer as far as is practicable (see Figure 4.12). By so doing, a constant supply of water can be expected, and the well will receive an increase of water during and after the wet season. The aquifer is usually underlain by an impervious layer of clay, shale, granite, etc. Such a layer may be tilted, or contorted and it may be cut by eruptive rocks. Hence underground there are unsuspected barriers (which may amount to dams) to intercept the movement of ground water.

It may be prudent and recommended to carry out an investigation of the area of a proposed well site in order to verify whether there is ground water present. The most practical approach to investigate a proposed well site is to put down a probe, using hand-boring equipment. Such equipment is designed and produced according to requirements in the form of lightweight or heavier models:

Light-weight hand boring equipment needed to put down a probe to 10 metres is as follows:

1 clay auger for stiff soil.
1 flat chisel for moderately hard ground.
1 'T' chisel for hard and broken ground.
1 shoe shell for bringing up sand and cleaning out the borehole.
1 worm auger for soft material.
1 pair tillers—these clamp on the rods and are for operating the string of tools (rods and bit, etc.).,
2 hand dogs to hold the rods when lifting or loosening the string of tools in the borehole.
2 lifting dogs for hoisting the rods and tools.
6 rods of 1·5 m in length.
1 swivel rod.
1 gin block.
1 spring hook and rope.
1 tripod with shackle.

If, as a result of probing, there are indications of water, the design of a well should then be considered. It may be possible to use hand-boring equipment to develop a bore-hole, lining the hole with light-weight steel or plastic casing if caving is likely to occur. The diameter of the casing should be large enough to accept a pump if it is required to test-pump the aquifer. If the rate of supply of water is sluggish, it may be expedient to sink a well of large diameter. Wells of 5 m dia. and 10 m deep are in existence. If the probe cuts a fissure in a rock and there appears to be a spring, a comparatively narrow well may be all that is needed. Some wells have a narrow shaft but bulge out in the water-bearing stratum so as to collect more water.

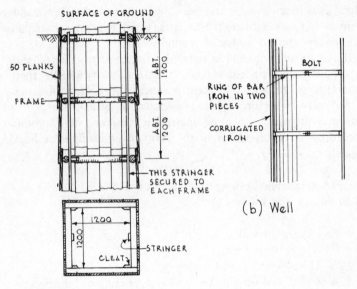

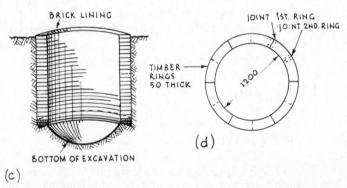

Figure 4.15 Hand-dug well construction.

4.4.6 Excavation of Hand-dug Wells

Wells should be dug in the dry season. Two considerations are important. First, and apart from hydro-geological requirements, the diameter of a hand-dug well must be sufficient for a man to work in comfort, and a minimum diameter would be 1 metre. Secondly, the safety of the people digging must be assured.

In loose soils the sides of the well must be supported during excavation. Timber can be used as in Figure 4.15(a). In formations which will stand of themselves, but from which small stones etc., are liable to fall, corrugated iron may be used as Figure 4.15(b). In hard formations support is unnecessary. Timber soon rots or is destroyed by white ants.

When excavating in wet sand or in sandy soils, a 'curb' is used. A 'curb' is not unlike a cart wheel without spokes as in Figure 4.15(d). It can be made of two or three rings of two-inch planks bolted one over another and broad enough to carry a ring of bricks or concrete blocks (see Figure 4.15(c)). The internal diameter of the curb must be at least 1·2 m. The curb is placed on the soil to be excavated where the well is chosen, and weighted with bricks, the soil is excavated from the centre, and the weight of the bricks presses the curb down. More bricks are added and the process is continued. Curbs are also made of reinforced concrete.

The difficulty is to keep the curb horizontal; excavation must be carried out carefully to maintain the verticality of the wall. Otherwise, if setting occurs, the lining will cease to follow the excavating. A curb may have a cutting edge on the bottom.

Alternatively, interlocking reinforced concrete rings are used instead of bricks in a manner similar to that described above. The first concrete ring to be 'dug in' has a cutting edge on the bottom.

When the digging has reached the water table, some form of pump will be required to extract water, thus depressing the water level so as to allow further excavation to continue. It is essential to penetrate below the original water level, or into the aquifer, as far as is practicable, to ensure the best possible yield of water.

4.4.7 Well Lining

The lining of a well may be of brick, stone, concrete blocks, reinforced concrete, concrete rings, corrugated iron, culverting, etc. Timber is not recommended as a 'permanent' lining, because it will rot and so contaminate the water supply. If the sides of the well have not been supported during excavating, and concrete lining is required then shuttering should be inserted with a space of a few inches clear of the sides of the wall. Concrete should be poured into this annular space and when set, the shuttering must be removed, to be positioned higher up inside the well, if it is necessary to cast the concrete in sections ascending from the bottom to the top.

Weep holes (slots) are made in the bottom section of a concrete lining, by positioning strips of wood in the annular space prior to pouring the concrete then removing them when the concrete has set, thus creating a void through which the water will flow into the well. Concrete rings can be obtained with weep holes incorporated in the design, for the intake section. In the case of a brick-lined well, bricks are left out, to provide weep holes.

Where the well is excavated in very solid formation, lining need only be carried down to 2·5–3 m below ground level in order to exclude the infiltration of surface water (see Figure 4.16) which could contaminate the well.

A task which often proves difficult to accomplish is to provide a sump below the area of infiltration in which sand and fine debris brought into the well by the water flow, can settle. There need be no weep holes in the sump which would measure from 0·5 to 1 m in depth. The bottom would be closed by a layer of concrete, stones or pebbles according to the design specifications of the well.

4.4.8 Well Head

The well head consists of a parapet, cover and apron as shown in Figure 4.16. The parapet is an extension of the well lining approximately 1 m in height and should be closed in by a cover. One or perhaps two openings may be made in the cover for water drawing purposes.

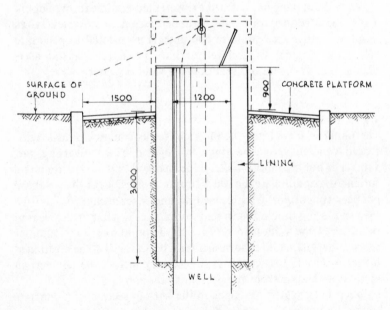

Figure 4.16 Well head.

For durability and protection of the water source it is recommended that concrete or steel plate is used for the cover. The openings should have a lid of durable material, to enable the well to be completely closed in when not in use. An apron should be cast in concrete for a distance of approximately 1·5 m around the parapet and sloping away in all directions to a peripheral drain leading into a major drain or soakage pit, to drain all surface water completely away from the well head. When casting the concrete apron, special attention must be paid to the sealing of the joint between the apron and the outside of the lining at the top of the well. One of the most common causes of contaminating well water arises from polluted surface water leaking through this joint. Another common cause of pollution stems from contaminated buckets and receptacles being used to extract water from the well. An obvious recommendation to minimize pollution of the well is to install a pump in the well, leaving one opening securely covered and locked, in case the pump is out of order.

4.4.9 Tube-Wells

The tube-well is most useful in areas which yield sub-surface water contained in gravels. The 'well' consists of lengths of tubes; the leading one is shod with a square steel point. Above the steel point a series of holes are drilled into the tube. The 'well' is driven into the ground by blows delivered on a driving cap.

The driving cap is a single block of steel secured to the top of the tube. The tube being of small diameter can only contain a small supply of water. When the stratum in which the water is found is porous (e.g., in gravel) the water flows freely into the tube. Where the water level can be established at less than 7 m below ground level, the water can be extracted from the tube by a bucket type of hand pump. There is a pump supplied with the tubes for this purpose.

4.4.10 Deep Wells and Bore-holes

In dense crystalline rocks, such as are encountered in Tanzania, deep-seated water is stored in cracks and fissures. A bore-hole sunk in crystalline rock may be a failure, even though it is close to a successful bore. It is reported that in one instance the unsuccessful bore was within 20 m of the successful bore.

Bore-holes sometimes yield a brackish water but, if the bore is lined and continued, fresh water may possibly be found below. Bore-holes and very deep wells should not be undertaken without expert advice. Deep wells are generally those which are sunk through impervious stratum or strata in order to tap the water held up by other deep seated impervious layers.

Drilling is expensive and it is therefore essential to find out as much as possible about the hydro-geology of a proposed site, to confirm the presence of potable groundwater at a feasibly exploitable depth. This may call for a geophysical survey with special equipment and professional operation and interpretation. Such a service can be costly, but it will be justified if it saves the greater cost of abortive drilling.

To be favourable for water, the material of the geological formation must be pervious (i.e., with pores which must be large enough to allow the water to drain out under the influence of gravity). The water may occupy cracks and joints in solid and otherwise impermeable rock, but commonly the water-bearing materials are granular such as sand, sandstone or weathered crystalline rock, and the water fills the spaces between the grains. In fine-grained silts the spaces between the grains or 'pore space' amounts to about 40 per cent, and in sand or gravels it is about 30 per cent. Water in traversing pervious materials obeys the ordinary laws of hydraulics. Gravity is the essential cause of all ordinary movement of bodies of water except capillarity which can raise water against gravity. The capillary water, though it may appear as moisture and dampness, is not available for springs and wells.

The basic fact is that at a distance which varies from a few metres to several hundred metres below the surface of the ground, pervious rocks or materials are more or less saturated with water. The upper surface of the saturated zone is called the water table; its position fixes the minimum depth to which wells must be sunk to obtain a supply of water. Generally the water table in a single pervious stratum is not dead level but has an undulating surface which follows roughly the contour of the land surface. It owes its irregularities of surface to the naturally uneven movement of underground water. There is a flow down the slopes of the surface. It is this fact which accounts for the 'flow' in wells and infiltration trenches.

The lower limit of the water-bearing zone is no doubt just as variable in position as the upper limit. From theoretical considerations, it has been concluded that water may occur in small quantities down to 1500 m. Experience generally supports this view. The world's deepest mine, Morro Velho, in Brazil, is perfectly dry below 1000 m but in some oil fields large quantities of water have been met at 900 m, and at least one deep well has struck water at over 1800 m.

4.5 WATER SUPPLY

4.5.1 Water Consumption Rates
The minimum quantity of water supplied per person per day in a hot climate should not be less than 10 l to ensure good health, but is often less than this in practice.
Typical consumption rates are shown in Table 4.10.

Table 4.10   Ranges of Daily Water Consumption

Type of Water Supply	*Litres per head per day**
Domestic	
Rural without standpipes or taps	1–25
Public standpipes	10–50
Household with single tap	15–90
Urban house with multiple taps	30–300

* Quantities given are derived from White, A., *Water Waste and Health in Hot Climates.*

Table 4.11 gives design criteria for some countries in East Africa. The data for Uganda, Kenya and Tanzania were published by the Bureau of Resource Assessment and Land Use Planning, University of Dar es Salaam in 1973. The data for Ethiopia were prepared by the Ethiopian Water Resources Authority in 1976.

4.5.2 Head and Pressure
The head of a particle of water with reference to a given point or datum is the energy which it contains by virtue of its height above the given point. A column of water standing 1 m high in a vertical pipe has a static head of 1 m above the base of the column. Particles at the upper surface of a column of water standing 1 m high in a vertical pipe have a static head of 1 m above the base. Moving down the column, particles lose static head but gain pressure from the weight of the water above them. At the base of the column there is no static head, but the pressure is the weight of the column of water 1 m high. Pressure and head are both expressed in units of length—metres.
In a water-supply system consisting of an elevated tank, supplied

Table 4.11   Some design criteria for water supplies.

		Litres per head per day
Uganda		
Rural	Trading centres	45
	Strictly rural areas	30
	Cattle	45
	Pigs, goats, sheep	20
Urban	Small centres	110–140
	Large centres	180–270
Hospital		180
Kenya		
Rural	Dry areas	8
	Communal standpipe	20
	Cattle	20
	Small livestock	5
Urban	Major towns	135–160
	Rural centres	110
Tanzania		
Rural	People	45
	Cattle	45
	School	25
	Hospital	90
	Communal standpipes	45
Ethiopia		
	Community populations: up to 2,500	20
	Community populations: 2500–10000	30
	Cattle, horses, mules, donkeys: highlands	20
	Cattle, horses, mules, donkeys: lowlands	15
	Camels: lowlands	2
	Goats, sheep: highlands	2
	Goats, sheep: lowlands	1

by a pump and delivering to a point of discharge (see Figure 4.17), the head or pressure at the point of discharge is the vertical height between the surface of the water in the tank and the point of discharge. The total static head on the pump is the vertical height that the water has to be lifted from the surface level in the well to the outlet of the rising main.

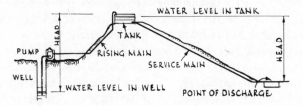

Figure 4.17 Static head.

Pressure Water weighs 1000 kg/m³; therefore a column of water 1 m high exerts a force of 1000 kg on a base area of 1 m² or a pressure of 0·1 kg/cm². Thus:

Head in metres = pressure in kg/cm² × 10

If water flows by gravity through a pipe from an elevated source to a point of discharge some of the total head is used in overcoming friction and other losses in the pipe. In small diameter pipes a great deal of head may be lost in friction (see Table 4.12). The pressure at the tap or point of discharge is the total head less losses, often described as the *residual* head.

Similarly a pump raising water through a pipe line has to overcome both the static head and the frictional and other losses.

4.5.3 Discharge of Pipes

The discharge or flow through a pipe depends upon its diameter, friction characteristics and the applied head. If A is the cross-section area of the pipe and v is the velocity of flow, the discharge Q is given by:

$$Q = Av$$

If the diameter of the pipe is d:

$$A = 0·7854 \times d$$

There are various formulae for calculating the discharge in a pipe, in relation to its size, length and the head difference between its ends. A rough formula is:

$$Q = 0·003 \, D^2 \, \frac{DH}{L}$$

where Q = discharge (l/sec); D = diameter of pipe (mm); H = drop in head along the pipe (m); and L = length of pipe (m).

This formula gives results which are too high in the case of small pipes with flat gradients. It does not take into account the different friction characteristics of different pipe materials.

In designing a pipeline the loss of head due to friction can be determined from charts or tables which give the losses per unit length for a range of discharges, pipe sizes and friction conditions. Table 4.12 gives the friction head loss in m/1000 m of pipe length, for small diameter galvanized iron pipes. The diameters in the table are the nominal internal diameters of pipes.

Table 4.12   Pipe friction head loss in m/1000 m length (for galvanized iron pipes.)

Flow	Pipe dia. (mm)									
l/sec	13	19	25	31	38	50	63	75	88	100
0·05	40·8	5·08	1·12	0·37	0·15					
0·10	162	20·2	4·70	1·48	0·60	0·14				
0·20	630	80·7	18·6	6·10	2.36	0·55				
0·30		181	42·0	13·8	5·30	1·23	0·38			
0·40		319	74·0	25·5	9·70	2·20	0·68	0·17		
0·50		500	116	39·0	15·0	3·50	1·05	0·28		
0·75			260	90·0	33·5	7·50	2·40	0·61	0·27	
1·0			465	161	60·0	13·5	4·30	1·08	0·48	0·25
1·5				372	136	30·2	9·50	2·47	1·10	0·57
2·0				670	242	53·0	17·0	4·40	1·95	1·00
2·5					380	83·0	26·6	6·99	3·10	1·58
3·0					525	119	38·0	10·1	4·45	2·28
3·5						165	51·0	13·7	6·10	3·12
4·0						210	67·0	17·8	8·10	4·08
5·0						325	107	28·5	12·6	6·50

Examples of the use of Table 4.12

(a) A cattle trough is to be supplied from a tank whose outlet is 14 m above the trough, through a pipeline 750 m long. The trough requires a constant supply of 1000 l/hour, which is nearly 0·3 l/sec. What size of galvanized iron pipe should be used? Try a 25 mm dia. pipe. From the table, the friction loss per 1000 m for a 25 mm pipe for a flow of 0·3 1/sec is 42 m. The loss in 750 m of pipe is 0·75 × 42 = 31·5 m. But only 14 m of head are available. Therefore try a larger sized pipe, say 31 mm. The loss is then 0·75 × 13·8 = 10·35 m. Hence a 31 mm pipe should be used.

(b) There is tank in the roof of a house and the bottom of the tank is 4 m above a bath. The bath is to be filled at the rate of 1 l/sec. Length of pipe between tank and bath = 12 m. There are four bends in the pipe. Bends introduce additional friction loss, and this can be estimated by adding 0·6 m to the length of the pipe for each bend. Thus 4 × 0·6 = 2·4 to be added to 12 giving 14·4 m total equivalent length. Examining the table and following the line for 1 l/sec, a 25 mm pipe will lose 465/1000 = 0·465 m/m length or 0·465 × 14·4 = 6·70 m friction head. But the available head is only 4 m, so try a 31 mm pipe. The friction loss will now be 0·161 × 14·4 = 2·3 m, and so a 31 mm pipe will be adequate. If a 25 mm pipe had been used, this does not mean that it would not fill the bath. It would fill it more slowly than required. In fact the rate can be calculated. The actual total head loss in 14·4 m of pipe is 4 m, and this is equivalent to 277·8 m/1000 m. In the 25 mm column in the table, 277·8 lies between 260 m for 0·75 l/s and 465 m for 1 l/s. By proportion the flow equivalent to 277·8 m loss is about 0·77 l/sec. This would be good enough to fill a bath. A flow of 1 l/sec will fill an ordinary bucket in about 10 sec.

4.5.4 Pipelines

Figure 4.18(a) shows three possible positions for a pipe to draw water from a reservoir and discharge at a delivery point.

In effect it matters very little whether the pipeline is laid as *ad, bd,* or *cd* in Figure 4.18(a), provided that the water level is maintained in the reservoir. The total head is the same at the end of each pipe. Pipes are laid so that they follow the contour of the ground as in Figure 4.18 (b).

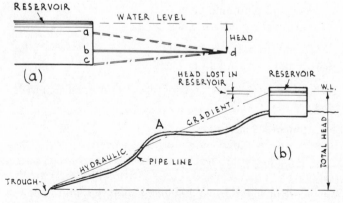

Figure 4.18 Pipe line from reservoir.

In this figure the line marked 'hydraulic gradient' is of great importance. It is a line which represents the energy head of the water as it passes down the pipe. As there are losses at the exit from the reservoir, the line starts below the water level in the reservoir. Along the length of the pipe, the slope of the line represents the friction loss (m/1000 m of pipe) and the height of the line above the discharge point represents the residual head at delivery.

If the pipeline rises above the hydraulic gradient as at A in Figure 4.18(b) there should, theoretically, be no problems provided that the pipe is kept free from air and constantly running full. In practice air entrained in the water may collect and obstruct the flow, so pipelines are generally laid in such a way that they do not rise above the hydraulic gradient.

4.5.5 Pipes

Pipelines can be classified into three categories of usage:

(a) Mains. For the conveyance of water (from a source to a reservoir or from a reservoir to a point of distribution, etc.). Generally of large diameter, 80 mm and above.

(b) Service. The individual supply to a house or building, taken from a main.

(c) Plumbing. The pipe-work within a building, for distribution to taps and other outlets.

Pipes for mains may be cast iron, spun iron, asbestos–cement, steel, pre-stressed concrete or rigid PVC. Service and plumbing pipes may be copper, steel, polyethylene and rigid PVC. Cast iron, asbestos-cement and concrete pipes are not available in the small sizes required for service and plumbing pipes.

Usual sizes for pipes for water services are:

(a) 20 mm to baths and sinks
(b) 13 mm to wash basins and WCs

Table 4.13 gives the weights of pipes of different materials.

4.5.6 Impurities in Water

These occur in three main forms: suspended solids, dissolved minerals and bacteria. The first may be derived from soil minerals or vegetable and animal matter. Some of these substances are harmful, most of them make water treatment more difficult. They can be removed by settlement or filtration. Many streams contain consider-

Table 4.13   Weights of pipes.
The internal diameters are nominal, and weights are given in kg/m of normal pipe. Cast iron and asbestos-cement pipes are Class B (tested to 120 m pressure head).

Int. dia. (mm)	Cast iron (kg/m)	Spun iron (kg/m)	Int. dia. (mm)	Wrought iron (kg/m)	Mild steel (kg/m)
50	14·66		13	1·32	1·35
75	21·03	16·41	19	1·87	1·91
100	26·97	21·36	25	2·70	2·75
125	34·94	27·90	38	4·75	4·85
150	43·61	36·08	50	6·04	6·16
			63	8·41	8·58
			75	9·91	10·11
			88	11·41	11·64

Int. dia. (mm)	Asbestos-cement (kg/m)	Int. dia. (mm)	Polythene (kg/m)
75	6·40	13	0·10
100	9·76	19	0·20
125	14·20	25	0·26
150	18·54		

able suspended solids, while subsoil water from springs or wells is relatively free.

Most disease organisms can be considered as suspended solids but they are so small that settlement or filtration are rarely 100 per cent effective in removing them, a disinfectation system may also be necessary to eliminate health risks. Dissolved mineral salts, another category of impurities, can occur in unpleasant or harmful concentrations in some wells and boreholes, and also in lakes which have no natural outlets. Water resources in hard insoluble mineral strata such as granites or basalts are usually free from dissolved salts. Chalk and limestones yield very hard water, deposits of salt and soda yield saline water, iron bearing soils often contaminate water to an objectionable extent. Certain toxic salts such as fluorides, arsenic and lead compounds can also be derived from soils and nitrates can also be present in concentrations harmful to small children. Standards have been published by WHO and others which indicate the maximum concentrations of mineral salts and other contaminants that can be tolerated without risking the health of consumers. Excessive concentrations of most mineral salts, with the exception of iron, and the substances causing excessive hardness are usually difficult to remove by simple technology and should therefore be avoided if better alternative sources can be found.

Dissolved organic matter can be found in many surface waters and may even penetrate into some wells. Figure 4.19 shows how groundwater can be polluted. Although much organic matter may be derived from decaying plants, certain organic substances indicate faecal contamination which implies the possible presence of harmful bacteria. Most of the health risks can be removed by slow sand filtration, and complete protection is possible with disinfection (chlorination).

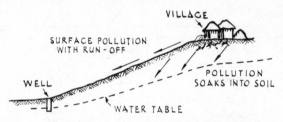

Figure 4.19 Contamination of groundwater.

4.5.7 Rough Tests for Water

Tests for water quality should ideally be made by trained chemists where possible, and guidance should be requested before samples are taken for analysis. If this is not possible rough tests can be made.

Four drops of a solution of potassium carbonate to a small glass of water; if decomposed organic matter is present, the colour turns pale or yellow. Six drops of sulphuric acid to a small glass of water; white precipitate will be formed if lead is present.

Eight drops of ammonia to a small glass of water; water turns blue if copper present. Six drops of ferro-cyanide of potassium to a small glass of water; water has a greenish colour if zinc present.

Cloudy turbid water may be cleared by adding a small quantity of Portland Cement or alum, if obtainable. The right amount of cement or alum is found by experiment—a spoonful to a barrel may be sufficient.

Simple test kits can be obtained that enable most field engineers to obtain satisfactory results for most of the more critical tests. Notable exceptions are: total dissolved solids (a precision balance is necessary) and chlorine demand. A test kit for free chlorine can be obtained and used to determine the minimum dose of chlorine (or hypochlorite) necessary to give 0·2–0·5 mg/1 free chlorine after 30 min reaction. If chlorination is not employed bacteriological tests are advisable. These should be carried out by experienced operators.

If commercial test kits are not available, simple kits can often be made up by the analytical laboratories of hospitals, schools or public health authorities.

Chlorine is used to disinfect water by destroying bacteria. Usually, chlorine in excess of that necessary to neutralize the bacteria is introduced into the water—the surplus is known as 'free chlorine', whose continued presence in the water therefore confirms the bacteria have been neutralized. Excessive chlorine is offensive, and so it is necessary to determine the amount of free chlorine in order to arrive at the minimum amount to be used. This minimum amount of chlorine needed to neutralise the bacteria is known as the 'chlorine demand'.

Testing for free chlorine and chlorine demand If test kits for free chlorine are not available a test for free chlorine can be made as follows:

(i) Take a sample of the chlorinated water, about 50 ml in a clean glass vessel will suffice.

(ii) Add a small crystal of pure potassium iodide and shake to dissolve.

(iii) Add a few drops of starch solution made by mixing a saltspoon-ful of clean starch with a little cold water to form a paste, then adding boiling water to make up the volume to about 50 ml. This solution does not keep for more than a few days.

(iv) If the water sample does not change colour no free chlorine is present. If a blue colour rapidly forms chlorine is present. The lowest concentration that will give a faint but clear blue colour is about 0·15 mg/l. Higher concentrations give deeper colours.

To measure the chlorine demand of water the multiple dilution test is easy to carry out and does not need an accurately standardized chlorine solution. It is essential however that the chlorine solution used for the test is the same as that used for disinfecting the supply. The stock solution can be prepared containing about 1% free chlorine by dissolving suitable quantities of hypochlorites in water:

(a) Bleaching powder (25% free Cl_2): 1 kg in 25 1 water gives approximately 1% free Cl_2.

(b) HTH (70% free Cl_2): 1 kg in 75 l water gives approximately 1% free Cl_2.

A series of 4 or 5 samples of the raw water must be taken, 1 litre each in clean glass bottles and dosed with the hypochlorite stock solution, one drop in the first, two drops in the second and so on. Each sample is mixed, stood in the shade for 30 min and tested for free chlorine with a test kit or by the starch iodide method to indicate the lowest dilution required to provide a concentration of $0.2 - 0.5$ mg/1. To chlorinate the supply to this level add 50 ml of stock hypochlorite solution per m^3 of water for every drop used in the lowest acceptable test.

4.5.8 Water Treatment

Water can be made bacteriologically pure by boiling. If boiled vigorously for five minutes, all forms of disease-producing organisms are destroyed. Although this may be expensive in fuel (roughly 1 kg of wood is required to boil a litre of water), a container of water can usually be boiled on the remains of a fire used for cooking a meal, and thus provide a limited supply of pure water daily. Water can also be purified by the introduction of a chemical disinfectant which destroys bacteria by oxidation. For small quantities of water, say 1 litre at a time, water purifying tablets can be used.

The installation of a domestic water supply depends on the selection of the best available source for both quantity and quality, and the application of appropriate treatment where necessary. Water treatment can be costly, and it is often cheaper to pipe good water from some distance rather than treat poor quality water that may be more easily available.

Water treatment processes are designed as a number of stages which are selected according to the requirements shown by the quality tests that have been made. It is important to place the stages in the correct order, and to ensure that essential operation and maintenance procedures, however small, are not neglected. Water treatment plants should adopt the general plan given in Table 4.14 using only those stages that are actually necessary.

The bottle tests used for designing or checking coagulation and settlement can be made by taking a 1 l sample of water in a clean glass bottle and allowing it to stand. The effectiveness of settlement can be roughly estimated by observation after at least 60 min. Settlement processes can easily last for many days and storage for this length of time may be necessary to ensure continuity of flow.

Table 4.14   *Simple treatment of non-saline water.*

Process and Purpose	Main design Parameters	Effect	Notes
Screening to remove coarse solids	Size and mesh of screen	Removes coarse solids, snails, etc.	Needs regular cleaning and removal of trash
Aeration if iron present using trickling filter	Flow rate 10–20 $m^3/m^2/d$. Number of layers of gravel used	Precipitation of oxidizable iron compounds	Needs occasional cleaning
Coagulation and flocculation to assist settlement of solids	Coagulant alum (aluminium sulphate). Dose may be 5–100 mg/l. Check by bottle test	Coarsens suspended solids to improve settlement	Regular supply of chemicals needed. Correct dosing procedure does not work in every case
Settlement and storage to remove suspended solids	Retention time check by bottle test	Removes settlable solids, parasite eggs	Needs regular desludging
Slow sand filtration to remove both settlable and unsettlable solids	Flow rate sand grading	Removes solids and many harmful disease organisms	Needs regular cleaning
Chlorine disinfection	Chlorine dose check by test. Retention time 30 mins or more	Destroys harmful disease organisms	Needs regular supply of chemicals and regular checking

Bottle tests for coagulation can be carried out in a similar way. Take a number, say three, 1 l samples of water in clean glass bottles. Using a stock solution of alum add 20 mg/l to one, 40 mg/l to the next and 60 mg/l to the third. Mix each bottle thoroughly and allow to stand in the shade, and while standing stir each bottle gently for a few seconds every 2 min. This enables a coarse floc to form and to settle. Select the lowest concentration of alum which produces a clear upper layer of water quickly. The test can be repeated to establish the dose more accurately if a different range of alum concentrations is used. Coagulation with alum in this simple way works well with many types of water but some may be found which are chemically unsuitable for coagulation. This test will establish this very quickly.

Suitable designs for simple settling tanks and sand filters can be found in *Water Treatment and Sanitation*, (see Ref. 19).

4.6 WATER LIFTING

4.6.1 Simple Methods of Raising Water

Figure 4.20 shows some simple traditional methods of raising water.
In Figure 4.20(a) the end of the bag is kept open by means of a hoop.
The bag is held by two ropes, one attached to the hoop, one to the
lower end or narrow neck of the bag. The ropes are so arranged that
when the hoop end of the bag reaches the top of the well, the narrow
neck has passed over the roller B. The water pours out in the trough
C. In India a bullock is trained to pull the ropes together by simply
walking away from the well.

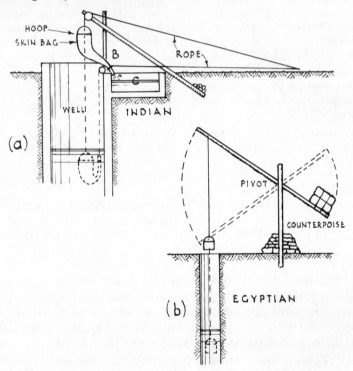

Figure 4.20 Simple water raising methods.

4.6.2 Pumps Generally

If at sea level the end of a long tube from which the air has been
exhausted is immersed in water, water will rise in the tube to a height
of about 10·3 m. The pressure of the atmosphere on the surface of
water causes the water to rise in the tube.

Suction pumps make use of this principle. For example in Figure 4.21(a) the pump bucket (or piston) has a valve A which permits the water to pass from the lower to the upper side of the piston. There is also a valve at B. During the up-stroke, when the pump bucket is ascending the valve A is closed and the air is partially exhausted in the pump barrel and suction pipe. Valve B is open. Therefore the pressure of the atmosphere causes some water to rise in the suction pipe. During the down stroke the valve B is closed and valve A opens. Some water will now pass through A. Repetitions of the strokes will gradually bring the water into the pump barrel and from thence to the discharge point.

As the mechanism of such a pump is not perfect and as a complete vacuum is not formed in the pump, it is unsafe to assume that water will rise more than 6–7 m at sea level. At levels much above sea level the atmospheric pressure is reduced so not even these lifts will be achieved. At sea level pumps will 'suck' from a depth of 6–7 m, at 1000 m from 5·5 to 5·8 m, at 2000 m from 4·8 to 5 m.

It should never be forgotten that all pumps need repairs, and that repairs are always a problem.

4.6.3 Positive Displacement Pumps
Figure 4.21(a)–(e) shows diagrammatically several types of barrel pumps also known as 'cylinder', 'plunger' or 'piston' pumps.

Figure 4.21(a) is a suction pump for use in shallow wells, from 5 to 7 m deep, according to the altitude. It delivers water from the spout of the pump.

Figure 4.21(b) is also for shallow wells. The pump barrel is from 5 to 7 m above the water level in the well. It will deliver the water to a much higher height than the surface of the ground as the barrel or cylinder is closed and a delivery pipe is fitted. There are numerous designs for this type of pump, some of which are horizontal. They have one, two or three barrels/cylinders; whatever the type, the principle is the same.

Figure 4.21(c) is a deep well pump. The working barrel is placed in the well itself so that the suction pipe is not more than 3–4·5 m long. The pump rods are carried up to the surface through guides and are connected to a mechanism which gives the necessary motion. In wells in which the water level fluctuates and rises above the barrels, or barrel, the guide tube is extended as shown by the dotted lines. In this type of pump an air vessel and a non-return valve are fitted. Air which is compressed in the air vessel by the normal action of the pump, equalizes the flow of water in the delivery pipe. If the air vessel is

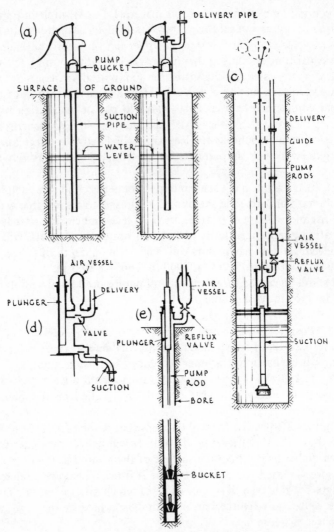

Figure 4.21 Barrel pumps.

omitted, water is delivered intermittently, and pipes and fittings may be damaged. An air vessel can be used with advantage in the type of pump shown in Figure 4.21(b) if the pump is to deliver water at a height. A non-return valve allows the water to pass into the rising main but will not allow it to flow back. Deep well pumps have one, two or three barrels. A 'three throw deep well pump' means a pump with three barrels.

Most of the problems with suction pumps occur through the failure to suck. The piston or the piston valve may be defective to the extent that the air leaks back during priming, or there may be leakage of air through joints in the suction pipe.

Figure 4.21(d) shows a force pump. In this type of pump a ram or solid plunger takes the place of a bucket. A force pump is used to work against high pressures as when it delivers water to a boiler which is under pressure of steam. Water enters through the lower valve during the upstroke of the plunger and is delivered through the upper valve during the down stroke—which also causes the lower valve to close.

Figure 4.21(e) shows a borehole pump. This is a common type. The barrel of the pump is screwed to the end of the delivery pipe. The barrel is of less diameter than the pipe so that the bucket and foot valve can be removed when necessary. (It is usually a tedious business fishing for the foot valve.) If the bucket and foot valve and the necessary rods, etc., were the only components in the pump, water would be delivered intermittently and on the upstroke only. In the larger types of pump this difficulty is overcome by fitting a solid plunger at the head of the delivery pipe as well as a bucket lower down. Both work on the same rod or rods. The plunger is made so that it has only one half the sectional area of the bucket, thus one half of the total discharge is made on the upstroke, and one half on the downstroke. The discharge is regular, not intermittent. In boreholes of any considerable depth balance weights are used to counter balance the weight of the pump rods, bucket and mechanism generally. They are attached to levers which are connected to the pump rods.

4.6.4 Discharge of Barrel Pumps

The theoretical discharge of a barrel pump is obtained by measuring the volume 'swept' or displaced in the barrel at each stroke and multiplying this by the rate of operation in strokes per minute or per hour. If: d = internal diameter of the barrel (mm); s = stroke (mm); n = number of strokes per minute; and Q = discharge (1/hour) then:

$$Q = \frac{0 \cdot 04712 \times d^2 \times s \times n}{1000} \text{ (l/hour)}$$

For the discharge in l/sec, divide this by 3600.

Table 4.15 gives figures for the value of Q/n for different pump strokes and barrel sizes. These figures, when multiplied by the number of strokes per minute, will give the discharge in l/hour.

*Table 4.15   Discharge factors (Q/n) for barrel pumps.**

Stroke	Diameter of pump barrel (mm)						
(mm)	50	63	75	88	100	113	125
100	11·8	18·7	26·5	36·5	47·1	60·2	73·6
150	17·7	28·1	39·8	54·7	70·7	90·3	110·5
200	23·6	37·4	53·0	73·0	94·2	120·3	147·3
225	26·5	42·1	59·7	82·1	106·0	135·4	165·7
250	29·5	46·8	66·3	91·3	117·8	150·4	184·1

* Multiply Q/n by strokes per minute (n) to give discharge in 1/hour

Example of the use of Table 4.15.

100 mm pump, with 225 mm stroke, pumping at 40 strokes per min. From Table 4.15 $Q/n = 106$ and $Q = 106 \times 40 = 4240$ l/hour (or 4240/3600 = 1·18 l/sec).

The size of pump for a particular situation will depend on the rate of delivery required, the safe yield of the source and the power available.

4.6.5 Semi-rotary Pumps

Semi-rotary pumps (Figure 4.22) are in common use for pumping water and other liquid, such as petrol, diesel etc. They are suitable for shallow wells and will deliver water at high levels (up to about 20

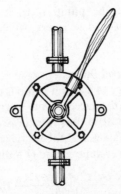

Figure 4.22 Semi-rotary pump.

m), though they can be damaged by impurities and may seize up if used infrequently. There are several makes and sizes. The all-brass type is recommended when the pump is only used occasionally.

Sizes range from 13 mm dia. suction and delivery pipes to 100 mm dia. In a test carried out on a range of sizes with 1 m suction and 1 m delivery, outputs ranged from 0·3 l/sec for the 13 mm size to about 2·5 l/sec for the 100 mm size.

4.6.6 Chain and Washer Pumps

This apparatus (see Figure 4.23) will lift water vertically from a well not less than 0·8 m dia., but cannot force water above the level of its outlet. The action of the apparatus is simple. On an endless chain rubber (or steel, or cast iron) discs are fitted. These pass through a rising pipe, so that when the discs are pulled up any water above a disc is also pulled up. The pipe is sometimes made in two sizes; in the

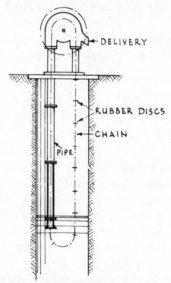

Figure 4.23 Chain pump.

upper section the discs are loose, in the lower they fit exactly. By this means excessive friction is reduced. There are several important points in this type of machine: it is comparatively easy to construct and maintain. It is fairly efficient. It is cheap. It does not get out of order quickly. Machines are made for lifts up to 20 m, though 10 m is more usual.

There is yet another type of chain pump in which buckets are fitted to a chain at frequent intervals. This type of pump predates both the chain and washer, and the barrel pump. It is the Persian wheel or 'chain of pots' and is usually animal or engine-powered.

Table 4.16   Approximate capacity of chain lift pumps at 30 revolutions of the handle per minute

	Diameter of tube (mm)				
	50	63	75	88	100
Litres per hour	2450	3860	5520	7545	9940

Under this head, although it is not a chain pump, may be mentioned the 'Bolton water elevator'. In place of a chain and pipes the apparatus is operated by means of an endless band of special construction, which does not require any fitting in the well itself. It is claimed that it will lift water from any depth up to 120 m.

Table 4.17   Capacity of Bolton water elevator at 55 revolutions of the handle per minute

	Size of band				
	00	0	1	2	3
Litres per minute	12	20	30	40	60

4.6.7 Centrifugal Pumps

Centrifugal pumps, which depend for their action on a special rotor revolving in an enclosed chamber, require power at high speeds. The speeds may be taken as from between 400–2000 rpm. In this type of pump (see Figure 4.24) the suction pipe is as short as possible. The pump must never be started or run unless it is full of water. Arrangements are made on all pumps for 'priming' (filling with water) either by hand or mechanically. Centrifugal pumps will work to heads of over 100 m but the pump must be specially designed for high lifts. It is difficult to apply power, other than electricity, to the ordinary type of centrifugal pumps if they are fitted in deep wells. They are, therefore, much used in shallow sources of supply and are invaluable in pumping out of reservoirs or from rivers.

There are many different types of centrifugal pump available to meet a very wide range of conditions. For high lifts the multistage centrifugal pump is used, which consists of several impellers and chambers clamped together in series. The maximum head for each stage is normally 80–100 m. The prime mover is a diesel or petrol engine; or an electric motor.

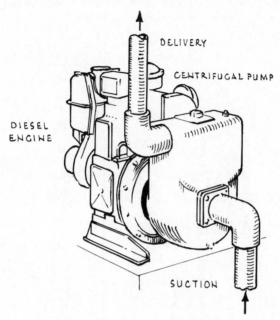

Figure 4.24 Centrifugal pump.

4.6.8 Submersible Pumps
The submersible pump is a special type of centrifugal pump consisting of a vertical spindle pump directly connected to an electric motor below it and the whole unit is suspended below lowest water level. There are various makes on the market; the chief difference between them is in the design of the motor. Submersible pumps are made to work in wells and boreholes. As they depend on electricity they can only be used in isolated situations with a generator.

4.6.9 Choosing a Pump
The following information will be needed when specifying a pump for a particular purpose:
(1) The rate of delivery required in litres per second or cu m per hour. (If the rate is likely to vary considerably, a range should be given.)
(2) The vertical distance in metres from the lowest expected water level of the source to the point of discharge of the delivery pipe (the static head).
(3) The expected variations in water level of the source, in metres.
(4) The nature of the source (e.g. well, river, lake, bore-hole etc).

Table 4.18 Characteristics of water lifting devices.

KEY TO SYMBOLS

Water Source	*Power Source*	*Use*
St = Stream, river, canal	H = Human	Do = Domestic
La = Lake, pond, tank	A = Animal	L = Livestock
Dw = Dug well	W = Wind	Ir = Irrigation
Bh = Bore-hole	IC = Diesel, Petrol	Dr = Land Drainage
	E = Electrical	
	Es = Solar-electric	

Other

Var. = Variable, FD = Free discharge, DL = Delivery lift

TYPE OF EQUIPMENT	WATER SOURCE				LIFT Approx. range m	OUTPUT Average m³/h	POWER SOURCE						USE			
	St	La	Dw	Bh			H	A	W	IC	E	Es	Do	L	Ir	Dr
Buckets and Scoops																
Swing basket	*	*			0·1–0·6	5	*								*	*
Scoop	*	*			0·1–1·0	8	*								*	*
Counterpoise lift (shadouf)	*	*	*		1·5–2·5	5	*								*	
Rope and bucket	*	*	*		1·5–10	1	*						*	*	*	
Rope and bucket (mohte)	*	*	*		4–9	12		*					*	*	*	
Water ladder	*	*			0·75–3·5	5	*	*							*	*
Chain and washer pump	*	*	*		1·5–6	18	*	*					*	*	*	
Persian wheel, saqia	*	*	*		1·5–9	14		*							*	
Noria	*	*			0·3–1·8	90									*	*

ground—Shallow well, FD	*	*		up to 6	var.	*		*	*	* *
" —Shallow well, DL	*	*		var.	var.	*		*	*	* *
Reciprocating, barrel below										
ground—Deep well, FD	*	*	*	var.	var.	*		*	*	* *
" —Deep well, DL	*	*	*	var.	var.	*		*	*	* *
Semi-rotary	*			var.	var.	*				
Archimedean screw	*			0·25-0·75	22	*				* *
Archimedean screw	*			3-10	var.					* *
Helical rotor ('Mono')	*	*		var.	var.	*		*	*	* *
Diaphragm	*			var.	var.	*		*	*	*
Rotodynamic Pumps										
Centrifugal, single stage	*	*		up to 100	var.	*		*	*	* *
Centrifugal, multi-stage	*	*		100-1000	var.	*		*	*	* *
Vertical spindle				var.	var.	*	*	*	*	* *
Propeller or axial flow	*		*	up to 30	var.	*		*	*	* *
Submersible			*	up to 1000	var.	*		*	*	*
Miscellaneous										
Hydraulic ram	*			up to 200	var.	*		*	*	
Air lift			*	var.	var.	*		*	*	

Sources: James Goodman, '*A Study of the use, efficiency and performance of simple water lifting devices used for irrigation*'. National College of Agricultural Engineering, Silsoe, UK., 1977.
Godofredo Salazar and Charles J. Moss, *An overview of the water pumping equipment available to small farmers*. International Rice Research Institute, Philippines, 1978.
A.C. Twort, R.C. Hoather, F.M. Law, *Water Supply*, (Chapter 12), Edward Arnold, 1974.
Appropriate Technology, Vol. 9, No. 1.

(5) Physical details of the site: depth of water, diameter and depth of a well or bore-hole, sketch with dimensions of river or canal bank or lake shore.

(6) Altitude of site above sea level.

(7) Power proposed for pumping: man, animal, wind, petrol, diesel, solar-electric etc.

(8) Weight which can be transported to the site and handled with ease.

Table 4.18 gives the characteristics of various water lifting devices which will need to be considered when choosing a pump.

In addition to this essential information, it is desirable to bear in mind other factors to ensure the eventual selection of a pump which will operate satisfactorily under the particular local circumstances:

—the presence of silt, sand or grit in high concentrations can be a major problem in certain situations; sediment in the water will wear down those moving parts of the pump with which it is in contact;

—salty or brackish water will corrode metal (particularly ferrous) parts more rapidly than fresh water;

—the ease of maintenance, the tolerance of the pump to wear and misuse, the availability of the tools and skills needed for repair, and the availability of spare parts, are in practice very important characteristics;

—the desired operating cycle—a few hours a day, or 24 hours a day —will affect the type as well as the capacity of the pump required.

—both the capital and running costs must be carefully calculated, in the specific local situation;

—above all, the people who are actually going to have to use the pump should be involved in the decision-making as far as possible.

4.6.10 Air-Lift System

This system can be used in deep bore-holes. The principle of action is simple. A pipe is immersed in a bore-hole for the greater part of its length. The upper end is curved so that the pipe can discharge into a tank. Air is pumped in at the lower end of the pipe, which is open. The air mixes with the water in the pipe forming in fact alternate bands of air and water. For this reason the water in the pipe must be of less weight (pressure) than the water outside it in the bore-hole. The excess of pressure in the bore-hole forces the water up the pipe to be discharged into the tank. The water is not blown up.

This system demands that the ratio of immersion of the pipe shall be properly proportioned to the lift. Some hold that this proportion

Table 4.19.
Lift and immersion
for air-lift pumping.

Lift (m)	Immersion (m)	Air pressure required (kg/cm^2)
7·5	12–15	1·2–1·4
15	25–30	2·3–3·1
30	45–60	4·6–6·1
45	70–90	6·9–8·4

should be 6:5 (e.g. 30m immersion: 25m lift). In any case the immersion of the pipe must be greater than the lift (or the bore-hole must always be much more than half full of water). Table 4.19 illustrates this point. It is only approximate and would be incorrect for high altitudes.

It will be seen that the air lift system is not suitable for small undertakings.

4.6.11 Hydraulic Rams
Figure 4.25 shows diagramatically a typical arrangement for the hydraulic ram, which has only two moving parts. It is powered by the flow of water passing through the pump body.

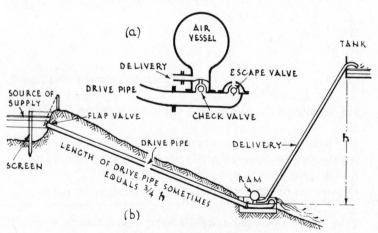

Figure 4.25 Hydraulic ram.

The water working the ram enters by the 'drive pipe' (Figure 4.25(a)) and flows out through the 'escape valve'. When the water has gained sufficient velocity it automatically closes the escape valve. There is not now a way of escape for the water which raises the check valve at the entrance to the air vessel. The water is forced up into the air vessel and finally from thence into the delivery pipe. By this process pressure is released at the escape valve which falls, water again gushes out, and the cycle is repeated. Each time the check valve prevents the water already raised from flowing back. Air is replenished in the air vessel by means of a small valve (snifter valve).

By the action of the ram, water falling from any height from 1m upwards is made to raise a portion of itself to any greater height between 10 and 40 times the height of the fall.

The drive pipe must be straight and must above all be strong, and made of a rigid material, and must not be less in length than five times the fall of the water (see Figure 4.25(b)). It is usually seven to 10 times the fall. (The delivery pipe on the other hand need not be so strong and may be about half the diameter of the drive pipe.) The diameter of any pipe depends primarily upon the discharge it has to carry. It is, above all, vital to remember that, depending on the site, the cost of construction can easily exceed the cost of the pump.

Hydraulic rams are made by which a falling stream of foul water can be used to raise a supply of clean water. This form of ram is less efficient than the simple type. Parts of it need renewal more frequently than parts of the simple ram.

Rams will force water considerable distances. One has been reported to be forcing water to a distance of 5 km and raising it to a height of 90 m. The working fall is 3 m.

When ordering an hydraulic ram the following information is required:

(a) Minimum amount of water available to operate ram (l/sec). See sections 4.1.7 and 4.1.8.
(b) Amount of fall available (m) from source of supply to site of ram.
(c) Distance from source to ram (m).
(d) Height above ram to which water is to be delivered (m).
(e) Distance from ram to point of discharge (m).
(f) Amount of water required to be delivered in 24 hours.

Table 4.20, reproduced from S. B. Watt's *Manual on the Hydraulic Ram for Pumping Water*, gives the quantity, in litres, of water raised

Table 4.20   Pumping performance of Blake's rams.

Supply head (m)	Delivery head (m)											
	5	7:5	10	15	20	30	40	50	60	80	100	125
1·0	144	77	65	33	29	19·5	12·5					
2·0		220	156	105	79	53	33	25	19·5	12·5		
3·0			260	180	130	87	65	51	40	27	17·5	12
4·0				255	173	115	86	69	53	36	23	16
6·0					282	185	140	112	93·5	64·5	47·5	34·5
7·0						216	163	130	109	82	60	48
8·0							187	149	125	94	69	55
9·0							212	168	140	105	84	62
10·0							245	187	156	117	93	69
12·0							295	225	187	140	113	83
14·0								265	218	167	132	97
16·0									250	187	150	110
18·0									280	210	169	124
20·0										237	188	140

every 24 hours, for each litre of supply flow used per minute, under the chosen conditions of delivery head and supply head. These figures have been obtained from field trials on Blake's rams, which can operate at efficiencies of about 65 per cent, providing the ratio of the working head to the driving head is in the order of 1 : 3.

4.6.12   Application of Power to Pumps

The power required to raise one litre of water per second against a head of 1 m is 9·81 watts, or if W = power in kW, Q = discharge (l/sec) and H = head (m):

$$W = \frac{9 \cdot 81 \times Q \times H}{1000} = \frac{Q \times H}{102}$$

This would be the power required for pumping if a pump were 100 per cent efficient. But there are losses due to friction, leakage etc., and in practice the hydraulic efficiency of pumps varies between about 60 per cent for small hand pumps to over eighty per cent for small modern centrifugal pumps. If e = efficiency, the power required to operate the pump is:

$$Wp = \frac{Q \times H}{102} \times \frac{100}{e}$$

Example

It is required to deliver 30 l/sec against a head of 60 m, with a pump efficiency of 75 per cent:

$$Wp = \frac{30 \times 60}{102} \times \frac{100}{75} = 23 \cdot 5$$

To convert kW into standard horsepower (hp) multiply by 1·34 and to convert into metric horsepower multiply by 1·36. Thus 23·5 kW is equivalent to 31·5 hp. In choosing a power source for a pump, the output of the motor should always be about 10 per cent greater than the maximum estimated input required at the pump, to allow for occasional overload conditions or loss of efficiency through wear. For details of some sources of power see Chapter 7.

CHAPTER 5
Sanitation

5.1 GENERAL

The chief objective of systematic sanitation is the replacement of casual or unsafe practices which allow faecal matter to be exposed to contact with flies and vermin, which may contaminate food, cooking and eating utensils, and drinking water sources. Much infectious disease is caused in these ways, and prevention is not only hygienically preferable but is also cheaper than medical treatment.

Two types of sanitation system can be distinguished. In urban communities faecal matter and waste water must be transported away from housing to a suitable site for treatment and safe disposal. In rural areas, on the other hand, where houses are farther apart a range of on-site disposal systems is possible. With all systems waste discharges must not be permitted to contaminate water supplies.

The effectiveness of every type of sanitation system depends on adequate design and construction and most emphatically on proper use and adequate maintenance. All systems must be kept clean at the user end to prevent a focal point for infection forming. All faecal wastes must be discharged to the sanitation system. If indiscriminate defecation or unsatisfactory sanitation is allowed to operate side by side with organized sanitation no real benefits can be gained. If water-borne sanitation is employed it is essential to flush the system regularly to ensure cleanliness in closets.

5.1.1 Water-borne Sewerage

The common system of sanitation in urban and semi-urban areas in temperate regions and many tropical areas is the conventional water-borne sewerage system. The capital costs of such systems are high, but they are particularly durable with a very low maintenance requirement and a high degree of hygiene protection. In rural areas with scattered population, costs can be prohibitive and a number of satisfactory alternative systems can be recommended. Waterborne sewerage must be backed by a systematic treatment system able to produce a final effluent of suitable quality for its eventual discharge to the sea, to rivers or for possible re-use as irrigation water. Re-use of treated sewage for irrigation requires special care in both the design of the treatment system and the operation of the irrigation scheme. If adequate care is not reliably available effluent re-use should not be considered.

In most cases sewerage systems should be designed for sewage only, and surface drainage systems should be separated. Rainfall in many tropical areas is very seasonal, and can also take the form of violent storms. Surge flows of surface water drainage cannot usually be economically accommodated in sewers, and can produce problems at treatment works that may be severe to the extent of complete washout. Combined drainage systems should only be used if these problems can be avoided.

If total sewage discharges are less than about 50 litres/head/day, or bulky anal cleansing materials such as corn cobs are used, special designs of sewerage are necessary to overcome the risk of blockages. All sewerage systems should be protected from casual discharges of rubbish.

5.1.2 Alternatives

The mid-1970s saw extensive reappraisals of the problems associated with providing both water supplies and sanitation to the majority of the people in the developing world, and it became evident that available world resources were quite inadequate to provide the western-type facilities universally. Large sections of the world's rural communities live in situations which are inaccessible to water supplies in the quantities enjoyed by urban communities and without liberal supplies of water, water-borne sanitation is impossible.

Attention is therefore now being directed to alternative systems of sanitation which are more appropriate to the real situations of the developing world. While a fully water-borne system is one of the options available, it is rarely a practical solution in rural situations, and this chapter is concerned with the more practical alternatives. Table 5.1 gives a list of seven available options together with a comparison of their principal features. Each of these systems will now be described.

5.2 PIT LATRINES

5.2.1 Description of the Pit Latrine

For most situations in remote areas with limited water supply, the pit latrine is the most practical solution to the sanitation problem.

*Table 5.1   Comparison of several sanitation technologies.**

Sanitation system	Rural application	Urban application	Construction cost	Operation cost	Ease of construction	Water requirement	Hygiene
Pit	Suitable in all areas	Not in high density suburbs	Low	Low	Very easy except in wet or rocky ground	None	Moderate
Bucket and cartage	Possible	Suitable	Low	High	Easy	None	Bad
Vault and vacuum truck	Not suitable	Suitable where vehicle maintenance available	Medium to high	High	Requires skilled builder	None	Moderate to bad
Aqua privies and soakaway	Suitable in most areas	Suitable	Medium to high	Low	Requires skilled builder	Water supply near privy	Very good
Septic tanks and soakaways	Suitable in most areas	Suitable for low-density suburbs	Medium to high	Low	Requires skilled builder	Water piped to privy	Excellent
Pour flush and soakaway	Suitable	Not suitable	Medium to high	Low	Requires skilled builder	Water supply near privy	Good
Sewerage	Not suitable	Suitable where it can be afforded	Very high	Medium	Requires experienced engineer	Water piped to to privy	Excellent

* After Feachem and Cairncross, *Small Excreta Disposal Systems*.

Construction is a relatively simple matter and with reasonable care in use and maintenance a moderate standard of hygiene is obtainable.

The essential features of a pit latrine are shown in Figure 5.1(a). Basically it consists of a hole in the ground over which is placed a squatting plate inside a simple shelter. The latrine works by *aerobic* decomposition (decomposition with air or oxygen), the excreta being digested by bacteria to kill off disease causing organisms.

5.2.2   Siting
Great care is necessary in siting a latrine. To ensure its regular use it should not be far from houses, but it should be at least 6 m away.

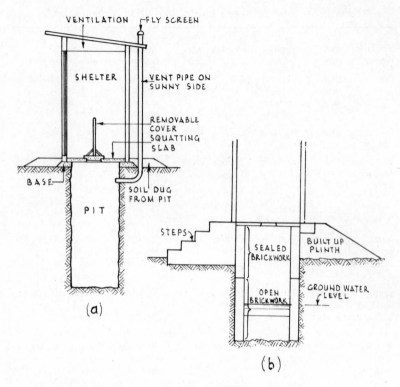

Figure 5.1 Section through pit latrine.

Contamination of ground water is a danger, and consideration should be given to the following guide lines:

(a) A latrine should always be sited at least 30 m from a water source, and wherever possible, downhill from the source. If downhill is impossible, then it should be sited at least 30 m away at the same level. It should never be uphill of a water source.
(b) Avoid areas subject to flooding—the site should be high and well drained.
(c) Ground water contamination is virtually nil if the bottom of the pit can be kept 1·5 m above the water table—this can sometimes be achieved by elevating the latrine as indicated in Figure 5.1(b).
(d) The contamination risk is especially high where there is fissured rock or limestone formation allowing free passage of ground water with little filtering provided by the sub-soil.

5.2.3 Design

A one-hole latrine is adequate for a family of up to six people. For communal latrines for markets or settlements, one hole should be provided for every 15 people.

The pit is usually round or square for the individual family installation and rectangular for communal latrines. The dimensions of the single family pit vary from 0·8 m to 1·2 m in diameter or width. The communal pit is also 0·8–1·2 m wide, its length depending on the number of squatting holes provided.

The depth of the pit depends on whether it is wet (i.e., penetrates the ground water table) or dry. Table 5.2 gives wet and dry pit volumes for design purposes. In general 2·5 m is the minimum desirable depth and the pit is full when the level of the contents reaches 0·5 m from the top.

Table 5.2   Volumes and depths for pit latrines
(see Ref. 21). Plan size 0·9 m × 0·9 m: suitable for family of five.

| | Personal cleansing material | | | |
| | Water/paper | | Bulky solids | |
Service life	volume m³	depth * m	volume m³	depth * m
Wet pit				
4 years (minimum)	0·74	0·90	1·13	1·40
8 years	1·47	1·80	2·27	2·80
15 years (maximum)	2·75	3·40	4·25	5·25
Dry pit				
4 years (minimum)	1·13	1·40	1·70	2·10
8 years	2·27	2·80	3·40	4·20
15 years (maximum)	4·25	5·25		

* Depth is effective pit depth and the total depth excavated should be about 0·5 m more than the effective depth.

If the soil is unstable, the pit will have to be lined. Lining may be of brickwork, masonry, timber or pre-cast concrete rings, and is generally required only for the top 1·0–1·5 m depth. The top section may have to be lined before further deepening. Below this the natural compaction of the soil usually ensures stability. With brickwork, masonry or concrete the best structural shape is circular (see Figure 5.2).

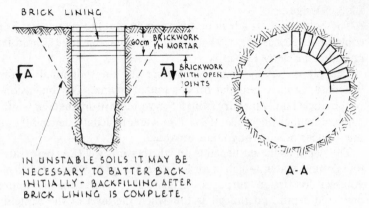

Figure 5.2 Pit latrine with brick lining.

The top 60 cm should be well bonded in cement mortar and below this, horizontal joints should be left open—using thin spacers of stone, slate etc. to provide for percolation into the soil. Good contact is essential in vertical joints between bricks or blocks to enable arching to take place.

With timber lining the easiest plan shape is square. A suggested method of lining and bracing is shown in Figure 5.3. All timber should be tarred and termite resistant if possible.

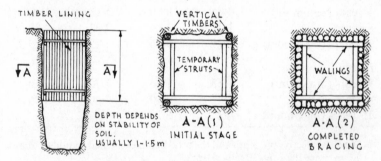

Figure 5.3 Pit latrine with timber lining.

5.2.4 Construction
The method of construction will depend on local conditions and available skills and resources, but standarization on the method, once selected, is desirable. Any excavation below 1 m deep may be dangerous work and pits more than 3 m deep should not be dug by inexperienced workmen.

The plan shape (circle, square or rectangle) should be marked on the ground for the excavation, and if several pits are to be dug a frame can be made to this shape. The sides of the excavation should be vertical, and to ensure constant cross section a form can be made to fit exactly inside the pit. If lining is required, it should be used as described in section 5.2.3 above.

When the pit is complete, the privy floor is constructed over it. The floor consists of a squatting plate with raised footrests and a central hole. It should be of an impervious durable material with a hard surface, strong enough to span the pit without flexing and easy to clean. Various materials may be used for the floor, including reinforced concrete, reinforced concrete with brick filler, ferrocement, wood and glass-reinforced plastic (GRP). If GRP, wood or metal floors are used, additional supports may be required to prevent flexing. Box seats can be provided instead of squatting plates when desirable.

Concrete slabs are most commonly used, are the most long-lasting and generally the most satisfactory. They are the easiest to clean. If wood is used it must be termite-proof.

Concrete slabs may be made on a mass-production basis using forms accurately constructed to detailed plans. With care these forms may each be used hundreds of times provided they are kept clean and well oiled. Typical floor and form designs are shown in Figure 5.4. Concrete slabs should always be reinforced with steel bars at least 8 mm in diameter spaced as shown in Figure 5.4.

The concrete mix should be 1 cement : 2 sand : 4 broken stone (maximum size 20 mm) by volume with just enough water to provide a stiff but workable mix. If mild steel reinforcement is not available, bamboo can be used. In this case, strips of good quality bamboo 25 mm wide with the inner weaker fibres stripped away are soaked overnight in water before use. Trials should first be made to prove their effectiveness.

Ferrocement has also been successfully used for the construction of slabs. In the trials undertaken, the slab thickness was 25 mm, the reinforcement consisted of two layers of chicken wire and the mortar mix was 1 cement : 3 sand by volume. An initial layer of mortar was first placed in a slab mould, spread and levelled to a uniform thickness of 6 mm. The first layer of chicken wire was then placed followed by more mortar to within 6 mm of the finished thickness. A second layer of chicken wire was then placed and the mould filled to the top and levelled.

Whichever cement-based solution is adopted, the slab should be

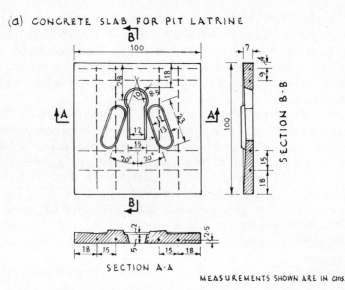

Figure 5.4 Privy floor details.

released from its mould after 24 hours and stored for at least 7 days in damp conditions under hessian or preferably immersed in water.

The slab is bedded on to a foundation base constructed of clay, soil-cement, masonry or preferably concrete. Figure 5.5 shows a suitable design for a base in soil-cement or concrete together with a suitable form for its construction.

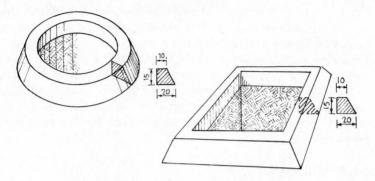

(a) TYPICAL ROUND AND SQUARE BASES
(BUILT WITH CONCRETE, SOIL-CEMENT OR CLAY)

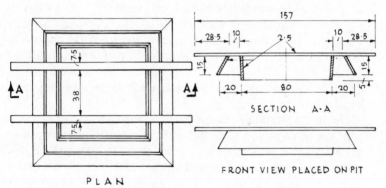

PLAN

SECTION A·A

FRONT VIEW PLACED ON PIT

(b) WOODEN FORM FOR CONCRETE OR SOIL-CEMENT
BASE TO USE ON 0·8m SQUARE PIT

Figure 5.5 Base for privy floor.

The shelter (Figure 5.1) should give protection from the rain and
privacy to the user. There should be no gap between the floor and the
walls and the wall cladding should stop short of the roof by 300 mm to
allow adequate ventilation. The design of the shelter will depend on
local building practices and the availability of materials (i.e., timber,
wattle and thatch, masonry, or brick with tile or corrugated iron
or asbestos cement roof). A roof is essential to shade the hole—flies
are less likely to enter a dark hole.

Insect problems in pit latrines can be reduced or eliminated in a
number of ways. A vent pipe (150–200 mm dia.) can be installed as
shown in Figure 5.1. If painted black and situated on the sunny side of

the latrine it will induce a draught of air down the hole in the squatting plate which reduces fly and odour problems. In some areas covers can be supplied for the holes in the squatting plates or seats, these however are not always acceptable. Traps can be fitted to the squatting plates; dry traps and water seal traps are possible but not in areas where bulky cleansing materials are likely to cause blockages. Adding a cupful of kerosene or waste oil once a week effectively reduces fly and mosquito breeding but does not reduce odour problems.

5.2.5 Maintenance
Where kerosene is used for control of insect breeding it should be repeated weekly. Most disinfectants will prevent decomposition of the waste in pits and may cause increased odour problems. They should not be used in the pit. Squatting plates must be kept clean, they should be roughly scrubbed with a coarse broom daily. If a teaspoon of bleaching powder, lime $(Ca(OH)_2)$ or cement is added to a gallon of water this will effectively disinfect squatting plates but do no lasting harm to the biological action in pits. These disinfectants are not effective if applied dry. The shelters and other wooden parts of latrines should be inspected occasionally for termite damage and repaired in good time.

Use of the pit should cease when the contents reach 0·5 m from the top. The pit should be backfilled with soil and left for a year, another pit being used meanwhile. After one year, the pit may (if this is socially acceptable) be re-excavated, the odour-free digested contents safely removed and used as fertilizer and the pit put back into service.

5.3 CARTAGE SYSTEMS

5.3.1 Bucket and Cartage
Bucket latrines are only acceptable where a well-organized collecting and disinfecting system exists and as this is rarely the case these days, their use should be discouraged on grounds of hygiene. For this reason details of their construction are not included here.

5.3.2 Vault and Vacuum Truck
Vacuum trucks are extremely costly, and require regular skilled maintenance. If this cannot be adequately and reliably supplied, then the system cannot function. The principle of this system is illustrated in Figure 5.6. It is more suited to high-density urban areas where access by truck is possible and truck maintenance facilities exist, and is therefore outside the scope of this book.

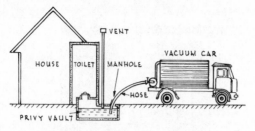

Figure 5.6 Vault system.

5.4 WATER-ASSISTED SYSTEMS

5.4.1 Aqua Privy

An aqua privy consists of a water-filled tank directly beneath a squatting plate, as shown in Figure 5.7. The tank is a form of septic tank (see section 5.5.1), in which the solid material settles at the bottom to be digested *anaerobically* (i.e., without air or oxygen) while the liquid effluent flows through an outlet to a soakaway system.

It is essential that effluents are free from solids in order to prevent clogging soakaways. The discharge from aqua privies is generally much smaller than that from septic tanks, but should not be permitted to fall so low that the tank starts to dry out.

The hole in the squatting plate is connected to a chute or drop pipe, the bottom end of which should be below water-level in the tank. This creates a water seal which prevents flies and mosquitoes entering the tank and smelly gases escaping into the latrines. For a family size aqua privy about 20 l of water (two buckets) a day are required to keep the tank topped-up and to flush the latrine. The accumulated sludge in the tank has to be emptied periodically, and a removable cover to the tank is provided for this purpose (Figure 5.7). Figure 5.8 shows a suitable arrangement for a two-family unit. Sludge must be removed from the tanks in time to prevent surplus sludge discharging with the effluents. Desludging can be carried out with vacuum tankers or by employing a diaphragm pump connected to a suitable tank on a truck. It is essential therefore that aqua privies are sited where access is possible for this purpose.

5.4.2 Pour Flush System

The pour flush system illustrated in Figure 5.9 uses the water-seal latrine bowl. The water-seal bowl is designed so that the contents can be flushed away with only 1–3 litres of water poured by hand. It can be used over an aqua privy as shown in Figure 5.9, or it can be connected

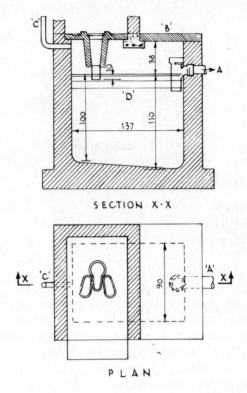

SECTION X·X

PLAN

'A'- OUTLET TO SOAKAGE TRENCH OF SOAKAGE PIT
'B'- REMOVABLE REINFORCED CONCRETE COVER SLAB.
'C'- 25mm DIAMETER PIPE VENTILATOR
'D'- CAPACITY OF TANK. 1340 LITRES

Figure 5.7 General arrangement of aqua privy.

to a soakaway (see section 5.5.2). Pour flush bowls can also be incorporated into pit latrines in well-drained areas.

5.5 WASTE DISPOSAL

5.5.1 Septic Tank

The septic tank is a water-borne sewage disposal system suitable for small communities or low-population-density areas. It consists of a covered settling tank into which raw sewage is led by pipe from latrines or dwellings. Other domestic liquid waste from bathrooms and kitchens can also be delivered to a septic tank without endangering its normal operation. Solid material settles at the bottom of the tank, forming sludge which is digested while the liquid

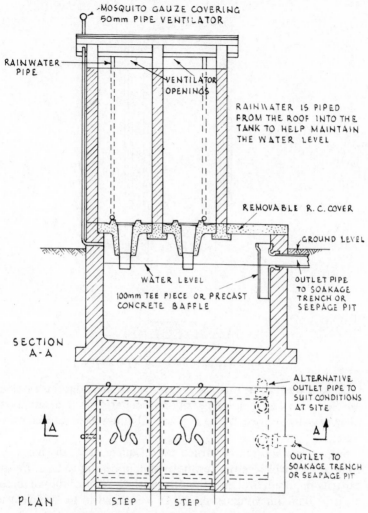

Figure 5.8 Aqua privy for two families.

effluent overflows through an outlet to a soakaway (or seepage pit). The general arrangement of a septic tank system for cistern flush latrines is shown in Figure 5.10.

5.5.2 Soakaway

A soakaway or seepage pit is a hole in the ground filled with stones through which waste water can seep away into the surrounding soil. Two kinds of seepage pit are shown in Figure 5.11.

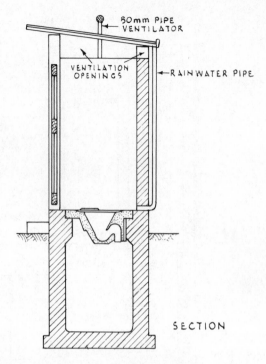

Figure 5.9 Pour flush and aqua privy.

Seepage pits can be used for the effluent from a pour flush system (see section 5.4.2) in a low-density housing area or rural situation. They can also be used for the disposal of bathwater or kitchen waste water.

Seepage pits must be constructed of adequate size to discharge the volume they will receive. Test holes should be dug to measure the capacity required. Broken stone-fill effectively reduces the volume of a pit to half. Pit volumes should be calculated to be sufficient to enable them to empty completely within 24 hours.

Most of the discharge from seepage pits or soakaway trenches flows through the floor of the excavation. This can easily become clogged if suspended solids are allowed to pass into them.

Seepage pits can only be used effectively in areas where the ground water table is at or below the floor of the pit. Where high water tables exist soakaway trenches are preferable. Soakaway trenches are ditches filled with open-jointed 100 mm dia. pipes laid on broken stone.

Soakaway trenches must be designed of adequate size for the

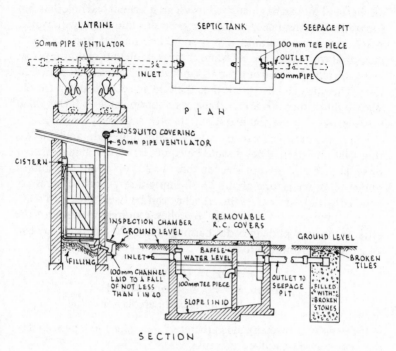

Figure 5.10 Septic tank system.

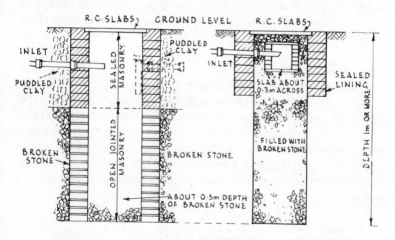

Figure 5.11 Seepage pits.

discharge. This can be calculated by digging a small test hole 300 mm square and 600 mm deep in the proposed site, and filling with water. After all water has drained out it should be refilled, and the depth measured with a dipstick. As water drains out the rate of drainage can be measured by measuring the fall in level in a convenient period of time. The rate can be expressed as the time in seconds taken for the level to fall 1 mm; this is called the percolation value V. If this value exceeds 140 secs the soil is not suitable for soakaway trenches.

Soakaway trenches can be dug 300–900 mm wide and not less than 500 mm deep. They should be equipped with drainage tiles or pipes laid to a slope not steeper than 1 : 200 on about 150 mm of gravel or broken stone about 20–50 mm grade. After the pipes are covered with more gravel the trenches can be backfilled with soil.

The floor area of soakaway trenches required to disperse the effluents from septic tanks discharging about 120 l/person/day can be calculated from the formula:

$$\text{Area } (m^2) = P \times V \times 0.25$$
$$\text{where } P = \text{no. of people served}$$
$$V = \text{measured percolation value}$$

If the volume discharged is greater or less than 120 l/person/day the area may be modified pro rata.

All seepage pits and soakaway trenches are sources of water pollution and should be sited at a safe distance from wells and other water sources. In most normal soils, 30 m is sufficient though in highly permeable gravels or fissured rock much greater distances may be required.

5.5.3 Piped Sewerage
The fully water-borne sewerage system which is used for high-density housing and large urban communities is expensive to construct and uses large quantities of water. It is generally not appropriate for rural areas where buildings are widely dispersed, or in situations where water supplies are scarce. If sewerage systems are used, sewage treatment is also required. The design of urban sewerage and sewage treatment systems requires expert supervision, and is beyond our scope here.

5.5.4 Incinerators
Many kinds of domestic rubbish can become health hazards if not properly disposed of. Incineration can be convenient, especially for rural hospitals. Incinerators should not be used for disposing of

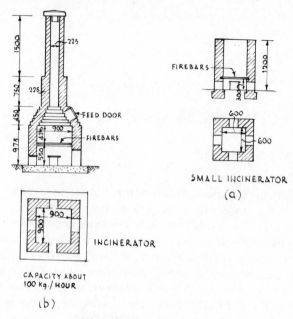

Figure 5.12 Incinerators.

excreta. There are numerous types of incinerators. A small square incinerator can be built of stone as in Figure 5.12(a). The inside dimensions are about 0·6 m × 0·6 m. The incinerator is built to any convenient height. Old angle iron, pipes, etc., are built in as firebars about 300 mm above the ground. Draught holes are formed in each face below the firebars. The incinerator is filled from the top.

A round incinerator is more efficient than a square one. The same dimensions can be used and at least four draught holes must be formed. Open incinerators are objectionable in that rain may put them out of action. A light shelter of corrugated iron cures this trouble.

Figure 5.12(b) shows a large incinerator suitable for a hospital.

CHAPTER 6
Roads and Bridges

6.1 ROADS GENERALLY

6.1.1 Low-cost Roads

These notes are concerned with earth roads, that is to say roads which have no other surface than the ground on which they are made. In many countries, such roads are likely to remain important as links of communication for many years. Cost considerations make it unlikely that more than a small proportion of roads can be provided with either a crushed rock or stone, much less a bituminous material, surface. Even surfacings of gravel or lateritic materials may only be possible in the, generally limited, areas where they occur naturally. Modern road construction is very expensive. Under savannah conditions in Zimbabwe, for example, the upgrading of earth tracks to gravel surfaced roads was estimated (in 1980) to cost about £18 000/km. For a 3·5 m bitumen-surfaced road the cost doubles. Under humid tropical rain forest or desert conditions both of these costs could well double or even treble again.

The sequence of road development is usually: first, a footpath or track which leads direct from place to place (although scarcely 50 m of it is likely to be in one straight line); second, the widening of the track; third, its gradual improvement by diversions, cuttings, embankments, and rough bridges over streams; finally, more attention is paid to drainage and surface treatment, until a passable road is created which can be used throughout most of the year.

6.1.2 Road Location

Where an entirely new road or a long diversion has to be made, the following points should be considered.

A good road location can only be obtained by the expenditure of much time and trouble. When looking for the trace of a new road, footpaths should be examined and particular note taken of all stream crossings, the extent of the areas liable to flood, of all hills and natural obstructions, and also the surface and sub-surface conditions of the area through which the road will pass.

Every opportunity should be taken to view the proposed line of the road from adjacent vantage points. The information obtained from an overview of the terrain is invaluable since the direction of the natural drainage can be studied; the best location for a road is obviously one which is not liable to flood.

The advantages of an aerial view of the terrain do not render unnecessary a most careful examination on foot. On all roads there are certain definite localities, or 'fixed points' through which the road must pass (e.g., a gap in a line of hills, the best point on a river for a bridge, on a stream for a ford, the points at which to avoid soft ground, and so on). The 'fixed points' are first determined, and the road is then designed to run as directly as possible between one fixed point and the next.

The roads will not necessarily run in a straight line between these points. Where the direction of the proposed road runs in the same direction as the watersheds, it should as a rule be aligned on the ridges, or along the backbone of the watersheds. By this means the natural drainage of the area falls away from the road, the cost of building bridges and culverts is reduced, and better formation is usually encountered.

Where hills, or spurs, obstruct or project into the line of the road, it is usually better to go round rather than over them. Some engineers allow a deviation equal to 20 units in length for every unit in height of the hill avoided. If a hill is 100 m high therefore, up to 2000 m might be added to the length of the road in order to avoid it. Otherwise the straightest and shortest road is the cheapest and best, though cuttings should be avoided if possible.

6.2   GRADIENTS AND SLOPES

6.2.1   Gradients

Gradients have a very severe effect on the operating costs of motor vehicles. They also limit the speed and payloads that can be achieved by animal transport. The effect of a given gradient on both motor vehicles and animals varies with altitude and the type of surface, being least severe on bitumen and progressively more severe on gravel and earth-surfaced roads respectively. For the latter reason short, very steep, sections of earth road are sometimes given a gravel or bitumen surface.

A gradient of 1 in 14 (see Figure 6.1), means a rise of one unit in the surface of the road for every 14 units of horizontal distance.

Gradients may also be expressed by percentage: a gradient of 1 in 25 equals 4 units in 100, or 4 per cent; 1 in 20 is 5 per cent, and so on.

6.2.2 Measurement of Gradients

In order to measure the gradient of a road it is necessary to use an instrument which will either measure the angle which the slope of the road makes with the horizontal, or the difference in height between two known points on the road. In increasing order of both price and

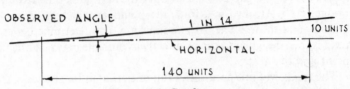

Figure 6.1 Gradients.

accuracy angles can be measured with a gradient template, clinometer or abney level. Differences in levels can be measured with a wide range of instruments which in approximate ascending order of price and accuracy are the flexible water tube level, line level, water manometer, road tracer, spirit level, Cowley and Abney levels.

6.2.3 Gradients Measured with Clinometer or Abney Level

Having observed the angle which the road makes with the horizontal, the gradient may be obtained approximately by dividing the value of the angle in minutes into 3434.

Example

$$\text{Observed } 4° = 240 \text{ (min)}$$
$$3434 \div 240 = 14 \text{ (about)}$$
$$\text{Gradient } 1 : 14 \text{ (roughly)}$$

The reverse process is also approximately correct:

Grade 1 : 15. What is the angle?

$$\frac{3434}{15} = 228 \text{ min} = 3 \text{ deg } 48 \text{ min } (3° \ 48')$$

Table 6.1 gives vertical angles for a series of gradients from 1 in 10, to 1 in 200.

Table 6.1 Angles of gradients.

Gradient	Approximate angle which road makes with the horizontal
1 in 10	5° 43′
1 in 15	3° 48′
1 in 20	2° 52′
1 in 25	2° 17′
1 in 30	1° 55′
1 in 40	1° 26′
1 in 50	1° 9′
1 in 100	0° 34′
1 in 150	0° 23′
1 in 200	0° 19′

Table 6.2 Gradient standards for minor unsealed roads.

Source of Data	Gradient standard	Terrain and Gradient (%)		
Brazil*		Undulating	Broken/hilly	
	Ruling	8	9	
	Maximum	9	11	
	Maximum length of grade (m)	250	150	
India†		Mountainous and steep over 3000 m altitude	Steep up to 3000 m altitude	
	Ruling	5	6	
	Limiting	6	7	
Kenya‡	Maximum	Not greater than 11; where a gradient greater than 11 is considered necessary then this gradient should not be exceeded for more than 100 m continuously.		
UNESCO§		Flat or rolling	Hilly	Mountainous
	Maximum	7	7–9	9–12
	Maximum length of grade (m)	None	None	1000 over 9%

For animals different figures apply¶

	Pack		Draught	
	Maximum	Ruling	Maximum	Ruling
Horse or pony	1 in 6	1 in 10	1 in 10	1 in 20
Mule	1 in 5	1 in 6	1 in 10	1 in 15
Camel	1 in 8	1 in 18		
Bullock	1 in 8	1 in 10	1 in 10	1 in 20

* † ‡ ¶ see Refs 26, 27, 28, 29, and 30 respectively.

6.2.4 Gradient Standards

There are a number of different ways of specifying gradient standards. The simplest is just a 'maximum' or 'limiting' gradient which may not be exceeded in other than the most exceptional circumstances: sometimes both the maximum gradient and its length are stipulated. More flexible standards specify a 'limiting' and a 'ruling' gradient which is the average maximum over the whole climbing section. Table 6.2 gives some examples of recommended gradient standards for minor earth- and gravel-surfaced roads intended for use by motor vehicles.

6.2.5 Slopes

The side slopes of embankments, cuttings, etc., are expressed in another manner (Figure 6.2). A side slope of 1 to 1 means a rise of one unit in every unit of horizontal distance, or the side slope makes an angle of 45° with the horizontal. 1·5 to 1 means a rise of one unit in every 1·5 units of horizontal distance.

Slopes can be measured in the same way and with the same instruments as gradients. Because slopes are relatively short, and less accuracy is normally required in their setting out, the simpler templates and levels will usually suffice. Table 6.3 gives angles of slopes, and Table 6.4 the natural slopes of earth materials (i.e., the maximum slope that the material will stand).

Table 6.3   Angles of slopes.

Slope	Angle
0.5 to 1	63° 26′
1 to 1	45° 00′
1.25 to 1	38° 40′
1.5 to 1	33° 42′
2 to 1	26° 34′

Table 6.4   Natural slopes of earth materials.

Material	Angle		
Gravel	about 40°	or approximately	1 to 1
Dry sand	about 35°	or approximately	1·5 to 1
Sand	about 22°	or approximately	2·5 to 1
Compact earth	about 29–50°	or approximately	2 to 1
Rubble	about 45°	or approximately	1 to 1
Clay, well drained	about 45°	or approximately	1 to 1
Clay, wet	about 16°	or approximately	3 to 1

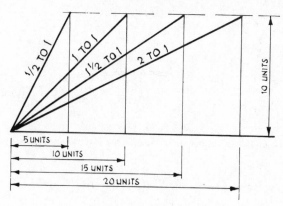

Figure 6.2 Slopes.

6.3 DESIGN AND SETTING OUT

6.3.1 Cross Sections

Figure 6.3 gives standard cross sections for rural access roads in Kenya, built by labour-based methods of construction. These roads have a gravel running surface. For earth-surfaced roads the cross-fall should be reduced to 3–4 per cent. A template can be made to give the correct crossfall to the surface of the road, as in Figure 6.4.

Figure 6.3(b) shows a road on side-long ground. In tropical countries, where roads cross flat plains, and where natural drainage facilities are slight, roads should be raised a minimum of 50 cm above the surface of the surrounding country. In black cotton soil, it is especially necessary to embank. The embankment should be 1 m higher than the plain, and through drainage, by culverts, bush drains, etc., is necessary.

6.3.2 Setting Out Roads

On fairly level ground, the road is set out by marking the centre line with a line of pegs. Side widths are then also set out and marked. On steep hillsides, it is usual to mark the line of the cutting, whether this happens to be the centre line or the edge of the completed road. In rocky ground white paint is useful in marking out the road.

6.3.3 To Set Out Curves

If for any reason it is required to set out a curve and it is not possible to set it out by striking from a centre, proceed as in Figure 6.5. The curve begins at *b*. Produce *ab* to *d*; let *bd* be any convenient length say 3 or 6 m.

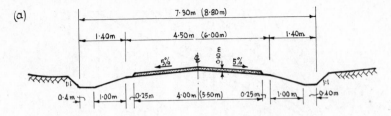

(a)

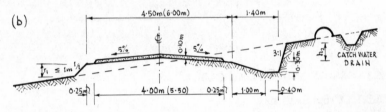

(b)

NOTES:
1. WIDTH OF EARTH ROAD FORMATION 4·50m FOR LESS THAN 30 VEHICLES PER DAY
   "   "   "   "   "   "   6·00m " MORE "   "   "   "   "   "

NOTES:
1. WIDTH OF EARTH ROAD FORMATION 4·50 FOR LESS THAN 30 VEHICLES PER DAY
   "   "   "   "   "   "   6·00 " MORE "   "   "   "   "   "
2. HEIGHT OF FILL LESS THAN OR EQUAL TO 1·00m.
3. H₂ HEIGHT OF CUT.

Figure 6.3 Cross sections.

$$\text{Now } \frac{dc = (bc)^2}{2\,r} \quad \text{where} \quad r = \text{radius}$$

Measure from b towards c the same distance as bd, and from d measure the distance dc as deduced from the foregoing formula. Where bc and dc intersect will be point c on the curve. Produce bc to e and proceed as before

$$\text{but } ef = \frac{(cf)^2}{r}$$

not twice the radius, as in the previous case. The subsequent offsets are calculated from this formula.

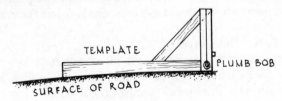

Figure 6.4 Cross fall.

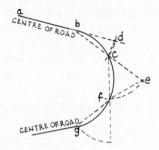

Figure 6.5 Setting out curves.

6.3.4 Drainage of Roads

The drainage of earth roads is of the utmost importance; proper drainage may turn a bad road into a good one. Not only is it necessary to dispose of the rain which falls on the surface of the road, but also to prevent rain which falls on the adjacent surfaces from washing across it. If the road is skilfully sited, the natural drainage of the land may be sufficient, as for example a road on a ridge. In any case, the natural drainage should be interfered with as little as possible. As the resistance of a road surface depends on the moisture content of the soil (the road must not be too wet or too dry) the degree to which drainage should be carried out has to be studied. Figures 6.3(a) and (b) and Figure 6.6 should be examined. The water passes from the curved surface of the road to shallow gutters, from thence through mitre drains to catchwater drains. In suitable country the catchwater drains need not be excavated, and the gutter can drain into the bush. Sandy soils, for example, do not need much surface drainage, for

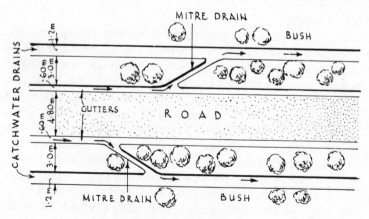

Figure 6.6 Road drainage.

moisture improves them. Where catchwater drains are necessary, and that is usually apparent, it is of vital importance that they should not be made at the edge of the road. Allow at least 3 m (or better 5 m) between the road and drain or ditch. Catchwater drains (ditches) should be wide and shallow, not deep and narrow. The soil from them should be spread well back so that it does not wash into the drain again. Catchwater drains must spill into streams or into low places which fall away from the road.

The gradient of the drains is also most important; if it is too steep the water will erode the drains into deep chasms, if it is too easy they will silt up.

If the gradient is too steep, walls (or steps), should be built across the drain as in Figure 6.7, at frequent intervals. Many roads have been destroyed because the side drains, which were meant to protect them, have been badly sited and levelled.

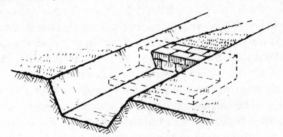

Figure 6.7 Drain check.

6.4 ROAD CONSTRUCTION

6.4.1 Clearing

In dry areas, trees will shade the road and thus preserve it; on hillsides they prevent erosion. Remove trees when they are on the line of the road, or when they will be dangerous if left at the side of a cutting. In wet areas, clear the trees far enough back from the road to keep the surface in sunshine. Trees can be destroyed by ring barking, by poisoning, by uprooting, or felling. Uproot rather than fell, since the subsequent removal of stumps is time-consuming and arduous work. Some trees can be pulled direct from the ground by animals, tractor or hand-operated winches. It is helpful if the main roots are first exposed and cut through, for the weight of the trees will often pull the remaining roots out. Old dried stumps can be destroyed by burning.

Clearing rock from the road formation can be a difficult operation. Some is sufficiently soft to be excavated with a pickaxe (e.g., chalk, coral). Other rock may be inherently hard, but sufficiently weathered or jointed to be broken up with a crowbar, or hammer and chisel.

There is a simple method for clearing isolated lumps of hard rock from the road formation. A fire is lit on top of the rock and water thrown on the hot ashes. This tends to fracture the rock, which can then be broken easily with a sledge hammer.

6.4.2 Embankments

Embankments ought to be constructed with care. First the 'profile' is erected, as in Figure 6.8. All clods of earth are broken up and distributed evenly over the surface. An embankment is built in shallow layers if settlement is to be avoided. The material for an embankment is obtained from a cutting or from pits (borrow pits) excavated near the road. Borrow pits should not be excavated closer than 3–5 m from the toe of the embankment, they should not be deep (0·6 m is enough), and they should not be continuous but broken up into sections of 6 m length or thereabouts. This is most important. Borrow pits interfere with the natural gradient of the country and if not properly regulated they may cause serious erosion.

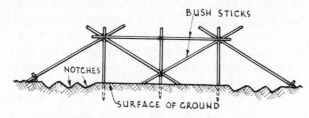

Figure 6.8 Embankment profile.

Ordinary loose earth shrinks about 0.17m/m, and black cotton soil about 0.25 m/m. Thus an embankment of black cotton soil 2 m high will settle down to 1·5 m, or even less. For a 6 m road, an embankment should be approximately 7 m wide when its height is from 1 to 1·5 m, and more than 7·5 m when it is over 1·5 m high. The side slopes should be 1·5 to 1, or 2 to 1 (see section 6.2.1).

A long embankment without culverts is much like a dam and is liable to destruction if unprovided with relief. Culverts of some form are a necessity in an embankment, especially in swampy ground.

6.4.3 Surface of Earth Road

Sand added gradually to a clay surface in wet weather, or clay added to a sand surface, makes a better earthen road. Laterite can be spread over the road surface where available. Crushed rock surfacing is normally too expensive to be carried out on minor roads.

In black cotton soil, where the road should be carried on an embankment, the surface of the road ought to be treated with a thick layer of sand.

6.4.4 Hill Roads

Hill roads are liable to damage from the water which washes down the hillsides. To prevent damage catchment drains are excavated on the upper side of cuttings as in Figure 6.9(a). The excavated material from the drain, which is a wide one, is spread on the road side of the drain, otherwise it will wash into the excavation. The water from catchment drains is discharged into culverts under the road. See Figure 6.9(b), which shows a plan and section of a culvert. Catchwater drains easily become blocked with vegetation, etc. and ought to be frequently inspected.

6.4.5 Road Surface on Hillsides

On re-entrant curves in road surfaces on hillsides, the surface of the road will slope away from the cutting and will drain naturally; on salient curves the surface will slope towards the cutting (Figure 6.10(a)). Where the road slopes towards the cutting it is usual to form a slight and shallow gutter as in Figure 6.10(b) and (c). Avoid long lengths of gutters, and let the water discharge into a culvert or away from the road as soon as possible.

The surface of hill roads, or any road on a slope, can be further protected by use of pole drains set diagonally to the road. By this means the water which ordinarily flows down the road itself, and erodes it, is diverted to the side. It also relieves the side gutter. A simple pole drain is shown in Figure 6.10(d). It is simply two saplings buried level with the surface of the road and held in their respective positions by iron dogs.

Figure 6.10(d) also shows a type of pole drain used in India. Here, a single sapling is used and it is not level with the surface of the road. This type is useful on hills where speeding must be restricted.

6.4.6 Zig-zag Roads

In mountainous country the necessary height can be gained by the construction of zig-zag roads (see Figure 6.11(a)).

Zig-zags make traffic difficult, and are expensive to maintain. The turning point on a zig-zag is sited on level or nearly level ground. The width of a hillside road for single-line traffic ought to be at least 4 m.

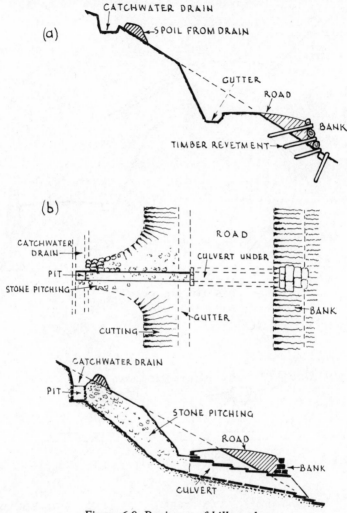

Figure 6.9 Drainage of hill roads.

The width of the road ought to be increased by one half at the turning points, and the outer edge of the road should be made higher than the inner. Allow 0·3 m higher in a 6 m road. The radius of the curves should not be less than 15 m generally (see Figure 6.11(b)) although in extreme instances 9 m radius has been used. Curves are improved by 'daylighting' them, as in Figure 6.11(c).

Zig-zag roads, and roads on hillsides, are cut into the side of the hill for at least part of their length, as in Figures 6.9(a), and 6.10(b) and

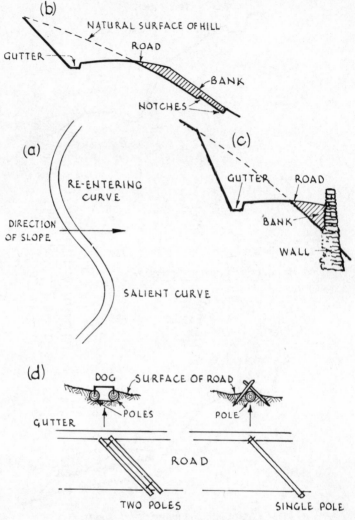

Figure 6.10 Roads on hillsides.

(c). Such roads, if the slope is fairly gentle, will be formed partly by cutting into the hill and partly by forming a bank, as in Figure 6.10(a). To give the embankment as good a hold as possible, notches are cut in the hillside to receive the toe of the embankment. In spite of such precautions, embanked roads on hillsides are liable to slip during the heavy rains and, where labour is plentiful, and where the soil to be removed is not heavy, it may be better to excavate the whole road in

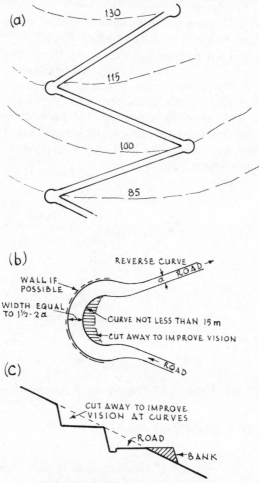

Figure 6.11 Zig-zag roads.

the side of the hill and to avoid embankments. The excavated soil can be dumped down the hillside. Under any circumstances it is better to use as little embankment as possible.

In order to avoid extremes and to keep the road as straight as possible, on the salient curves the road should be cut well into the side of the hill, and on the re-entrant curves more embankment should be used (see Figure 6.10(a)).

The slopes of the cuttings should be as steep as the material in which they are excavated can stand (see section 6.2.5).

6.4.7 Revetments

At frequent intervals on embanked hillside roads some form of revetment will have to be constructed. Roughly squared stone built into a wall is a good and most durable form of revetment. The wall can be built dry (i.e., without mortar). Long bondstones (see section 2.3.3) must be introduced at frequent intervals.

The usual proportions of a wall are 0·75 m wide at the top. Add 0·25 m of thickness for every 1·0 m of height as shown in Figure 6.12.

Timber revetment is constructed as in Figure 6.9(a). A combination of timber and stone is often used, but timber is very liable to attack by white ants where these are active.

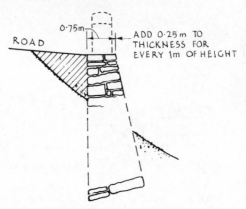

Figure 6.12 Proportions of revetment wall.

6.5 MAINTENANCE OF ROADS

6.5.1 Maintenance Generally

The main purpose of maintenance is to conserve the assets represented by the roads, by preserving the road structure and its associated drainage systems in good condition. Maintenance can be organized in one of two ways: either to 'prevent' or to 'remedy' damage to a road. Obviously preventative maintenance is to be preferred because, whilst it may require more regular attention, the overall amount of work is likely to be less than if repairs are only carried out when their effect is sufficient to draw attention (i.e., to remedy serious failures in the road's structure).

There are two main elements to be maintained: the running surface and shoulders; and the drainage ditches and structures. Both the running surface and shoulders must be kept free of potholes, ruts, and low spots, where water may stand and soften the material leading to further damage by traffic. To prevent this the profile of the road must be maintained so that the water drains rapidly away.

Light raking and hand ramming is useful for local irregularities. More extensive irregularity, such as 'corrugations', can be reduced by use of a simple road drag. A simple wooden type is illustrated in Figure 6.13(a). Figure 6.13(b) illustrates the design and use of a stronger metal drag which can be made from short lengths of 'I'-beam, or scrap railway line. The frequency with which drags should

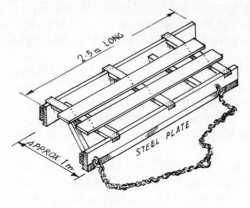

(a) Wooden Drag

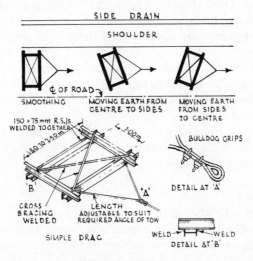

(b) Metal Drag

Figure 6.13 Road drags.

be used must be determined locally since it depends on the type of surfacing material and the amount of traffic.

Potholes should be filled with suitable material which should be thoroughly compacted with a hand rammer. Whenever possible, the material used should be the same as that used in the road structure. To fill a hole with a loose gravel will lead to further deterioration as the hole will continue to act as a reservoir for surface water run off. Material removed from drainage ditches, frequently of a silty or clayey nature, may be useful as a binder for gravel surfacings. In this case it should be conserved in stockpiles for future use. Grass on the surface of an earth road helps to preserve it; cut the grass rather than uproot it.

Erosion gullies formed in the edges of the shoulders should be cut out and made good with suitable material well consolidated with rammers. Grass on the shoulders should never be allowed to grow so tall as to obscure vision or to hide objects, such as boulders or tree branches, which might cause damage to vehicles driving on to the shoulder.

Drainage is of paramount importance. Drains, ditches, culverts, etc. must be kept clear. They need to be inspected regularly and silt or other debris removed. Evidence of erosion or scour ought to be checked and appropriate preventative measures taken. In hilly terrain side and catchwater drains are particularly likely to suffer from erosion. These effects can be checked either by building check dams across the drain at intervals (see Figure 6.7) or by placing vertical barriers of sticks, at intervals of about 10 m, across the drain to slow the velocity of storm water. The height of these barriers must be less than the top of the drain, otherwise water may overflow onto the road. Check dams must be solid, on sound level foundation, and keyed well into the sides of the ditch to prevent water finding its way round the dam.

Culverts and causeways are more prone to scour: appropriate stone aprons on the downstream side (see Figure 6.15 and 6.16) ought to reduce this tendency.

6.5.2 Tools

Much useful maintenance can be undertaken with basic or improvised handtools. The mobility of maintenance teams can be increased by equipping them with wheelbarrows or bicycles and trailers.

The tools required for road maintenance are axes, crowbars, pickaxes, mattocks (similar to pickaxes but with one edge like a hoe), shovels, rammers, sledge hammers, wedges both wood and iron, ordinary hammers, string, nails, chalk, baskets or earth pans, hoes, ranging rods or bamboos and spirit and other levels.

6.6   MINOR RIVER CROSSINGS

6.6.1   Fords

The best position for a ford is shown in Figure 6.14. The passage of fords by vehicles in sandy rivers stirs up the sand and increases the depth. The approaches to fords should be made with as gentle an inclination as possible, 1 in 20 is allowable, and they ought to be wide enough to allow two vehicles to pass so the ford is not blocked if a heavy vehicle sticks. The approaches should be gravelled when possible. Vehicles carry water up the slopes, if they are ungravelled they become slippery.

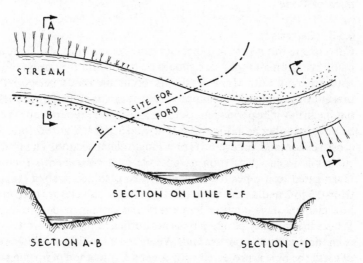

Figure 6.14 Location of ford.

Where the river only brings down a small quantity of water for the greater part of the year, it is more economical to build a paved ford or Irish bridge than a bridge. The ford may be paved with concrete, stone, or even timber. It is good practice to build a wall on the down river side of the ford as in Figure 6.15. The wall prevents the action of the water from scouring underneath the paving. The surface of the paving is kept a little below the bottom of the river for the same reason. The paving will become covered with a surface of sand which will help to bind the structure together.

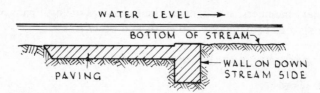

Figure 6.15 Paved ford.

6.6.2 Causeways

If stone is available in the neighbourhood, causeways can sometimes be built. A causeway is raised above the normal flow of the river, the flood waters pass over it. The normal flow passes through gaps or culverts which are built at frequent intervals. The gaps are bridged with flat stones or concrete slabs. The causeway is constructed of a mass of stone.

6.6.3 Culverts

Culverts are water passages through banks or under roads. There are many types. In all types care should be taken with the design of the entrance and exit. Many washouts occur on roads because this precaution is omitted. The simplest culvert can be built of bush sticks, but it can never be permanent. A more satisfactory type of culvert can be built in timber as in Figures 6.16(a) and 6.16(b); Figure 6.16(a) is a cross section and Figure 6.16(b) a longitudinal section. The timber culvert is replaced as soon as possible by a permanent structure. Corrugated iron pipes for culverts can be obtained in sizes ranging from 0·3 to 2 m dia., but often corrugated iron culverts are used in an intermediate stage between temporary and permanent construction. Where the capacity of one pipe is not sufficient for a culvert, two or even three rows of pipes are laid. Where there is only a shallow cover of earth the pipe is protected with concrete. A method of forming the entrance and exit from corrugated iron pipe is to build a wall at right angles to the pipeline. However, in rough work the entrance and exit are not specially treated. Culverts can be built of stone and covered with large flat stones as in Figure 6.9(b). Figure 6.16(c) shows a more elaborate stone culvert which is standardized in India and illustrates the method of dealing with the entrances and exits of culverts. The splayed walls, or 'wing walls', protect the bank from flood waters, and some such arrangement is necessary in all permanent work. Some authorities advocate that the bottom of the culvert should have the same fall as the stream which it carries. The water as it leaves a culvert is liable to erode away the channel; to prevent erosion an 'apron' of

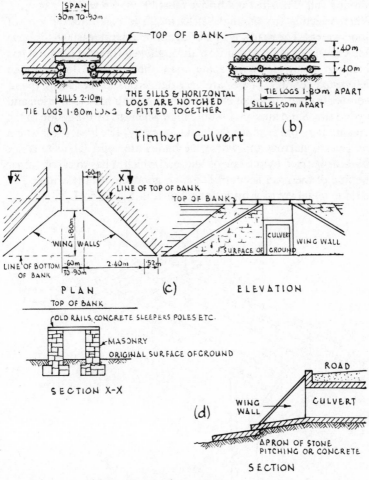

Timber Culvert

PLAN (c) ELEVATION

Masonry Culvert

Figure 6.16 Culverts.

stone or concrete is laid as in Figure 6.16(d). Culverts are one of the most important features in road construction. Care in construction will save many washouts.

6.7 BRIDGES

6.7.1 Bridges Generally

A bridge should carry a road across a stream or gap with the minimum interference to the natural waterway when the river is running full. The site for a bridge must be chosen with this in view. When selecting the site make strict inquiries regarding the level of flood waters. The roadway of a bridge should be at least 0·6 m above flood level. Streams which flow through well-forested land are less likely to come down in spate than those which flow through deforested country. Spates are very dangerous to the usual type of wooden bridge. Steep-cut banks often indicate a hard formation and a good site. Sand appears to stand high when cut by the action of the stream, therefore examine the banks carefully. The ideal site is where the river is narrow and where the banks are solid. The site is not necessarily fixed by the line of the road which it has to carry, rather the line of the road is controlled by a good site for the bridge. The various members of a bridge are shown in Figure 6.17.

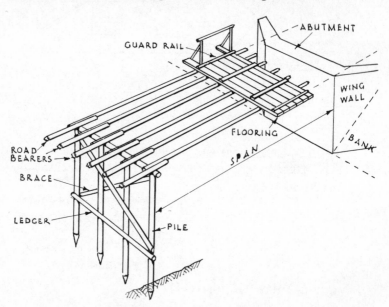

Figure 6.17 Bridge members.

6.7.2 Choice of Type of Bridge

The material available for road bearers (e.g., locally cut unseasoned timber, squared seasoned timber, rolled steel joists or old rails) will decide the type of bridge to be built (i.e., whether it shall be of single span or a bridge with intermediate supports, or some type of framed or trussed bridge). The simplest type will naturally be chosen. Provided that the material available is sufficiently strong and is treated skilfully 'single span bridges' (i.e., bridges without intermediate support), can be constructed to span great widths; however, 6 m can be considered the limit for the rough material available in the field.

6.7.3 Loads on Bridges

In order to understand the construction of bridges it is important to remember the following points. The loads which a bridge must carry are:

(a) The weight of the members of the bridge.
(b) The weight of any material—such as road metal, earth, etc., which is spread over the bridge in order to assist traffic.
(c) The weight of the traffic, vehicles, or people which pass over the bridge.

Points (a) and (b) are termed 'dead loads', as they are inert, and point (c) is termed a 'live load', a 'moving load' or a 'rolling load'. A live load, weight for weight, produces greater stresses in bridge members than a dead load—especially when it is suddenly applied as when a loaded lorry rushes a bridge. In field engineering it is usual to multiply the live load by 2 in order to convert it to an equivalent dead load. This is in order to simplify calculations.

6.7.4 Distributed and Concentrated Loads, Bending Moments, Shear, Deflection

The loads which any beam in a bridge has to carry may be distributed over it (as the earth in (b) above) or they may be concentrated at points on the beam. When a laden motor vehicle passes over a bridge the weight of the vehicle is supported by the four wheels, and the wheels at any moment are supported by the flooring planks or spars on which they stand, the planks are supported by the road bearers. At any instant, therefore, there are concentrated loads on the road bearers at a distance apart equal to the wheel base of the vehicle. In a bridge of short span the front wheels of a loaded lorry may be off the bridge when the back wheels (which carry the greatest weight) are in the centre of the span. The maximum stress in the bridge is then caused by a concentrated load in the centre of the span and the load equals the weight on the back wheels of the lorry. The bearers are supported by the abutments or the transoms. Whether the load on the bearer is distributed or concentrated, the load on the transom is assumed to be distributed.

When a beam is loaded it tends to curve downwards under the load in the shape of a bow. When in this state the lower fibres of the beam are stretched or are in tension, and upper fibres are compressed, there is also a place in the beam where the greatest bending moment occurs. The bending moment at any section of the beam measures the tendency to bend the beam at that section. It is important to know at what point in the beam it is at a maximum and what is its intensity.

The bending moment (written Mff) is counterbalanced by the moment of resistance (see Appendix IV). The position of Mff and its value is given in Figure 6.18 and Appendix IV.

Except for very short spans a beam that is strong enough to resist bending is strong enough to resist shear. Shear is not considered in rough field calculations. However, in very short timber beams if the depth of the beam does not exceed one tenth of the span under a distributed load, or one fifth of the span under a central concentrated load, the beam is strong enough if it can resist bending. The stiffness or deflection of a beam under a load is also of importance in long spans but it too is not taken into account in rough field work (see Appendix IV).

The decking should be strong enough to spread a concentrated load over at least two road bearers. In a calculation for the strength of road bearers, if there are six bearers the weight to be carried by each is one-fifth of the total load to be carried by the bridge, if there are five bearers then one-fourth of the total load and so on.

6.7.5 Factors of Safety

The strength of wood, steel, etc. is determined by experiment, the results of which are given in tables. They are usually expressed as 'the ultimate resistances' either in compression, tension, or shear. This means that the values given in a table show the stress under which the material will fail. The material cannot be used in a structure under stresses which cause collapse or obviously the structure itself will fail. A fraction of the ultimate resistance is taken as the limit to which the material shall be stressed. This fraction is termed the 'factor of safety'. A factor of safety of 2 means that the tabulated ultimate resistances of the material must be divided by 2 in order to get the working stress. In the construction of rough bridges the material is used under unfavourable conditions and a factor of safety of 4, 5 or 6 should be adopted.

6.7.6 Dimensions of Timber Road Bearers

The points outlined above have been considered in calculating the size of the wooden beams given below. The dimensions are for

MAXIMUM BENDING MOMENTS = M_{ff}			
MEMBER & LOADING	M_{ff}	POSITION OF M_{ff}	δ
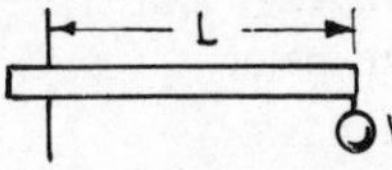	$W.L.$	AT POINT OF FIXING	$\dfrac{WL^3}{3\,EI}$
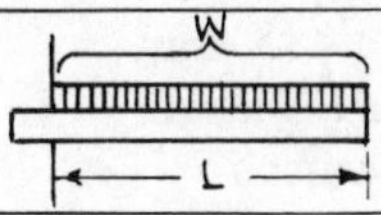	$\dfrac{WL}{2} = \dfrac{\omega L^2}{2}$	AT POINT OF FIXING	$\dfrac{WL^3}{8\,EI}$
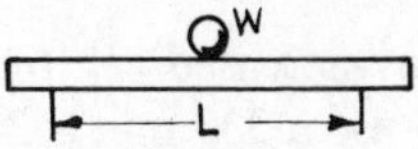	$\dfrac{WL}{4}$	AT CENTRE	$\dfrac{WL^3}{48\,EI}$
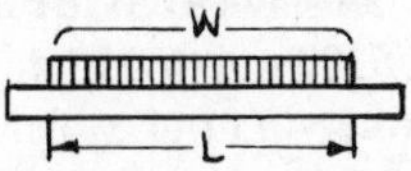	$\dfrac{WL}{8} = \dfrac{\omega L^2}{8}$	AT CENTRE	$\dfrac{WL^3}{76.8\,EI}$

LENGTH OF MEMBER = L   TOTAL LOAD = W.   DISTRIBUTED LOAD W = ωL.   ω WEIGHT PER UNIT LENGTH.
DEFLECTION = δ

I = MOMENT OF INERTIA

E = YOUNG'S MODULUS

MODULI OF SECTIONS			
SECTION	$Z = \dfrac{I}{y}$	y	I
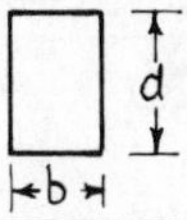	$\dfrac{bd^2}{6}$	$\dfrac{d}{2}$	$\dfrac{bd^3}{12}$
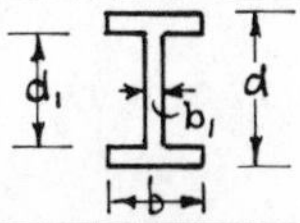	$\dfrac{bd^3 - (b-b_1)\,d_1{}^3}{6d}$	$\dfrac{d}{2}$	$\dfrac{bd^3 - (b-b_1)\,d_1{}^3}{12}$
	$.0982\,D$	$\dfrac{D}{2}$	$.0491\,D^4$

Figure 6.18 Maximum bending moments and moduli sections.

bridges 3·2 m wide, with six road bearers as in Figure 6.19—a bridge to carry the traffic on a district road for moving loads of up to 10 tonnes.

Up to 3 m clear span
Rectangular	255 mm × 150 mm
Square	215 mm × 215 mm
Round	255 mm mean

Up to 4·5 m clear span

Rectangular	300 mm × 150 mm
Square	240 mm × 240 mm
Round	300 mm mean

Up to 6 m clear span

Rectangular (outside)	300 mm × 150 mm
Square (inside)	300 mm × 300 mm
Round	400 mm mean

These dimensions, of course, can be increased. If timber is available it would obviously be better to use a 300 mm × 300 mm beam even for a bridge of 3 m span. If less than six bearers are used the dimensions must be increased. If a beam of 300 mm × 150 mm is not available two beams each 150 mm × 150 mm will not be of sufficient strength to take its place. The invariable rule is that the strength of each beam must be calculated separately. Following the rule given in

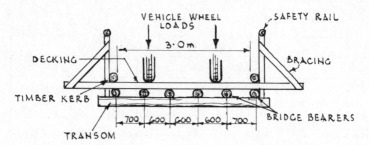

Figure 6.19 Timber bridge with six road bearers.

section 2.6.5, for a 300 mm × 150 mm beam, $300 \times 300 \times 150 = 13\,500\,000$, and for two 150 mm × 150 mm beams, $150 \times 150 \times 150 \times 2 = 6\,750\,000$. The comparative strength of the first to the second is as $13\,500\,000 : 6\,750\,000$ or $2 : 1$. If two 150 mm beams are bolted together, one above the other, the total strength of the composite beam will hardly be affected for the bolts may tear the fibres of the timber. On the other hand timber beams are stiffened by bolting two deep and narrow beams together and introducing a piece of wrought-iron plate between them. Such beams are used as lintels and not in bridge work.

Bearers can be stiffened by introducing struts which run down at an angle of 45° to the abutments and trestles (see Figure 6.20).

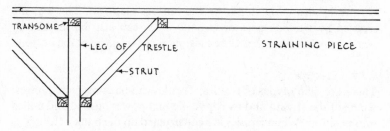

Figure 6.20 Stiffening for bearers.

6.7.7 Rolled Steel Joists and Steel Rails as Road Bearers

The following rolled steel joists can be used as road bearers:

3·0 m span, 4 joists, each 225 mm × 95 mm × 30 kg/m
4·5 m span, 4 joists, each 250 mm × 125 mm × 52·5 kg/m
6·0 m span, 4 joists, each 300 mm × 150 mm × 66 kg/m

Steel rails weighing 25 kg/m will span up to 1·5 m if used as road beams.

6.7.8 Intermediate Supports

Figure 6.17 shows how timber road bearers are placed in a bridge with intermediate supports. The ends of all bearers must rest on a support. A road bearer which stops short of a support and which is lashed to a projecting bearer is of no structural value though local builders put great faith in such expedients.

In shallow streams with slow currents crib piers can be used as shown in Figure 6.21. At the bottom of each crib a rough platform of bush poles is constructed. The crib is put together wholly or in part on

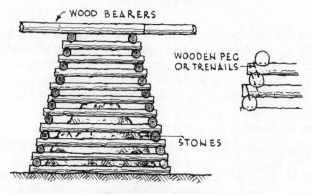

Figure 6.21 Crib pier.

the bank and towed or pulled in position by ropes. When in position it is sunk by dropping stones on the bottom platform. The logs are secured by wooden pegs or trenails. They can also be secured by twisting ropes about them; the twisting is commenced at the bottom.

6.7.9   Trestles

There are many types of trestles. Trestles can be constructed on the banks of the stream and by ropes and manpower pushed and pulled into position. When trestles are constructed on the bank a 'ledger' is added to the bottom of the frame (see Figure 6.22(a)). The ledger distributes the weight over the bottom of the river.

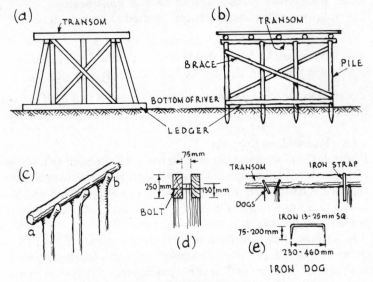

Figure 6.22 Trestles.

In pile trestles which are not constructed on the bank (see Figure 6.22(b)), it is well to introduce a ledger where possible. When there is little or no water in the stream this is an easy matter. In order to prevent debris washed down by the stream from becoming entangled in the piles and blocking the waterway, the piles may be cased with boarding for a portion of their height.

In the construction of rough field bridges where pile drivers are not available, the legs of the pile trestles are let into holes excavated in the bed of the stream and then bumped into position. If the legs are to carry the transom in their forks this method is troublesome for it is difficult to get the bearing surfaces of the forks level (Figure 6.22(c)).

Better methods of securing the transoms than by resting them in the forks are shown in Figures 6.22 (d) and 6.22(e). Where dogs, or spikes or tools are not available, the transom must rest in the fork. The transom must not press unduly on the sides of a fork or the weight when applied will split the leg (see Figure 6.22(c)). The transom must be properly fitted into its resting place by means of packing as at *a* and *b* shown in Figure 6.22(c). Do not cut the transom. Transoms should be of 250–300 mm dia.

Legs up to 3·0 m high,   200–230 mm dia.
Legs up to 4·5 m high,   250–300 mm dia.

The strength of a leg decreases rapidly with its height.

6.7.10 Decking

The decking or flooring consists of planks, bush poles, or stout bamboos. It may be spiked or nailed to the bearers or bound to them with wire or even rope. Figure 6.23 shows how the floor planks can be secured by wire. Where the flooring consists of bush poles and the bridge is designed for motor traffic, it should not be covered with a coating of earth under any circumstances. The earth disguises any weakness in the bridge. It holds the rain which in turn rots the timbers, and it encourages greater speed on the part of drivers than the bridge is built to withstand. It is better to have a rough surface on a bridge as this compels a driver to approach cautiously.

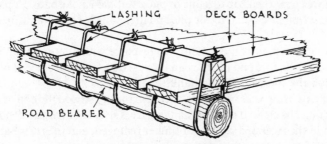

Figure 6.23 Decking.

Where prepared planks are used, the thickness of the planks is 50–75 mm. The decking of a bridge, particularly that of poles, is much improved by nailing two stout planks across so as to form a wheel track for lorries and cars. The planks are 300 mm wide and 1·3–1·5 m apart centre to centre. In any bridge a pole or timber guard rail (or curb) should be secured to the edges of decking as shown in Figure 6.19. Figures 6.17 and 6.19 show the construction of the handrail.

6.7.11   Abutments

Bridges fail through the action of the stream which washes out their shore ends. An abutment is a structure of stone, brick, concrete or timber which actually carries the shore ends of the road bearers (see Figures 6.17 and 6.24). In order to defend the abutment from the action of the stream, walls are built which run back into the bank and form, as it were, a funnel to pour the stream through the bridge (Figure 6.17). These walls are also termed wing walls as in culverts. The thickness of masonry abutments at their base should be two-fifths of their height.

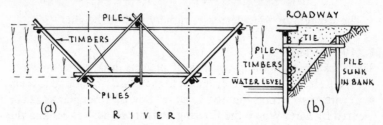

Figure 6.24 Timber abutment.

The principles of construction of timber abutments are shown in Figure 6.24, where (b) is a section of (a). Behind the piles timbers are laid to form the wall of the abutment and wing walls. The timbers are notched or dovetailed together where they join. The piles are anchored near their top to a pile or piles sunk well in the bank. A piece of stout timber secured to the pile and to the anchor pile is a sufficient tie.

In some instances it is possible to dispense with abutments and to support the shore end of the road bearers on a transom set well back beyond the top edge of the bank.

When a bridge has been constructed in the dry season the bed of the river must be cleared up. Overhanging trees should be trimmed, holes filled in the river bed, all bits of timber removed, and the river banks attended to. If these precautions are not taken when the river comes down in flood all sorts of swirls and eddies will be set up. They may, and often do, wash out the abutments or the bank ends of the bridge.

6.7.12   Short Span Bridges

For light bridges the designs in Figures 6.24 and 6.25 can be used if the materials are available. Figures 6.25(a) and 6.25(b) show a sling bridge. Deep and solid banks are required for this type which can be made to span up to 15 m. It will be observed that there are three

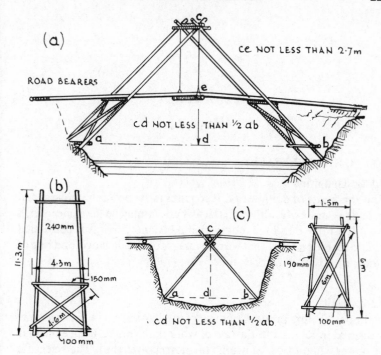

NOTE : THE DIMENSIONS GIVEN ARE MEAN DIAMETERS FOR SELECTED ROUND TIMBER AND MUST BE INCREASED FOR UNSELECTED TIMBER

Figure 6.25 Short span bridges.

transoms and the total span is thus divided into four bays. Short road bearers can be used.

Figure 6.25(c) is a single-lock bridge for spans up to 9 m. The data figured on the sketches must be carefully followed. The section diameters shown are for selected timber and must be increased for unselected timber.

CHAPTER 7
Power

7.1 POWER GENERALLY

7.1.1 Definition
Power is a rate of doing work. It requires more power to move a load quickly than slowly, although the work done may be the same in each case. If a force or a load moves over a distance, energy is consumed and work is done. In other words work = force × distance, and rate of work, or power = work ÷ time.

7.1.2 Units
In the past, before the development of mechanical engines, power was measured in relation to the rate of work of the horse. Hence the unit of power came to be known as the horsepower (hp). The scientific unit of power is the watt (W), and because this is small it is very often expressed as the kilowatt (kW). The unit of work or energy corresponding to the watt is the joule (J), which is defined as the work done when a force of one newton (1N) moves through a distance of one metre (1 m). Watts = joules per second.

$$J \ = N \times m$$
$$W \ = J/s$$
$$kW = 1000 \ W$$

The horsepower, which was originally defined in terms of pound-foot units, is equivalent to 746 W. The metric hp is 735.5 W.

7.1.3 Brake Horsepower
The brake horsepower of a power unit defines its power output. The name derives from the original method of measuring the output power of an engine by causing it to work against a brake whose loading could be measured. The efficiency of an engine is the ratio of its power output to its power input.

7.2 LIVE POWER

7.2.1 Human Power
While the human physique is capable of short bursts of intense power, the sustained energy output over a prolonged period, such as might be required for pumping or load haulage or other similar labouring activity, is about 60 W.

7.2.2 Animal Power
Draught animals can provide power for ploughing and other agricultural operations, transport and water lifting. Table 7.1 gives the power output of some animals.

Table 7.1   Animal power.

Animal	Weight (kg)	Draft force (kg)	Ave. speed (m/sec)	Power (W)
Heavy horse	680–1200	50–120	0·7–1·25	350–1500
Light horse	400–700	45–78	0·8–1·40	370–1080
Mule	350–500	50–60	0·9–1·00	450– 600
Donkey	200–300	30–40	0·7	250
Cow	400–600	50–60	0·7	350
Bullock	500–900	60–80	0·6–0·80	360– 640

Source: Reproduced from *Economics and Power Requirements of Small Irrigation Pumps in Bangladesh and Egypt,* by David Birch, Institute of Irrigation Studies, University of Southampton, 1979. *Sources of information:* (1) S. B. Watt, *Chinese Chain and Washer Pumps,* IT Publications; and (2) *Civil Engineers* in *Management in the Community,* a Conference at N.E. London Polytechnic.

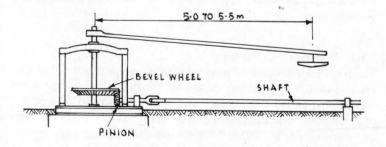

Figure 7.1 Horse gear.

It is often assumed that an animal working on a circular track can exert a force of one tenth of its weight at a speed of 0·7 m/s. To enable an animal to walk in a circular track the diameter of the walk should not be less than 7·5 m; 9–10 m would be still better. Figure 7.1 gives a sketch of animal gear suitable for water raising.

7.3   WIND POWER

7.3.1   Power in the Wind

The power which can be extracted from the wind by a windmill is, theoretically:

$$W = 0·373 \, AV^3 \text{ W}$$

where A is the swept area of the rotating blades in square metres and V is the velocity of the wind in metres per second. A well-made propeller or rotor will extract 30–40 per cent of the wind energy; if the efficiency is, say, 0·35, the power is given by:

$$W = 0·131 \, AV^3 \text{ W}$$

7.3.2   Windmills

Although the initial cost of a windmill is higher than the equivalent powered petrol or diesel engine, having no fuel costs and minimal maintenance, running costs are very low. A well-designed windmill will start in a light breeze of under 2 m/sec velocity, and must be able to withstand winds of up to 30 m/sec. A moderate breeze is about 7 m/sec, a strong breeze is about 12 m/sec and 15 m/sec is a near gale. Towers are usually from 6 to 20 m in height, and the top of the tower must always be at least 5 m higher than any surrounding obstructions to wind flow.

7.3.3   Windmills for Pumping

The most common use of windmills is for pumping water, but they are also used for generating electricity. When used for pumping, the pump must be matched to the wind machine. Storage capacity for pumped water is necessary as winds are variable and the machine may not work every day. Table 7.2 gives some wind pump performance figures for Kijito windmill pumps manufactured in Kenya.

*Table 7.2 Wind pump performance.**

| Rotor dia. | Total head (m) | | | | | | | | | |
(m)	15	30	45	60	90	120	150	180	210	240
3·7	45	20	13	9	6	4	—	—	—	—
4·9	75	30	20	15	10	6	4	3	—	—
6·1	125	55	35	25	17	11	7	5	3	—
7·3	180	80	52	38	24	16	11	8	5	3

* Output in m^3/day for an average wind speed of 3.5 m/sec.

7.4 WATER POWER

7.4.1 Power from Water

The theoretical power in kilowatts developed by a flow of water of Q l/sec falling through a vertical distance H m is given by:

$$W = \frac{QH}{102} \text{ kW}$$

In practice energy is lost through mechanical and electrical friction, and sometimes, through leakage of water. The actual power output is less than the theoretical power, and the ratio of actual to theoretical power is the efficiency of the system converting the power. If k = efficiency, then actual power is given by:

$$W = k \cdot \frac{QH}{102} \text{ kW}$$

7.4.2 Water Wheels

There are several types of water wheel, as shown in Figure 7.2. The overshot wheel is the most efficient, with efficiencies (k) from 0·6 to 0·65. For a breast wheel the efficiency is about 0·5 and for an undershot wheel about 0·25.

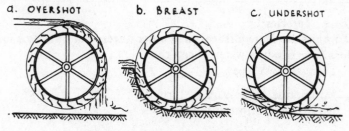

Figure 7.2 Types of water wheel.

Figure 7.3 shows the proportions of the buckets in overshot and high breast wheels. Overshot wheels have diameters up to 7·5 m. The diameter should be as nearly as possible equal to the height of the fall, or head, available, if the wheel is to be efficient.

The depth of the shrouding is from 300 to 400 mm. The number of buckets to a wheel = 7–8 times the diameter of the wheel in metres (see Figure 7·3).

Table 7.3 gives the appropriate power in kilowatts of well-constructed iron overshot wheels of various diameters. Figure 7.4 shows an undershot wheel.

FOR WHEELS UP TO 7·5m DIAMETER
b = 300 - 400 mm
a = ½ b, c = b
d = ABOUT 0·9 c

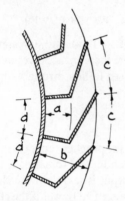

Figure 7.3 Bucket proportions for overshot and breast wheels.

Table 7.3   Output of overshot wheels (kW).

Width of wheel (m)	Discharge (l/sec)	Diameter of wheel (m)					
		1·0	2·0	3·0	4·0	5·0	6·0
0·6	100	0·66	1·31	1·97	2·63	3·28	3·94
0·9	200	1·31	2·63	3·94	5·26	6·57	7·88
1·2	300	1·97	3·95	5·91	7·89	9·86	11·82

7.4.3   Turbines

Turbines are more efficient than water wheels, but cannot be made locally as easily as water wheels can.

There are two types:

(a) Impulse or pressureless turbines.
(b) Reaction or pressure turbines.

In (a) above the water is passed through fixed guides or nozzles, to

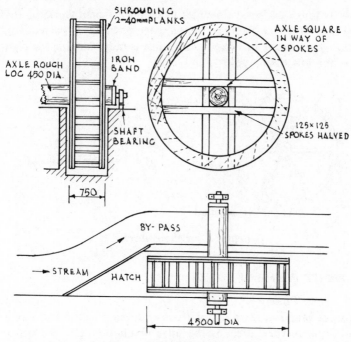

Figure 7.4 Undershot wheel.

discharge as a free jet, impinging on curved vanes mounted in a wheel, thus causing the wheel to revolve.

In (b) above the water passes through fixed guides as in (a) above but its pressure is used to react on moving blades to cause rotation. The wheel passages must always be full, whereas in (a) above they need not be filled. A reaction turbine will work equally well if it discharges into the atmosphere or in water.

The power developed by a turbine can be calculated from the formula in section 7.4.1. The maximum overall efficiency to be expected from a small water turbine is about 60–70 per cent. The power output of a turbine depends upon its operating head, flow of water and speed of rotation, and machines are manufactured to meet a wide range of conditions. Speeds of rotation for different machines may be from 100 r.p.m. or less to over 1000 r.p.m.

7.4.4 Pelton Wheel
Figure 7.5 gives a diagrammatic sketch of a type of impulse turbine known as a pelton wheel. The water under pressure from the jet or nozzle impinges on blades which are fixed to the rim of a wheel and

power is thus developed. In order to obtain efficient working, the water must enter the blades without impact, or energy is wasted. The pelton wheel works at various heads but is most suitable for high heads and low discharges.

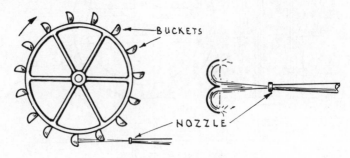

Figure 7.5 Pelton wheel.

7.5 OTHER FORMS OF POWER

7.5.1 Solar Power
The most practical form of solar power development for use on a small scale in rural areas is the solar or photovoltaic cell which transforms sunlight directly into electrical energy. In this system, silicon solar cells, usually 100 mm dia., are connected in groups known as modules, several modules being mounted in a panel known as an array.

Under a solar irradiance of 1 kW/m^2 a single cell will give about 2 ampères (A) at 0·5 volts (V), or 1 W of electrical energy. An array of 144 cells will therefore produce about 100–120 W for an irradiance of 1 kW/m^2.

7.5.2 Solar Pumping
Solar pumps have been used successfully in a number of countries. Initial costs are high and in 1982 were about US$20 per peak watt electrical output. Operation is very cheap because there are no fuel costs, and very little maintenance is required.

7.5.3 Petrol and Diesel Engines
The small petrol and diesel engine is still popular as a power unit in rural areas. Rising fuel costs make operation expensive. The brake horsepower of an engine is the power developed at its drive shaft, under normal operating conditions.

Engines are usually rated by the manufacturers at sea level and at an ambient temperature of 15°C. If engines are used at higher altitudes or higher ambient temperatures, the power output is reduced. The percentage reductions to be applied to diesel engines are given in Table 7.4.

Table 7.4 Diesel engine reduction of power with altitude and temperature.*

| Metres above | Temperature (°C) | | | | | | |
sea level	15	20	25	30	35	40	45
500	1·9	2·8	3·7	4·6	5·5	6·4	7·3
1000	6·9	7·8	8·7	9·6	10·5	11·4	12·3
1500	11·9	12·8	13·7	14·6	15·5	16·4	17·3
2000	16·9	17·8	18·7	19·6	20·5	21·4	22·3
2500	21·9	22·8	23·7	24·6	25·5	26·4	27·3

* Percentage reduction of power for heights above sea level and temperatures above 15°C.

For continuous use, reduce the normal rating by 25 per cent.

Example
A diesel engine rated at 18 bhp is to be used at an altitude of 2000 m above sea level, during daylight hours when the average ambient temperature is 22·5°C. From Table 7.4 the percentage reduction is between 17·8 and 18·7, which, by interpolation is 18·25, and the reduced output is therefore $(100-18·25) \times 18/100 = 0·8175 \times 18 = 14·7$ hp. If the engine is to be run continuously, this should be reduced by a further 25%, giving 11 hp.

Specific fuel consumption for a diesel engine is 0·25 l/bhp/hour at full load. At threequarters load it is 0·26 l/bhp/hour and at half load, 0·27 l/bhp/hour.

7.5.4 Electric Motors
Wherever electric power is available, electric motors can be used. Power supply is usually alternating (a.c.), and motors are rated in kilovolt amps (kVA). Power in kilowatts = kVA × *power factor*. A very wide range of electric motors is available commercially and professional advice should be sought in choosing a motor for a particular purpose. It is very important to specify the frequency of an a.c. supply, together with the operating voltage, and whether the supply is single-phase or three-phase.

7.6 MECHANICAL AIDS

7.6.1 Buoyancy

The buoyancy of a floating object is its resistance to sinking and is measured by the minimum weight required to sink the object, so that it is totally immersed. The uplift on a body immersed in water is equal to the weight of the volume of water which it displaces.

The buoyancy of a closed cylindrical drum of circumference C and length L, both in metres, is approximately $80\,C^2L - W$ in kilogrammes, where W is the weight of the drum in kilogrammes. In practice the safe buoyancy is 90 per cent of the total buoyancy.

7.6.2 Mechanical Advantage Gained by Blocks

The theoretical gain achieved by a hoist consisting of a fixed block and a moveable block is the number of ropes leading to or from the moveable block. In practice energy is used in overcoming friction in the blocks and the actual force P required to lift a weight W is given by:

$$P = \frac{W}{G}(1 + fn)$$

where G is the theoretical gain as above, f is a friction coefficient equal to 0·17 for tackle in average condition, or 0·2 or more for tackle in poor condition, and n is the total number of sheaves (wheels in the blocks) in the tackle.

Glossary

Abney Level	See 1.2.8.
Aeration	Bringing water into contact with air.
Aerobic	In contact with air or oxygen.
Ambient	Surrounding.
Amorphous Material	Material composed of particles without crystalline form.
Anaerobic	Without air or oxygen.
Aneroid Barometer	An instrument for measuring atmospheric pressure without the use of mercury or other liquid.
Aquifer	Water-bearing ground material or stratum (layer).
Argillaceous	Of clay or clay-like.
Bitumen	Naturally occurring tar substance.
Calcareous	Containing lime or calcium.
Clinometer	See 1.2.9.
Coagulation	The conversion of a liquid or a semi-liquid impurity into solid materials by introducing chemicals.
Concrete cast in situ	Concrete poured and cast in its final position in a structure.
Contour lines (or contours)	Lines on a map joining points of equal height.
Dead load	The weight of permanent immovable components, see 6.7.3.
Evaporation	The change of water from liquid to atmospheric vapour, see 4.1.4.
Evapo-transpiration	The evaporation of water through the leaves of vegetation.
Faecal	Of human excrement.
Filtration	The passage of water through a porous material, which stops and separates suspended solid particles.
Flocculation	The building up of coagulated particles to a larger size, which can be removed by filtration or settlement.
A Fortin barometer	A common type of mercury barometer, in which the atmospheric pressure is balanced

	against the weight of a column of mercu vertical tube.
Gypsum	A form of calcium sulphate found in clays and limestones.
Hafir	Excavated earth reservoir (originally developed in the Sudan).
Homogeneous	Of similar constituents, uniform in consistency.
Infiltration trench	Excavated trench in a water-bearing formation, to collect water.
Kunkar	Nodular limestone, common in India.
Lateritic	Derived from laterite, a soil material consisting essentially of hydrated iron oxides, usually associated with silica.
Line of collimation	Horizontal line of sight in the telescope of a surveying instrument.
Magnetic bearing	The angle between a line or direction and magnetic north.
Magnetic North	The direction near to true North, towards which a pivoted or magnetized needle points when allowed to swing freely.
Micro-Wave	Very short-wave electro-magnetic radiation.
Organic material	Material from living matter.
Photogrammetry	The science of mapping from aerial photographs.
Phreatotypes	Plants which indicate the presence of a permanent ground-water table.
Precipitation	Fall of rain, sleet, snow or hail.
Prism	A solid, triangular-shaped glass body for deflecting light rays.
Reduced levels	Heights to a common datum (such as mean sea level, or an assumed datum), calculated from survey observations.
Run-off	See 4.1.6.
Sub-tended angle	The angle between two lines from the ends of a short base line, which intersect at a distant object.
Tacheometry	See 1.3.8.
Tamping	Soft material such as earth used to fill a hole in rock in which explosive has been placed for blasting.
Tripod	A three-legged stand (for an instrument).
True North	The direction towards the north pole (the axis of rotation of the earth).
Watershed	See 4.1.5.

References

General

1 Blake, L. S. (Ed.), *Civil Engineer's Reference Book,* Newnes-Butterworth, London, 1975.
2 Thurston, A. P. (Ed.), *Molesworth's Handbook of Engineering Formulae and Data*, E. & F. N. Spon, London, 1951.
3 Dancy, H. K., *A Manual of Building Construction*, Intermediate Technology Development Group, London, 1973.

Chapter 1   Survey

4 Williamson, J., *Surveying and Field Work*, Constable, London, 1952.
5 Bannister, A. and Raymond, S., *Surveying*, Pitman, London, 1972.
6 Collett, J. and Boyd, J., *Eight Simple Surveying Levels*, Intermediate Technology Publications, London, 1977.

Chapter 2   Engineering Materials

7 Knight, B. H. and Knight, R. G., *Builders' Materials*, Edward Arnold, London, 1955.
8 Reynolds, C. E., *Reinforced Concrete Designer's Handbook*, Concrete Publications, London, 1964.
9 The Indian Standards Institution has published a wide range of standards dealing with all aspects of lime production, kiln construction, and the use of lime. Their address is: Indian Standards Institution, Manak Bharan, 9 Bahadur Shah Zafar Marg, New Delhi 110002, India. Copies of the Indian Standards are also available from the British Standards Institution, 2 Park Street, London W.1.
Note especially:

IS 1849	1/1 — 1976	(Kiln construction)
IS 1861	1/1 — 1975	(Lime manufacture)
IS 712	1973	(Lime specifications)
IS 2541	1974	(Lime concrete)
IS 1625	1971	(Lime mortar)

10 *Steel Designer's Manual*, Crosby Lockwood, London, 1972.

Chapter 4   Water Development

11 Stern, P. H., *Small Scale Irrigation*, Intermediate Technology Publications, London, 1979.

12 Doxiadis Ionides Associates, *Land and Water Use Survey in Kordofan Province of the Republic of the Sudan*, London, 1966.

13 *Handbook of Basic Instructions for Dam Construction*, Engineering Branch, Department of Conservation and Extension, Government of Zimbabwe.

14 Wood, A. D. and Richardson, E. V., *Design of Small Water Storage and Erosion Control Dams*, Department of Civil Engineering, Colorado State University, 1975.

15 Stern, P. H., 'Gabions for hydraulic structures', *Appropriate Technology*, Vol. 7 No. 4, London, 1981.

16 Wagner, E. G. and Lanoix, J. N., *Water Supply for Rural Areas and Small Communities*, World Health Organization, Geneva, 1959.

17 Twort, A. C., Hoather, R. C. and Law, F. M., *Water Supply*, Edward Arnold, London, 1975.

18 Watt, S. B. and Wood, W. E., *Hand Dug Wells and their Construction*, Intermediate Technology Publications, London, 1979.

19 Mann, H. T. and Williamson, D., *Water Treatment and Sanitation*, Intermediate Technology Publications, London, 1979.

20 McJunkin, F. E., *Handpumps, International Reference Centre for Community Water Supply*, Leidschendam, The Netherlands, 1977.

Chapter 5   Sanitation

21 Wagner, E. G. and Lanoix, J. N., *Excreta Disposal for Rural Areas and Small Communities*, World Health Organization, Geneva, 1958.

22 Feachem, R. and Cairncross, S., *Small Excreta Disposal Systems*, The Ross Institute of Tropical Hygiene, London, 1978.

23 Mann, H. T. and Williamson, D., *Water Treatment and Sanitation* Intermediate Technology Publications, London, 1979.

24 Feroze Uhmed, M., *Report on the Study of Ferro-Cement Slabs for Water Sealed Latrines*, University of Engineering and Technology, Dacca, Bangladesh.

25 Howard, J. and Jaques, R., *The Oxfam Aqua Privy*, Oxfam, Oxford.

Chapter 6 Roads and Bridges

26 Cross, W. K., *Designs and Estimates for Low Cost Roads in North-East Brazil*, Proceedings of the Institution of Civil Engineers, London, November, 1973.

27 Indian Roads Congress, *Recommendations about the Alignment, Survey and Geometric Design of Hill Roads*, New Delhi, 1973.

28 De Veen, J. J., *The Rural Access Roads Programme: Appropriate Technology in Kenya*, International Labour Organisation, Geneva, 1980.

29 UNESCO, *Low Cost Roads: Design, Construction and Maintenance*, Butterworth, London, 1971.

30 *Military Engineering, Vol. II. Field Engineering: Pamphlet 8A Roads*, Ministry of Defence, January 1971, London.

Chapter 7 Power

31 Birch, D., *Economics and Power Requirements of Small Irrigation Pumps in Bangladesh and Egypt*, University of Southampton, 1979.

32 McGuigan, D., *Small Scale Water Power*, Prism Press, Dorchester, 1978.

33 McGuigan, D., *Small Scale Wind Power*, Prism Press, Dorchester, 1978.

APPENDIX I

Units, Abbreviations and Conversion Factors

METRIC AND ENGLISH UNITS

Table I.1 gives factors for converting units from Metric to English and *vice versa*. To convert *from* the unit column multiply *by* the appropriate conversion factor.

OTHER MEASUREMENTS OF LENGTH

1 fathom	= 6 ft. = 1·829 m
1 shackle	= 12·5 fathoms
1 nautical mile (UK)	= 1·853 km
1 cable	= $\frac{1}{10}$ nautical mile = 185·3 m
1 knot	= 1 nautical mile per hour

1 degree of latitude is about 111 km
1 degree of longitude is about 111 km at the equator and about 56 km at 60°N or S of the equator.

ANGULAR MEASUREMENT

60 seconds (60 sec or 60″) = 1 minute (1 min or 1′)
60 minutes (60 min or 60′) = 1 degree (1 deg or 1°)

The radian is the scientific unit of angle, and is the angle at the centre of a circle subtended by an arc equal in length to the radius.

$$\text{Angle in radians} = \frac{\text{Length of arc}}{\text{Radius}}$$

$$2 \pi \text{ radians} = 360°$$

$$1 \text{ radian} = \frac{180}{\pi} = 57.296 \text{ deg.}$$

$$1 \text{ degree} = \frac{\pi}{180} = 0.017453 \text{ radian}$$

$$\pi = 3·14159$$

Table I.1 Units of measurement and conversion factors.

Metric			English		
Unit	Abbr.	Conversion Factor	Unit	Abbr.	Conversion Factor
Length					
millimetre	mm	0·0394 in	inch	in	25·4 mm
centimetre	cm	0·394 in		in	2·54 cm
metre (= 1000 mm)	m	3·281 ft	foot (= 12 in)	ft	0·3048 m
	m	1·094 yd	yard (= 3 ft)	yd	0·914 m
kilometre (= 1000 m)	km	0·621 mile	mile (= 5280 ft) (= 1760 yd)	—	1·609 km
Area					
square centimetre	cm^2	0·155 in^2	square inch	in^2	6·45 cm^2
square metre	m^2	10·76 ft^2	square foot	ft^2	0·0929 m^2
	m^2	1·196 yd^2	square yard	yd^2	0·836 m^2
hectare (= 10 000 m^2)	ha	2·47 ac	acre (= 43 560 ft^2)	ac	0·405 ha
square kilometre (= 100 ha)	km^2	0·386 square mile	square mile (= 640 ac)	—	2·59 km^2
Volume					
cubic centimetre	cm^3	0·061 in^3	cubic inch	in^3	16·4 cm^3
litre (= 1000 cm^3)	l	0·220 imperial gallon	imperial gallon (= 1·20 US gallon)	—	4·55 l
	l	0·264 US gallon	US gallon (= 0·833 imperial gallon)	—	3·79 l
	l	0·0353 ft^3	cubic foot	ft^3	28·32 l
				ft^3	6·23 imperial gallon
				ft^3	7·48 US gallon
cubic metre (= 1000 l)	m^3	35·31 ft^3		ft^3	0·0283 m^3
	m^3	1·308 yd^3	cubic yard	yd^3	0·765 m^3
			acre-foot (= 43 560 ft^3)	—	1233·5 m^3
Weight					
gramme	g	0·0353 oz	ounce	oz	28·35 g
kilogramme (= 1000 g)	kg	2·205 lb	pound (= 16 oz)	lb	0·454 kg
tonne (= 1000 kg)	t	0·984 ton	ton (= 2240 lb)	—	1·016 tonne
Velocity					
metre per second	m/s	3·281 ft/s	foot per second	ft/s	0·3048 m/s
Rate of flow					
litre per second	l/s	0·0353 ft^3/s	cubic foot per second (= 2 acre-feet per day approx.)	ft^3/s	28·32 l/s
	l/s	13·21 imperial gallon per minute			
	l/s	15·85 US gallon per minute			
cubic metre per second (= 1000 l/s)	m^3/s	35·31 ft^3/s		ft^3/s	0·0283 m^3/s
Density					
gramme per cubic centimetre	g/cm^3	0·0361 lb/in^3	pound per cubic inch	lb/in^3	27·68 g/cm^3
kilogramme per cubic metre	kg/cm^3	0·0624 lb/ft^3	pound per cubic foot	lb/ft^3	16·02 kg/m^3
Pressure					
kilogramme per square centimetre	kg/cm^2	14·22 lb/in^2	pound per square inch (psi) (= 2·31 ft water)	lb/in^2	0·0703 kg/cm^2
	kg/cm^2	0·968 atm		lb/in^2	0·068 atm
	kg/cm^2	10 m water			
atmosphere (= 1·033 kg/cm^2)	atm	14·7 lb/in^2			
Power					
kilowatt	kW	1·341 hp	horsepower	hp	0·746 kW
metric horsepower	—	0·986 hp	(= 550 ft lb/sec)	hp	1·014 metric horsepower

PAPER

24 sheets	= 1 quire
20 quires	= 1 ream
2 reams	= 1 bundle
10 reams	= 1 bale

'A' sizes

A0	841 mm × 1189 mm
A1	594 mm × 841 mm
A2	420 mm × 594 mm
A3	297 mm × 420 mm
A4	210 mm × 297 mm
A5	148 mm × 210 mm

SHIPPING MEASUREMENT

Gross tonnage = Total cubic space below deck and total cubic contents of closed spaces above deck in units of 100 ft^3 or 2·83 m^3

Net tonnage = Gross tonnage less all space not available for freight (i.e., crew space, engine room, coal bunkers, water ballast etc.)

Deadweight tonnage or carrying capacity is the number of UK tons (2240 lb or 1016 kg) that a vessel is capable of carrying when loaded to load line. Displacement tonnage is the weight of sea water displaced by a vessel when loaded to a load line (i.e., the weight of the vessel and its contents).

Shipping tonnage is a measure of cubic capacity. Freight is paid for by the freight ton of 40 ft^3 or 1·13 m^3 of cargo space.

COMPARISON OF THERMOMETERS

F = temperature Fahrenheit
C = temperature Centigrade

$$F = \frac{9C}{5} + 32$$

$$C = \frac{5(F-32)}{9}$$

APPENDIX II
Areas of Figures

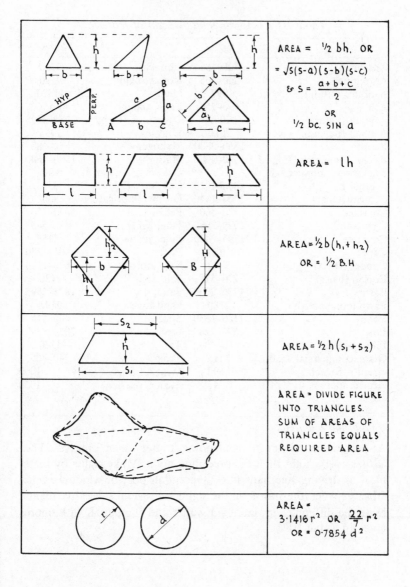

	AREA = $\frac{1}{2} bh$, OR $= \sqrt{s(s-a)(s-b)(s-c)}$ & $s = \frac{a+b+c}{2}$ OR $\frac{1}{2} bc. \sin a$
	AREA = lh
	AREA = $\frac{1}{2} b(h_1 + h_2)$ OR $= \frac{1}{2} B.H$
	AREA = $\frac{1}{2} h(s_1 + s_2)$
	AREA = DIVIDE FIGURE INTO TRIANGLES. SUM OF AREAS OF TRIANGLES EQUALS REQUIRED AREA
	AREA = $3.1416 r^2$ OR $\frac{22}{7} r^2$ OR $= 0.7854 d^2$

APPENDIX III

Miscellaneous Data

Table III.1   Approximate weight of materials

	kg/m³		kg/m³
Acacia	705–785	Iron, cast	7200
Aluminium	260–265	Iron, wrought	7690
Asbestos (crude)	897	Lead	11370
Ash	690–750	Lime, slaked	800–960
Asphalt (natural)	1009	Limestone	2230–2595
Asphalt (paving)	2080	Mortar	1905
Basalt	2850–2880	Mahogany	560–280
Bricks, commercial English	1600–2000	Mud, dry	1280–1600
Brickwork, commercial		Oak, dry, African	990
English	1860–1920	Oak, dry, English	930
Cement (loose)	1200–1440	Oil fuel, lubricating	900
Charcoal	320–560	Petrol	690–770
Clay, solid	1920–2080	Pine, white	430–545
Concrete	1795–2400	Pine, yellow	515
Copal	1040	Pitch	1105–1230
Copper (sheet)	8800	Salt, loose	800–1120
Cotton (bales)	270–575	Salt, solid	2130
Earth (dry)	1230–2000	Sand, dry	1875–2595
Earth (compacted)	2180	Sandstone	2195
Ebony	1185–1330	Spruce	400–515
Elm	575–720	Steel	7850–8330
Fibre board	160–400	Tar	1230
Glass, commercial window	2515	Teak	740–865
Granite, Scotch	2690	Water, fresh	1000
Gravel, loose	1745	Water, sea (av.)	1030
Ice	913		

Regulating a watch

Any fixed star crosses the same point at intervals of 3 min 55·91 sec
earlier every night than the preceding night. Make sights by fixing
pins, or driving fine nails into a verandah post or window frame.
Observe when the star is on the sights on several successive nights.
Note the difference in time by a watch and compare it with figures
given in Table III.2.

Table III.2. Sun's rising and setting

Latitude	40°N. rises	40°N. sets	30°N. rises	30°N. sets	20°N. rises	20°N. sets	10°N. rises	10°N. sets	Equator rises	Equator sets	10°S. rises	10°S. sets	20°S. rises	20°S. sets	30°S. rises	30°S. sets	40°S. rises	40°S. sets
Jan. 1	7 23	4 43	6 56	5 10	6 35	5 31	6 16	5 50	5 59	6 7	5 42	6 24	5 23	6 43	5 2	7 4	4 35	7 30
,, 16	7 21	4 58	6 56	5 21	6 37	5 41	6 21	5 57	6 5	6 13	5 49	6 29	5 33	6 45	5 14	7 4	4 49	7 28
Feb. 1	7 10	5 16	6 50	5 35	6 35	5 51	6 22	6 4	6 9	6 17	5 56	6 30	5 43	6 43	5 28	6 58	5 8	7 18
,, 16	6 54	5 34	6 40	5 48	6 29	5 59	6 19	6 9	6 10	6 18	6 1	6 27	5 51	6 37	5 40	6 48	5 26	7 2
Mar. 1	6 34	5 50	6 26	5 58	6 20	6 4	6 14	6 10	6 8	6 16	6 2	6 22	5 57	6 27	5 50	6 34	5 42	6 42
,, 16	6 13	6 5	6 10	6 7	6 9	6 10	6 7	6 11	6 5	6 13	6 3	6 15	6 1	6 17	5 59	6 19	5 57	6 21
April 1	5 46	6 23	5 50	6 18	5 54	6 14	5 57	6 11	6 0	6 8	6 3	6 5	6 6	6 2	6 10	5 58	6 14	5 53
,, 16	5 23	6 37	5 33	6 27	5 42	6 18	5 49	6 11	5 56	6 4	6 3	5 57	6 10	5 50	6 19	5 41	6 29	5 31
May 1	5 1	6 53	5 18	6 36	5 31	6 23	5 42	6 12	5 55	5 59	6 6	5 48	6 15	5 39	6 28	5 26	6 45	5 9
,, 16	4 46	7 6	5 7	6 45	5 24	6 29	5 38	6 14	5 52	6 0	6 6	5 46	6 20	5 32	6 37	5 15	6 58	4 54
June 1	4 35	7 21	5 0	6 56	5 20	6 36	5 38	6 18	5 54	6 2	6 10	5 46	6 28	5 28	6 48	5 8	7 13	4 43
,, 16	4 32	7 30	4 59	7 3	5 21	6 41	5 40	6 22	5 57	6 5	6 14	5 48	6 33	5 29	6 55	5 7	7 22	4 40
July 1	4 36	7 32	5 3	7 5	5 24	6 44	5 43	6 25	6 0	6 8	6 17	5 51	6 36	5 32	6 57	5 11	7 24	4 44
,, 16	4 45	7 27	5 10	7 2	5 29	6 43	5 46	6 26	6 2	6 10	6 18	5 54	6 35	5 37	6 54	5 18	7 19	4 53
Aug. 1	4 58	7 14	5 18	6 54	5 35	6 37	5 49	6 23	6 2	6 10	6 15	5 57	6 29	5 43	6 46	5 26	7 6	5 6
,, 16	5 12	6 56	5 27	6 41	5 40	6 28	5 50	6 18	6 0	6 8	6 10	5 58	6 20	5 48	6 33	5 35	6 48	5 20
Sept. 1	5 27	6 33	5 36	6 24	5 43	6 16	5 50	6 10	5 56	6 4	6 2	5 58	6 8	5 52	6 16	5 44	6 25	5 35
,, 16	5 41	6 9	5 44	6 6	5 47	6 3	5 49	6 1	5 51	5 59	5 53	5 57	5 55	5 55	5 58	5 52	6 1	5 49
Oct. 1	5 56	5 44	5 53	5 47	5 50	5 50	5 48	5 52	5 46	5 54	5 44	5 56	5 42	5 58	5 39	6 1	5 36	6 4
,, 16	6 11	5 21	6 2	5 30	5 55	5 37	5 48	5 44	5 42	5 50	5 36	5 56	5 29	6 3	5 22	6 10	5 13	6 19
Nov. 1	6 29	4 59	6 14	5 14	6 1	5 27	5 50	5 38	5 40	5 48	5 30	5 58	5 19	6 9	5 6	6 22	4 51	6 37
,, 16	6 46	4 44	6 26	5 4	6 9	5 21	5 55	5 36	5 41	5 49	5 28	6 3	5 13	6 17	4 56	6 34	4 36	6 54
Dec. 1	7 3	4 35	6 38	5 0	6 18	5 20	6 1	5 37	5 45	5 53	5 29	6 9	5 12	6 26	4 52	6 46	4 27	7 11
,, 16	7 17	4 35	6 50	5 2	6 28	5 24	6 9	5 43	5 52	6 0	5 35	6 17	5 16	6 36	4 54	6 58	4 27	7 25

This table shows the approximate mean local times of the sun's rising and setting for the latitudes given. The times for intermediate dates and latitudes can be found by interpolation.

Example: Required time of sunset of Lat. 4°S. on 1st May. On 1st May 10°S. sun sets 5h.48m. On 1st May Equator sun sets 5h.59m. therefore difference for 10° = 11 mins. and difference for 1° = 1·1 mins. difference for 4° = 4·4 mins. this amount subtracted from 5·59 (= 5·54 mins.) is the time of sunset on 1st May. (From "Field Service Pocket Book", 1914).

Calculations for Beams and Columns

BEAMS SUBJECT TO BENDING

The following information gives the basis for calculation of the dimensions of beams subject to bending.

The general expression for the moment of resistance (Mr) of a beam is $Mr = PbZ$ where Z is known as the section modulus. Its value depends solely on the size and shape of the beam and has nothing to do with the nature of the material of which it is made. The value of Z for three of the sections most likely to be encountered is given in Figure 6.18.

Note that these values are only correct for the 'I' beam and the rectangular beam, when they stand vertically on their bases 'b'. An approximate formula for steel joists is $Z = ad$, where a = effective sectional area of one flange and d = depth of the section.

The value of Pb, the permissible working stress for the component materials likely to be encountered will depend very much on the particular situation to be considered and the advice of a qualified engineer should be sought if at all possible.

If this is not possible, the following values are recommended:

Table IV.1   Permissible stresses.

Material	Bending tension (N/mm^2)	Bending compression (N/mm^2)	Direct compression (N/mm^2)
Mild steel	165	100*	100†
Cast iron			120
Wrought iron			60
Larch	4·5	4·5	4·5
Oak	7	7	7

* Limit (length/breadth) to 40 } where the breadth is the least lateral dimension.
† Limit (length/breadth) to 15 }

To design a beam, the first step is to calculate the maximum bending moment *Mff* resulting from the applied loading and span condition. Values of *Mff* for the conditions most likely to be encountered are shown in Figure 6.18. The maximum bending moment is then equated to the moment of resistance *Mr* and as *Mr* = *PbZ*, knowing the permissible stress *Pb* for the material of which the beam is constructed, a value of *Z* can be calculated. Suitable dimensions for a beam are then selected to give the desired value of *Z*.

In making calculations of this sort, the same units must be used throughout.

Under the new SI (Système Internationale) system, forces are measured in Newtons (N), bending moments in Kilonewton-metres (kNm) and stresses in Newtons per square millimetre (N/mm²).

Example
Calculate the bending moment caused by a load of 50 kg/m over a simply supported span of 15 m.

From Figure 6.18

$$Mff = \frac{wl^2}{8} \text{ and } 1 \text{ N} = 100 \text{ kg}$$

Therefore

$$Mff = \frac{50}{100} \times \frac{15^2}{8} = 14 \cdot 06 \text{ kNm}$$

A beam is generally considered stiff enough for deflection calculations to be ignored if the ratio of its span to depth does not exceed 20 : 1. If, however, deflection calculations are to be made, Figure 6.18 gives the formulae for the most common loading/span conditions likely to be met and the following are some values of *E*:

$$\begin{aligned} \text{Steel} &= 210 \times 10^3 \text{ N/mm}^2 \\ \text{Oak} &= 8 \times 10^3 \text{ N/mm}^2 \\ \text{Larch} &= 7 \times 10^3 \text{ N/mm}^2 \end{aligned}$$

The following table gives safe load-carrying capacities over simply supported spans for some of the more common steel beams and joists in use in Britain.

Table IV.2   Properties of some British steel universal beams and rolled joists.

Size (mm)	Weight (kg/m)	Safe distributed loads in tonnes for spans in metres*										
		2 m	3 m	4 m	5 m	6 m	7 m	8 m	9 m	10 m	11 m	12 m
Beams												
762 × 267	147							64·6	46·6	33·0	23·6	20·2 16·7
686 × 254	125							48·5	35·2	24·8	18·7	15·4
610 × 229	101						43·6	31·0	21·1	15·2	12·1	
533 × 210	82					40·6	28·5	19·3	12·8			
457 × 152	52					14·1	8·5	6·1				
406 × 140	39					7·9	4·8					
356 × 127	33				9·4	5·0						
305 × 102	25			7·8	3·5	2·1						
203 × 133	25	15·3	9·9									
Joists												
254 × 114	37·2			15·2	8·6							
203 × 102	25·33	14·9	8·2	4·4								
178 × 102	21·54	11·3	6·2	3·3								
152 × 127	37·20	15·8										
152 × 76	17·86	7·3										
127 × 76	13·36	4·8										

* These loads will not cause overloading of the unstiffened web, nor deflection exceeding span/360 and do not assume any lateral support to the beams.

WOODEN COLUMNS

Gordon's rule for round or rectangular wooden columns is as follows, where P = total working load on column, A = area of column, r = safe intensity of stress (in same units as P and A), L = length of column, d = its least dimension in same units as L and a = a coefficient.

$$P = \frac{rA}{1 + a \dfrac{(L)^2}{d}}$$

The values for a are as shown in Table IV.3

Table IV.3

Type of column	Ends flat or fixed	Ends round or hinged	One end round other end fixed
Solid round	$\dfrac{1}{190}$	$\dfrac{1}{48}$	$\dfrac{1}{108}$
Solid rectangular	$\dfrac{1}{250}$	$\dfrac{1}{62}$	$\dfrac{1}{140}$

The following rough rules for the strength of columns, piles, struts, etc., is also given where r = safe compression in N/mm² on a column where there is no buckling, where L = the length of the column in mm and d = the least dimension in mm:

(a) when L is not greater than $8d$ (i.e., when the length of the column does not exceed 8 times its least dimension) then safe stress = r.

(b) When L is between $8d$ and $12d$ the safe stress = $5/6r$.

(c) When L is between $12d$ and $24d$ the safe stress = $\frac{1}{2}r$.

(d) When L is between $24d$ and $36d$ the safe stress = $\frac{1}{4}r$.

(e) When L is between $36d$ and $48d$ the safe stress = $\frac{1}{6}r$.

Here r is taken as the safe compression in N/mm² of the timber used.